FAITH - BASED OUTCOME INDEPENDENT

LIVING BY FAITH

Dr. Michael H Yeager

(Some of the teaching in this book is taken from the Adam Clarke Commentary, and other non-copyright material found on the internet)

ISBN: 9798417846335
Imprint: Independently published

DEDICATION

All the Scriptures used in this book: **"FAITH-BASED OUTCOME INDEPENDENT"** are taken from the original 1611 version of the King James Bible. I give thanks to **GOD** the **FATHER**, **JESUS CHRIST**, and the **Holy Ghost** for the powerful impact the Word has had upon my life. Without the Word Quickened in my heart by the **Holy Ghost**, I would have been lost and undone. I am eternally indebted to the Lord of Heaven and Earth, for His great love and His mercy, His protection and His provisions, His divine guidance, and overwhelming goodness. The Price He PAID for my Healing! To Him be glory and praise forever and ever: Amen

---

WE CANNOT BE DEFEATED WHEN WE ARE WALKING & MOVING WITH A **FAITH** THAT WILL NOT TAKE NO FOR AN ANSWER!

To Obtain the Kingdom of GOD, its blessings, and provisions, you need to rise up with a Radical, No Matter What, Aggressive, no matter what kind of FAITH. The author has apprehended many of GOD's blessings because he Took by No Matter What FAITH what GOD had promised him. He would not let go of GOD's Promises no matter what the outcome looked like. This book is filled with many radical stories of the author, who knew the will of GOD and did not care if he lived or died, to obtain what GOD said He Had Given to him. Remember, GOD is not a respecter of persons. What HE has done for others HE will do for YOU!

CONTENTS

ACKNOWLEDGMENTS

*To our Heavenly **FATHER** and His wonderful love.

*To our Lord, Savior, and Master — **JESUS CHRIST**, who saved us and set us free because of His great love for us.

*To the Holy Spirit, who leads and guides us into the realm of truth and miraculous living every day.

*To all of those who had a part in helping me get this book ready for the publishers.

*To my Lovely Wife Kathleen, and our precious children: Michael, Daniel, Steven, Stephanie, our precious daughter-in-law Catherine Yu, and Naomi, who is now with the Lord.

Important Introduction!

FAITH - BASED OUTCOME INDEPENDENT

FAITH-Based Outcome Independent causes us to become free of fleshly barriers and limitations common to the natural man.

FAITH-Based Outcome Independence is an essential tool in terms of growing spiritually and living a life that is aligned with the truth of **God**'s word. If we only ever define ourselves on what 'happens' to us or on the results that we get – instead of our trust and **FAITH** in **God** and his word – then we end up being swallowed up by what's happening to us physically, and emotionally.

FAITH-Based Outcome Independence means that "we give our best and let **God** take care of the rest" and that whatever happens, you know you'll be okay because you're in **God**'s hands. You will enter a place of not being able to be shaken. You will experience the Scripture that declares:

Romans 8:27 And he that searcheth the hearts knoweth what is the mind of the Spirit, because he maketh intercession for the saints according to the will of God.28 And we know that all things work together for good to them that love God, to them who are the called according to his purpose.29 For whom he did foreknow, he also did predestinate to be conformed to the image of his Son, that he might be the firstborn among many brethren.

Understanding **FAITH**-based outcome independence means that we actively live a life that is based on nothing but **FAITH** in **God** and his will. Because we are not moved by what it should look like, we simply trust **God** and his word.

__1 Thessalonians 5:18In every thing give thanks: for this is the will of God in Christ Jesus concerning you.__

Remember: it is not what comes to us that makes us or breaks us but our response to our **Circumstances**. We need to continue to trust **God** no matter what happens. Will we continue to agree with him even if it looks like he is not hearing our prayers or responding to our **Circumstances**?

By no means do the following stories account for all the Provisions and Miracles that I have seen and experienced in my life. If I were to recount every single answer to every single prayer and every wonderful healing, miracle, and blessing - there would be no end to this book!

What I share with you in this book are simply some highlights of what I have experienced in the Lord. Some of these experiences will seem incredulous. However, they are all true! This is not a testimony of how spiritual I am, but of how wonderful and marvelous the **FATHER**, the Son, and the **Holy Ghost** are.

I share these experiences to the best of my recollections and understanding. Not every conversation is exactly word for word; I would love to name every person that was a part of these wonderful occurrences, but privacy laws do not allow this. If you are reading this book and you either saw, experienced, or were a part of these events, please do not be offended because your names are not mentioned. This book was written in order to HELP Believers see how **FAITH** walks, Talks, Acts, Responds to the **Circumstances** of Life.

CHAPTER ONE

The name of this book is called **Faith Based Outcome Independent**. I ran into that declaration as I was on YouTube. I did not realize that that the world is using this terminology: outcome independent. I think this is a missing reality when it comes to the subject of **Faith** in the modern-day church.

AN ASPECT OF FAITH THAT MOST ARE MISSING!

Faith Based Outcome Independence = Submitting yourself to nothing but the will of **God** in every area of your life! Being authentic and sincere in this endeavor. There are multiple ways to say this, but for the believer in **Christ** the concept is always the same. You put yourself out there as an act of **FAITH** based on what you know to be the known will of **God**, without knowing what will happen and without knowing the exact outcome of your commitment. What I am talking about is Living by **Faith**.

Romans 1:17 For therein is the righteousness of God revealed from Faith to Faith: as it is written, The just shall live by Faith.

Galatians 3:11 But that no man is justified by the law in the sight of God, it is evident: for, The just shall live by Faith.

Hebrews 10:38 Now the just shall live by Faith: but if any man draw back, my soul shall have no pleasure in him.

OUTCOME = Definition of outcome: something that follows as a result or consequence, after effect, aftermath, backwash, conclusion, consequence, result.

INDEPENDENCE = Freedom from outside control or support: the state of being independent. For the believer it is Freedom from being controlled by the flesh, the world or the devil.

Living life with no fear of man or **Circumstances**!

Isaiah 51:7 Hearken unto me, ye that know righteousness, the people in whose heart is my law; fear ye not the reproach of men, neither be ye afraid of their revilings.

Psalm 10:6 He hath said in his heart, I shall not be moved: for I shall never be in adversity.

Psalm 16:8 I have set the Lord always before me: because he is at my right hand, I shall not be moved.

Psalm 46:5God is in the midst of her; she shall not be moved: God shall help her, and that right early.

Psalm 62:2He only is my rock and my salvation; he is my defence; I shall not be greatly moved.

Psalm 62:6He only is my rock and my salvation: he is my defence; I shall not be moved.

Psalm 121:3He will not suffer thy foot to be moved: he that keepeth thee will not slumber.

FAITH BASED OUTCOME INDEPENDENT

*** SONG: Well I'm on my way to heaven**
We shall not be moved
On my way to heaven
We shall not be moved
Just like a tree that's standing by the water side
We shall not be moved
We shall not we shall not be moved
We shall not we shall not be moved
Just like a tree that's standing by the water side
We shall not be moved
On the road to freedom

This type of **Faith** will produce Joy in every situation! We are talking about total dependence upon **God** dear regardless of the **Circumstances**! There are many stories within the Bible revealing this truth in the lives of **God**'s saints. The fact is that we to trust in **God**. We are required to depend upon **God**. The Scriptures command us to look to **God**. We're going to rely upon **God**, no matter what the outcome is. Like I said, there's many examples throughout the Scriptures.

One major example we will look at in the beginning of this book is the three Hebrew children who stood before Nebuchadnezzar. They had decided that they were not going to worship the idle that Nebuchadnezzar had set up. They told the king, we're not bowing our knees, no matter what, we know that **God** is able to deliver us, but we're not bowing our knees even if he doesn't.

In this book I will share with you many of my own personal experiences. Many times, when it looked like I should've compromised, quit bowed my knees to the **Circumstances** by **Faith** in **Christ** I refused even as the three Hebrew children. In all these situations **God** has never failed me. At the time it looked like I was a goner, and that **God** was not going to come through for me. That doesn't mean the outcome was always positive, or it happen the way I was expecting, but **God** was faithful.

When I knew what the will of **God** was, I had decided within my heart, within my mind that I was going to obey **God**, whether the results or the outcome was going to come in line with what I wanted or not. I think that's what Paul meant when he says:

Philippians 4:10 But I rejoiced in the Lord greatly, that now at the last your care of me hath flourished again; wherein ye were also careful, but ye lacked opportunity. 11 Not that I speak in respect of want: for I have learned, in whatsoever state I am, therewith to be content. 12 I know both how to be abased, and I know how to abound: every where and in all things I am instructed both to be full and to be hungry, both to abound and to suffer need.

FAITH IN GOD DOES NOT MEAN IT ALWAYS TURNS OUT THE WAY, YOU WANT IT TO!

Paul said: *Romans 14:8For whether we live, we live unto the Lord; and whether we die, we die unto the Lord: whether we live therefore, or die, we are the Lord's.*

Now this is an aspect of **Faith** I think many are missing in the modern-day church. Modern-day believers have been deceived into thinking that if you are walking by **Faith**, living by **Faith**, speaking by **Faith**, moving by **Faith**, that the outcome will always be the way you wanted to be. But that just, isn't true.

Almost 40 years ago when I started the church that I am pastoring, I knew that it was the will of **God** for me to be here. But to be honest with you I did not want to be here. Through the years, many times, many times, I wanted to leave. If I had been moved by the **Circumstances**, but what it look like, but what was happening, I would have left in a nanosecond.

But I knew I was in the will of **God**. So, I put it into the hands of

FAITH BASED OUTCOME INDEPENDENT

God. Now the word **outcome** or the definition of **outcome** means something that follows because of decisions you have made. It's a conclusion, or a result.

Independence means freedom from **Circumstances**. When we are truly living, walking, moving by **Faith** we will not be looking at the **Circumstances**.

A LOOK AT SMITH WIGGLESWORTH

Smith Wigglesworth, often referred to as 'the Apostle of Faith,' was one of the early pioneers of the Pentecostal revival that occurred a century ago.

Without human refinement and education, he was able to tap into the infinite resources of God to bring divine grace to multitudes.

Thousands came to Christian **Faith in his meetings, hundreds were healed of serious illnesses and diseases as supernatural signs followed his ministry.**

A deep intimacy with his heavenly Father and an unquestioning Faith in God's Word brought spectacular results and provided an example for all true believers of the Gospel.

May this stir your Faith and deepen your vision for the glory of God in our generation.

Smith Wigglesworth: This Is the Place Where God Will Show up!

You must come to a place of ashes, a place of helplessness, a place of wholehearted surrender where you do not refer to yourself. You have no justification of your own regarding anything. You are prepared to be slandered, to be despised by everybody. But because of His personality in you, He reserves you for Himself because you are godly, and He sets you on high because you have known His name (Ps. 91:14). He causes you to be the fruit of His loins and to bring forth His glory so that you will no longer rest in yourself. Your confidence will be in **God**. Ah, it is lovely. "The Lord is the Spirit; and where the Spirit of the Lord is, there is liberty" (2 Cor. 3:17).

Born June 10th, 1859

Died March 4th, 1947

***There have been times when I have been pressed through Circumstances and it seemed as if a dozen road engines were going over me, but I have found that the hardest things are just the right opportunities for the grace of God to work. We have such a lovely Jesus. He always proves Himself to be such a mighty Deliverer. He never fails to plan the best things for us.**

*All things are wonderful with our wonderful **Jesus**. If you would dare rest your all upon Him, things would take place and He would change your whole **Circumstance**. In a moment, through the name of **Jesus**, a new life can be realized.

FAITH BASED OUTCOME INDEPENDENT

* I am moved only by what I believe. I know this for a fact that no man who was walking by Faith looks at the Circumstances if he believes. No man considers how he feels if he believes. The man who believes God has victory in every situation. Every man who comes into the fullness of the spirit can laugh at all things and believe God.

---

*"The man who wants to work the works of **God** must never look at conditions or **Circumstances** but only at **Jesus**."

---

*"Never listen to human plans. God can work mightily when you persist in believing Him in spite of discouragement from the human standpoint. ... I am moved by what I believe. I know this: no man looks at the Circumstances if he believes."

---

* It was the purpose of **Jesus** to die for His Bride. Oh, dear saint, will it ever be spoken thru your lips or your mind that you will ever have a desire to serve **Christ** like that? Will you and I, under all **Circumstances** take up your cross so fully, to be in the place of any ridicule, any surrender?

YOU MUST TAKE YOUR HEALING!

(Many are waiting for God to heal them, but that is not the way to get healed) Faith never considers the Circumstances!

Faith will take what **God** has made available! When real **Faith** comes into operation you will not say, "I don't feel much better."

Faith says, "I am whole." **Faith** doesn't say, "It's a lame leg." **Faith** says, "My leg is healed." **Faith** never sees the problem, but it sees **Jesus** as the solution.

A young woman with a goiter came to me to be prayed for.

In a testimony meeting, she said, "I do praise the Lord for healing my goiter." (before she saw any change) She went home and said to her mother, "Oh Mother, when the man prayed for me, **God** healed my goiter."

For 12 months she went about telling everybody how **God** healed her goiter. Twelve months afterward I was in the same place and people said, "How big that lady's goiter is!" There came a time for testimony. She jumped up and said, "I was here 12 months ago, and **God** healed me of my goiter. Such a marvelous 12 months!"

When she went home her folks said, "You should have seen the people today when you testified that **God** had healed your goiter. They think there is something wrong with you. If you go upstairs and look in the glass you will see the goiter is bigger than ever it was."

She went upstairs, but she didn't look in the glass. She got down on her knees and said, "O Lord, let all the people know just as you have let me know, how wonderfully you have healed me." The next morning her neck was as perfect as any neck you ever saw. The goiter was completely gone! **Faith** never looks. **Faith** praises **God** that it is done!

Be not afraid, only believe

[Mk 5.22]

This is one of those marvelous truths of the scriptures that is written for our help, that we may believe as we see the almightiness of **God**; and also our privilege, not only to enter in by **Faith**, but to become partakers of the blessing he wants to give us. My message is based on having **Faith** in **Christ**. Because many are not hearing in **Faith**, the Word profits them nothing. There is a hearing of **Faith**, and a hearing which means nothing more than listening to mere words. I beseech you to see to it that everything that you do may bring not only blessing to you but strength and character. That you may be able to see the goodness of **God** in this message.

I want to impress upon you the importance of believing what the scripture says, and I have many things to relate about people who dared to believe **God** and his word until it came to pass. This is a wonderful reality. In fact, all of the word of **God** is a wonderful reality. It is an everlasting word, a word of power, a word of health, a word of substance, a word of life. It produces life into the very nature, to everyone that lays hold of it, if he believes. I want you to understand that there is a need for the word of **God** that brings us the blessing.

What am I here for? Because **God** delivered me when none other could do it. I stand before you as one who was given up by everybody, when no one could help. I was earnest and zealous for the salvation of souls. If you were in Bradford [England], you would know. We had police protection for nearly 20 years in the best thoroughfare in the city, and in my humble way with my dear wife, who was full of fire for **God**, we were ministering in the open air. Full of zeal? Yes.

 But one night, 30 years ago, I was carried home helpless. We knew very little about divine healing, but we prayed through. It is 30 years and more since **God** healed me. I am 68 years old and fresher, in better health, and more fit for work than I was at that time. It is a most wonderful experience when the life of **God** becomes the life of man. The divine power that sweeps through the body, cleansing the blood, makes the man new every day. The life of **God** is resurrection power.

When they brought me home helpless, we prayed all night. We did all we knew. At 10 o'clock the next morning, I said to my wife, "This must be my last roll call." We had five children around us. I tell you it was not easy in our **Circumstance**. I told my wife to do as she thought best, but the poor thing didn't know what to do. She called a physician who examined me, shook his head, and said, "It is impossible for anything to be done for your husband; I am absolutely helpless. He has appendicitis and you have waited too long. His system will not stand an operation. A few hours, at best, will finish him."

What the doctor said was true. He left her and said he would come back again, but he couldn't give her any hope. When he was gone out of the house an old lady and a young man who knew how to pray came in. The young man put his knees on the bed and said: "Come out, you devil, in the name of **Jesus**." It was a bold declaration, we had no time for argument, and instantly I was healed. Oh, hallelujah! I was as free as I am now, 30 years later. I never believed that any person ought to be in bed in the daytime, so I jumped up and went downstairs. My wife said: "Oh, are you up?" "I'm all right, wife; it is all right now," I said.

I had some men working for me and she said none of them had turned up that morning, so I picked up my tools and went to work. Then the doctor came. He walked up the stairs and my wife called, "Doctor, doctor, he is out!" "What?" he said. "Yes," she said, "he is out at work." "Oh," he said, "you will never see him alive again. They will bring him in a corpse." Am I a corpse? Oh, when **God** does anything, it is done forever! And **God** wants you to know that he wants to do something in you forever. I have laid my hands on people with appendicitis when the doctors were in the place, and **God** has healed them.

UNMOVABLE Faith

FAITH BASED OUTCOME INDEPENDENT

Are we children of Circumstances, or children of Faith?

If we are on natural lines, we are troubled at the wind blowing, as it blows it whispers fearfulness; but if you are rooted and grounded you can stand the tests, and it is only then that you prove what is the breadth and length and depth and height and know the love of **Christ**. [Ep 3.18-19] It is an addition sum to meet every missionary's needs, to display **God**'s power, enlarging that which needs to be quickened. Breadth: The whole man seeing **God** is sufficient in every state.

The length of things. **God** is in everything. Oh, the depths! But **God** is in the depths! The heights! **God** is always lifting you, and the revelation of the mind in that verse is enough for any in any **Circumstances** to triumph, able to do exceedingly abundantly above all that you can ask or think, [Ep 3.20] not according to the mind of Paul but according to the revelation of the Spirit.

Filled unto all the fullness of God. [Ep 3.19] The natural capacity when filled with simplicity has within it an enlargement of itself, but this fullness is an ideal power of **God** in the human soul; every part of you is enlarged by the Spirit. **God** is there instead of you to make you full, and you are full as your **Faith** reaches out to the measure. "Filled unto all the fullness of **God**."

    ***We should be able under all Circumstances to triumph because we have no confidence in ourselves, [Pp 3.3]** . But our confidence would be only in **God**. It is always those people who are full of **Faith** that have a good report, that never murmurs, that is in the place of victory, that is not in place of human order but of divine order, since **God** has come to dwell in them.

    ***We that handle the Word of life ought to be well built on the lines of common sense, judgment, and not given to anything contrary to the Word of God. There should be in us all the time such deep reverence towards God and His Word**

that under all Circumstances we would not forfeit our principles on the lines of Faith that God had revealed unto us by the truth.

*** "And as I prophesied there was a noise, and behold, a shaking, and the bones came together, bone to his bone." [Ek 37.7]** There is something worth your recognition in this. It is only the Spirit that can make the crooked straight, raise the dead, and perform miracles.

Some of you, no doubt, have thought some of your neighbors are a bit crooked and were, in fact, some of the most crooked of-the-way bones you ever saw in your life, and it would be impossible for them to get saved. That is nothing to do with you. It is for you to live in the Holy Ghost, and he can change the whole **Circumstance**, and you will be amazed at the way the crooked bones will be straightened. Nothing can change such **Circumstances** as **God** can.

"Bone to bone," no crooked places now; but it takes **God** to do that. Man has been trying to do it all along, but as soon as a man has been truly baptized with the Holy Ghost, **God** does it. There is power in the Holy Ghost to transform, renew, and change the whole **Circumstances** of life. You must submit and let **God** take hold of you. Don't be troubled because you have not reached the place. You have reached somewhere, but the best is in store. Only yield so that he may have full control of all you are.

*** One of the reasons why Jesus came was to make in the world new orders in the Spirit. We must this morning see our vocation in the Spirit. We must under all Circumstances understand that God has something far over that day when we first saw the light. You must see that he took your sins only for one purpose: That you might be channels for the covenant of promise.**

***God** would not have us under any **Circumstances** to think that we are in the place of blessing when we are not in the place of humiliation and humbleness. It cannot be. **Jesus**, our blessed Lord, was the meekest, the loveliest, and the most beautiful in character. You never find him with that said: **"Stand aside now. I am a man who has the gifts!"** You never find that in **Jesus**, but he was so moved with compassion that he could raise the widow's son. [Lk 7.11-17] We will not have had compassion except by the inward power of **God** moving us. Everybody can be humble. It costs nothing except your pride and ugly self to be put out of the way.

*** No matter what ship I travel on people are always saved on that ship. And if I go on a railroad journey, I am sure there is someone saved before I get through. It isn't possible for me to live without getting people ready for dying. I believe we have to live in a new spiritual realm of grace where all our mind, our walk, and everything is in the Holy Ghost. Beloved, the Spirit alone can do this. You can never reach these attainments under any Circumstances in the flesh: "Ye are not in the flesh but the Spirit." [Ro 8.9] May God help us to see our destined position.**

*It may be a blessing for you to know that if ever I have trouble and my peace is destroyed on any line, I always know it is satanic; it is never **God** under any **Circumstances**.

If I am not at peace, there is something wrong somewhere, and I must get to know what it is because they that keep their minds stayed upon **God** shall be kept in continual peace. [Is 26.3]

When I find where the leakage is I shall be able to put my hand upon it and say, "That is healed." Beloved, **God** wants to take us into that solid peace. It will make a difference in our prayers; it will make a difference in our reading and our conversation when we are at peace with **God** and with one another. All the blasts of hell's furnace whenever they come, cannot touch you.

FAITH QUOTES FROM WIGGLESWORTH

"The way of **Faith** is the **Christ** way, bringing us to a place where there is always an Amen in our hearts to the will of **God**."

"Feed on the living **Christ** and the **Faith** of **God** will spring up within you!"

"You can never pray 'the prayer of **Faith** by looking at the **Circumstance**. There is only one place to look, and that is to **Jesus Christ**."

"**God** rejoices when we manifest a **Faith** that holds Him to His word no matter what the **Circumstances** may be."

"Great **Faith** is the product of great fights. Great testimonies are the outcome of great tests. Great triumphs can only come out of great trials."

"**Faith** is the audacity that rejoices in the fact that **God** cannot break His own Word!"

"Without **Faith** in **Jesus Christ**, you have absolutely nothing. You cannot be saved without it. You cannot be healed without it. **God** would not be able to lead you or guide you "

"What is **Faith**? It is the very nature of **God** at work in you. **Faith** is the Word of **God**...the personality Flowing through you, the character of **Jesus** in manifested in you."

"Believers were designed to operate in what is called: the law of **Faith**"

"There is only one way to all the treasures of **God** discovered in **Christ Jesus**, and that is the way of **Faith**. By **Faith** and **Faith** alone do we enter a knowledge of the attributes of **Christ** and become partakers of His beatitudes and participate in his resurrection. All His promises are Yea and Amen to them that believe."

"**Faith** is a divine act; **Faith** is **God** at work your soul. **God** operates in us and through us by **Faith** in His Son and transforms the natural into the supernatural. **Faith** is always moving, never dormant; **Faith** lays hold of **God**'s promises, **Faith** is the hand of **God**, **Faith** is the power of **God**, **Faith** never fears, **Faith** thrives in the greatest conflict, **Faith** moves even things that cannot be moved. **God** fills us with His divine power by **Faith** in **Christ**, and sin is dethroned by **Faith**."

"I believe that all lack of **Faith** is due to not feeding, drinking, thinking, speaking, singing **God**'s word!"

"To the man of **Faith** everything that is contrary to the will and the word of **God** is nothing but an opportunity to prove that **God** is true."

By Dr. Michael H Yeager

Faith-Based Outcome Independence means I am free. I'm free to obey **God**. I'm free to serve **God**. I'm free to follow **God**. I'm free to do the will of **God**, no matter what the outcome or **Circumstance**.

Most Christians when it comes to healing, will say: I know that by his stripes I am healed make the mistake of getting their mind, eyes, and heart upon the manifestation of their healing. This is where they are completely missing the target. They say they are looking to **God**, but they are looking for the manifestation. True **Faith** never considers the **Circumstances**. When their healing does not manifest the way they wanted, they begin to waiver in their **Faith** and in their confidence with **God**. I think that's what it means in Hebrews chapter 10:

Hebrews 10:36

36 For ye have need of patience, that, after ye have done the will of God, ye might receive the promise. 37 For yet a little while, and he that shall come will come, and will not tarry. [38] Now the just shall live by Faith: but if any man draw back, my soul shall have no pleasure in him. [39] But we are not of them who draw back unto perdition; but of them that believe to the saving of the soul.

And because people are not getting the outcome that they're wanting or they're expecting, or they're demanding, or they're desiring, they walk away from the will of **God**. I think a perfect example is what is happening right now in our society. This is especially true in the church.

Now **God** has given to us specific directions. He has told us what we are to do. For instance, we are to come together. If you study the global church history, you will discover that governments were upset and are upset because they could not and cannot get the believers to stop gathering.

This has brought much persecution. China currently is a very good example. You will end up going to prison if you refuse to listen to the government and gathered together with your brothers and sisters in **Christ**. Many believers are sitting in prison today in China because they said: we will come together even as **God** commanded us.

Hebrews 10:24 and let us consider one another to provoke unto love and to good works: 25 not forsaking the assembling of ourselves together, as the manner of some is; but exhorting one another: and so much the more, as ye see the day approaching.26 For if we sin wilfully after that we have received the knowledge of the truth, there remaineth no more sacrifice for sins,

Back in 2015 I wrote a book entitled:

Why We (MUST) Gather! 30 Biblical Reasons

In this book I share 30 Dynamic reasons of why we as Believers

FAITH BASED OUTCOME INDEPENDENT

must be gathering. You will discover that Amazing Miracles happen when Lovers of **Christ** come together in **Faith** and obedience to Gods Will. The best example we have of this is revealed to us in the book of ACTS. Everything that **God** did in the early church, will still happen today when each of us take our rightful place in the Body out of obedience to **God**'s Word and **God**'s will. Hopefully this book will not only open your eyes to the Amazing Possibilities that **God** has in store for YOU, but the truths in this book will be used as a wonderful tool for those in leadership to combat the lies of the enemy!

(This book is available on Amazon if you are interested)

https://www.amazon.com/dp/1495957713

MOST PASTORS FAILED THE TEST IN 2020

When the governments of the world declared that we could not come together because of a manufactured pandemic, what did most pastors do? The problem, the **Circumstance**, moved them, and they shut down their church services. They were not, **Faith**-Based Outcome Independent. In their hearts, they did not say: **God**, I am going to do your will, even if it means that I will be persecuted, prosecuted, and suffer.

I believe that history will look back at 2020 as one of the greatest failures of church leaders in America. It could have been one of the greatest moments for the church to shine. While huge box stores stayed open, liquor stores still selling booze, the doors of most churches were locked. If the pastors had a love for **Christ**, obedience to the word, and unmovable **Faith** in **God**, they would have stayed open.

Possibly if the Pastors would have had a spiritual backbone, the election of 2020 would not have been stolen by the wicked. If tens of thousands of churches had refused to bow their knees by closing their church services, the hype of having to mail in your ballots because of the plague would have failed. But because the spiritual leaders of our nation went along to get along, the enemy succeeded in turning our nation over to the wicked. **Faith** without action, without works, is dead.

What did I do as a pastor? I had decided that I would obey **God** no matter what man did to me. If it meant that I was going to have a jail ministry, then so be it. It was not a matter of pride but simple **Faith** and obedience in **Jesus Christ** and his word. **Jesus** declared: all that live righteously will be persecuted. I think that much of the Western church run from persecution. This book will is filled with many examples of men and women who have stood their ground no matter what the results would be. Hebrews 11 gives us a perfect example.

Hebrews 11:35 Women received their dead raised to life again: and others were tortured, not accepting deliverance; that they might obtain a better resurrection: 36 and others had trial of cruel mockings and scourgings, yea, moreover of bonds and imprisonment: 37 they were stoned, they were sawn asunder, were tempted, were slain with the sword: they wandered about in sheepskins and goatskins; being destitute, afflicted, tormented; 38 (of whom the world was not worthy:) they wandered in deserts, and in mountains, and in dens and caves of the earth. 39 And these all, having obtained a good report through Faith, received not the promise:

MANY BIBLICAL EXAMPLES

The Bible is full of examples from Genesis to Revelation where people were not moved by the **Circumstances**. Here is a list of some of them: Noah building the ark, Abraham forsaking his homeland, Abraham offering up Isaac, Jacob wrestling with **God**, Joseph and his dreams, the parents of Moses putting him in the Nile River, Moses' forsaking Egypt, Sampson in the Philistine temple, Gideon facing the Midianites, Samuel giving the people a king, David facing the lion, and the bear, Goliath, and running

FAITH BASED OUTCOME INDEPENDENT

from king Saul. Elijah and Elisha facing the false prophets and evil kings. The four lepers in Samaria. The three Hebrew children standing against Nebuchadnezzar. Daniel disobeying the king's edict. Mordechai refusing the bow before Haman.

This is just a small example of those who lived in the place of what I call: **Faith-Based Outcome Independence**! This is not including all the saints in the New Testament up to the present time. One of our greatest examples is **Jesus Christ** who obeyed his **Father** even to the point of all the sins of the world being placed upon him. In another chapter we will deal with nothing but what **Jesus** went through for his bride.

Think about Joseph and what he went through because of his **God-** given vision and dreams. When it was sold as a slave and ended up in Egypt.

Genesis 39:1And Joseph was brought down to Egypt; and Potiphar, an officer of Pharaoh, captain of the guard, an Egyptian, bought him of the hands of the Ishmeelites, which had brought him down thither.

For 10 years it is estimated he was a slave, but **God** prospered him. Then out of the blue the master's wife decided to seduce Joseph, but he refused her. He would not give into her seductions. This is a perfect example of: **Faith-Based Outcome Independence!**

Genesis 39:7And it came to pass after these things, that his master's wife cast her eyes upon Joseph; and she said, Lie with me.

Genesis 39:10And it came to pass, as she spake to Joseph day by day, that he hearkened not unto her, to lie by her, or to be with her.

Because Joseph refused to compromise with her, he was falsely accused and thrown into prison.

Genesis 39:20And Joseph's master took him, and put him into the prison, a place where the king's prisoners were bound: and he was there in the prison.

But even in prison Joseph would not let go of **God**'s promises. He did not grow bitter or revengeful. He was operating in the **Faith** in **God** that simply refused to be moved by his **Circumstances**. **Jesus** talks about the widow lady who walked in the same type of **Faith**.

And on just judge who did not know **God** and did not respect men would not give her justice. But she would not be moved by this wicked judge. She just kept coming back to him over and over. Finally, this judge relented and gave her justice. **Jesus** said this was an example of how the kingdom of **God** works. But he made a rather frightening statement.

Luke 18:8 I tell you that he will avenge them speedily. Nevertheless when the Son of man cometh, shall he find Faith on the earth?

PAPER BAG OVER HIS HEAD
Amazing Healing from Incurable Cancer

Back about 40 years ago, I was given a cassette tape with a wonderful testimony on it. It was about this man who was a song leader in a church. Now, this was a man who was what I call: **Faith-Based Outcome-Independent.** He began to experience strange symptoms in his head. From what I understand, he went to find out what was going on at the hospital.

After thoroughly examining him they informed him that he had a rapidly spreading cancer that manifested with tumors. They told him even if they began radiation treatments, most likely, he would still die. He went before the Lord in prayer, and the Lord

FAITH BASED OUTCOME INDEPENDENT

impressed upon him the Scripture that declared :

1 Peter 2:24 who his own self bare our sins in His own body on the tree, that we, being dead to sins, should live unto righteousness: by whose stripes ye were healed.

At that moment, he knew, that he knew, that he knew in his heart that **God** had spoken to him. He decided that he was not going to be moved by the **Circumstances**, the symptoms, or the pain no matter what the outcome. He was not simply ignoring them, but he was declaring that they had no right to exist. He spoke the word of authority over the cancer and then acted upon the word of **God**.

Philippians 4:6Be careful for nothing; but in every thing by prayer and supplication with thanksgiving let your requests be made known unto God.

 So began a very long journey of **Faith** that refused to be moved by the **Circumstances**. Tumors began to spring up all over his face and head. His head began to swell. His head and his face became so grotesque to where people could not stand to look at him. During this whole time, it was a great fight of **Faith**, but he would not be moved off of **God**'s truth. In his heart, he had decided that no matter what the outcome, he would trust **God**. The Scripture became real:

Romans 14:8 For whether we live, we live unto the Lord; and whether we die, we die unto the Lord: whether we live therefore, or die, we are the Lord's.

 One Sunday morning, his pastor came to him. he told him: brother, I am so sorry, but I cannot let you lead worship any longer. I know that you are trusting **God** for your healing, but to be honest, you have become so ugly that it is distracting everybody. Amazingly this man was not offended.

 He said: pastor, I understand, but could I suggest something? The pastor asked him: what would that be? The man said: would you let me lead worship if I put a paper bag over my head? The pastor said: you must be kidding me, right? No, I am very serious. I will put some holes in the paper bag for my eyes and my mouth. I know that **God** wants me to continue to lead worship for as long as I can. The pastor agreed to permit this man to lead the worship services with a paper bag over his head. From that moment forward he led worship with the paper bag over his head at every service until **God** supernaturally healed him.

Weeks went by, and everything said in the natural that he was getting worse, and that he would die from this terrible cancer. Now, he worked as a janitor and repairman at a local office building. At night when everybody went home, he would clean the offices, empty the garbage, and fix everything that was wrong. Because he was all alone, he had all night to pray, sing, and talk to the Lord.

One night he went into one of the closets to get some supplies and equipment. As he was in there, the door accidentally closed. Now this was a problem because these doors only opened up from the outside in, and now he was locked in this closet with no one to help get him out. Now he knew That there was space between the walls, the ceiling, and the second floor.

He would have to remove the ceiling tile and climb up between the ductwork and the electrical wiring. He climbed up on the shelving and removed one of the ceiling tiles. Then he began to position himself as he struggled to climb over the wall and out into the hallway.

As he was Squeezing his way past the wall and the ductwork, his head became wedged. His head had swollen so large that it could not fit between the top of the wall and the ductwork. His head was securely stuck.

In the natural, you would think he would break down and start crying and feeling sorry for himself, but the opposite happened. You see he knew, that he knew, that he knew he was healed no matter what the **Circumstance** said, or what people said, or what the doctors said. At that moment, he began to laugh hysterically.

Supernatural joy hit his heart, and began to flow. Eventually, he was able to wiggle through and get to the other side.

 It was not too long after **God** instantly supernaturally healed him. He went to be One night with his head swollen, ugly and covered with tumors. The next morning, he woke up completely healed. As he looked in the mirror, his head and face were completely ordinary, exactly like it was before the cancer had come. **God** had completely healed him in one night with all the symptoms gone. He was operating in **Faith-Based Outcome Independence!**

GOD SENT ME BUT

I cannot tell you how many people have come to me through the years and said: pastor Mike, I know that **God** sent me here. I know he wants me here. I know this is his will. I wish I could say that I get all excited, but I know how easily people are moved out of Gods will!

We had a young man in his 30s who came to us just about a month ago. He said he wanted to be discipled, and that **God** had sent him to us. He swore up and down that he would be with us for at least three years. I think he lasted two weeks. I am not saying that **God** did not speak to him, but he was moved by the **Circumstances**. This is illustrated to us in the book of James chapter 1.

James 1:5 If any of you lack wisdom, let him ask of God, that giveth to all men liberally, and upbraideth not; and it shall be given him. 6 But let him ask in Faith, nothing wavering. For he that wavereth is like a wave of the sea driven with the wind and tossed. 7 For let not that man think that he shall receive any thing of the Lord.

We need a **Faith** that is outcome independent. One that is built on nothing but **Christ** and his word. The test and trials of life are going to come. If we are not grounded and rooted in **Christ**, we will be like a shooting star. Here and gone within a blink of an eye.

Why do people leave so quick? I am talking about people who swore up and down that **God** had sent them. It is because they do not have **Faith** based on nothing but **God** and his word. They're looking at the size of the crowd. They're looking at the physical building. At the natural **Circumstances** all around them. They are being moved by the **Circumstance**. Of course, the satanic realm will use everything they can to get people out of the will of **God**.

Why Pastors Come and Go

Back in 1979 I was pastoring my second church. I was with the Assembly of **God** denomination. Back then I was told that the average pastor among the Assembly of **God** only stayed in the same church for about two years. Whether or not this statistic was true I'm not sure. I read another article as I was writing this book that says the average pastors stays for about four years at a church as a senior pastor. Youth pastors last about three.

Now, there are many reasons why pastors leave churches. I think one of them is because these churches are not based on biblical principles of leadership. The pastors are under the thumbs of a controlling group of the carnally minded Christians. Spiritual pastors hands in these situations many times are tied. They cannot obey **God** even if they wanted to. The evidence of this is the fact there is very few churches anymore that move in the gifts of the Holy Ghost. Most churches have a program, timetable that they are locked into.

Of course, there are pastors who simply leave because of the **Circumstance** does not suit their fleshly desires. This constant leaving makes churches doubt pastors. Small churches feel like they are steppingstones to larger churches. Many church attending Christians do not take the pastor seriously because they all know will be leaving to greener pastures.

We must question whether these are true pastors or simply hirelings. This moving on to another church every time things get rough reveals that pastors are not solid in **Jesus Christ**. Pastor turnover also undermines any teaching on reaping and sowing, patient endurance, perseverance, longsuffering, love, solid **Faith** or any such topics. **God** says that he will never leave you nor forsake you. The action of the pastor contradicts this reality. True pastors will never move on until the spirit of **God** requires them to.

CHAPTER TWO

If Only GOD's People Would Take Him at His Word, He Would Have Delivered Them Speedily!

Isaiah 58:7-8 Then shall thy light break forth as the morning, and thine health shall spring forth speedily: and thy righteousness shall go before thee; the glory of the Lord shall be thy reward.9 Then shalt thou call, and the Lord shall answer; thou shalt cry, and he shall say, Here I am. If thou take away from the midst of thee the yoke, the putting forth of the finger, and speaking vanity;

If you study the four gospels, you will discover that **JESUS** operated in unwavering **FAITH**! He was waging a battle against demonic powers, and it took a bold, audacious, and determined **FAITH** to win over the enemy.

*Acts 10:38 How **GOD** anointed **JESUS** of Nazareth with the **Holy Ghost** and with power: who went about doing good, and healing all that were oppressed of the devil; for **GOD** was with him.*

*1 John 3:8 He that committeth sin is of the devil; for the devil sinneth from the beginning. For this purpose the Son of **GOD** was manifested, that he might destroy the works of the devil.*

***JESUS** Said That the Strong And Forceful Ones Claim It For Themselves Eagerly.

MY OWN PERSONAL EXPERIENCE
Elders All Forsake Me (1983)

The elders called a special meeting with me because of their meetings with a divisive person. The four Elders and their wives sat down at a table with me. I could tell they were out for blood! They told me that they did not like the Constitution and bylaws that I had written. I reminded them that they asked me to put together these documents. That they all had agreed upon them.

They said that they had gone over them and discovered that basically, the pastor's word was law. I told them I could see where they were coming from because I had simply copied another Word of **Faith** churches bylaws. I told them that I would agree to change these bylaws to agree with the word of **GOD** to the greatest degree we could! They basically told me that not only were they going to change the bylaws, but that they would tell me when I could preach and teach, and what I could preach and teach.

I simply put my Bible down in front of me, and I told them I would submit to the word of **GOD**. They said what? I said I would submit to the word of **GOD**. Show me in **GOD**s Word my position and I would submit to that.

At that very moment, they all began to attack me, husbands, and wives. They said that I was egotistical and full of pride. During this whole terrible affair, I did not raise my voice once even though they were making terrible accusations. They accuse me of stealing money, which was ridiculous.

Everybody had agreed that I would be paid $500 a week, but up to that time I had only been receiving about $200 a week. That was my choice, which my wife and I made because as a new church we wanted the money to stay in the account to get ready for the new building and the new property.

Since 1983 up to 2022 I only received $500 a week one year. Then from 1999 to this present moment of 2020, I have not cashed a paycheck from the church. I have simply **Trust**ed and **Believe**d **GOD** for our finances, and he has always met our needs. We have given way more to the church than what the local church had given to us.

When they began to accuse me, I simply smiled at them. I told them that the Bible says contention only cometh by pride. I said to them who is it that is full of contention and strife in this meeting? Of course, that was like putting gasoline on the fire.

Proverbs 13:10 Only by pride cometh contention: but with the well advised is wisdom.

They must've had this planned out because suddenly, they all stood up and declared boldly: We are out of here! I said what do you mean? They said we are quitting! Let's see how long you can keep this church together after we are gone.

I truly **Believe** that they thought that when they walked out the door, that was the end of the church, but, that was just the beginning. 37 years have come and gone, and the Church is still going strong. Thank you, **JESUS**!

Proverbs 13:10 Only by pride cometh contention: but with the well advised is wisdom.

I Just Kept Visiting Him No Matter How He Treated Me!

One of the main Elders of our church who had left was Bill L------l. Now, Bill was a real good guy who was approximately 10 years older than me. I hated to see him leave the church simply because a man had deceived him in who he thought I was. Now, Bill was over the full Gospel businessmen's gathering in

FAITH BASED OUTCOME INDEPENDENT

Thurmont, Maryland. He had me speak numerous times at this gathering. Plus, we had cut firewood together and went on numerous adventures with our motorcycles.

Bill was one of these kinds of guys who had a hard time forgiving. Yet it was laid upon my heart to try to reach out to him. I knew what his work schedule was and when he would be home. I would drive over to his house which is about 5 miles away for my home in the evenings. If his vehicle was there, I would park my car and go up to his house and bring his doorbell. He would come to the door and look out the window, and when he saw that it was me, he would walk away. But I was not in any way discouraged because I knew it would take some time.

There were times when I went to his house, and he would be sitting out on the front porch enjoying the weather. I would pull into his driveway and when he would see that it was me, he would get up off his chair and go into the house. This continued week after week, but I never got discouraged.

There are times when I went to his house and his wife Barbara was outside with him. As I would go to park my vehicle in his driveway, he would go into the house, but his wife would stay outside. So, I would get out of my vehicle and simply go talk to her for a little bit. I never talked about what had happened with the elders, or what was happening at the church. I would just talk small talk as friends normally do. I continued this routine for numerous weeks.

One day I pulled up into his driveway and he was sitting outside with his wife. This time he did not get up to leave. I simply walked up the stairs to his porch and began to talk with him. His wife Barbara I **Believe** brought out a glass of ice-cold tea for me and Bill. We began to talk like we used to in the good old days. The wall that was between us came crumbling down.

From that moment forward until he went home to be with the Lord, we were good friends. The Bible says that love covers a multitude of sins. There are times we just must be persistent if we know that **GOD** is calling us to bring healing in a relationship in which the devil somehow divided us.

2 Timothy 2:24 And the servant of the Lord must not strive; but be gentle unto all men, apt to teach, patient, 25 in meekness instructing those that oppose themselves; if GOD peradventure will give them repentance to the acknowledging of the truth; 26 and that they may recover themselves out of the snare of the devil, who are taken captive by him at his will.

GOD Supernaturally Sent Hungry People

After the split with the previous elders, our attendance went way down to less than 40 people. To be honest I became extremely discouraged because we were on the backside of the mountain, out in the countryside. One day in prayer the Scripture came to me that said: When the wolf comes the hireling will flee!

I decided within my heart on that very day that I would not flee from this church with its small congregation no matter what. That was back in 1984, and here I am in 2022 still pastoring the same church.

The Scripture also declares: Do not despise small beginnings. The Scripture also says; Be Faithful over the little things, and **God** will make you ruler overmuch. From that moment to now **God** has allowed us to reach many people around the world.

This is a brief bio of my life: Dr. Michael met and married his wonderful wife (Kathleen) in 1978. As a direct result of the Author and his wife's personal, amazing experiences with **God**, they have had the privilege to serve as pastors/apostles, missionaries, evangelist, broadcasters, and authors for over four decades.

By **God**s Divine Grace, Doc Yeager has published over 180 books, ministered over 10,000 Sermons, and has helped to start over 25 churches. His books are filled with hundreds of their amazing testimonies of **God's** protection, provision, healing's, miracles, and answered prayers. They also have a broadcasting network that reaches around the world called the: Word Broadcasting Network.

Back to my story: So here I was with a small handful of people, just plugging away the best I knew how. Slowly but surely people began to come from the north, south, east, and west. Miracles began to happen everywhere. Eventually, our attendance including all the weekly services added up to approximately 700 people.

Most of them were coming from a long distance on the backside of the Allegheny Mountains about seven miles west of Gettysburg Pennsylvania. Dear True Ministers of **God** we should never be moved by how it looks but be sensitive to the leading and the guidance of the **Holy Ghost**.

Hearing the Voice of God Very Clearly, Agreeing with Him, and Obeying No Matter the Circumstance.

(1983)

As I was in prayer one day, the Lord quickened to my heart to build a church that would seat eight hundred people. At the time, the size of our congregation was only about seventy people, plus we had no money. I knew the members of our congregation well, and as far as I could tell, none of them were wealthy. When the Lord quickened my heart, I immediately acted upon on what he spoke to me. I went to the land that we owned which was nothing but an empty cow field. I began to walk that field declaring by the word of the Lord we would have a church upon this property that would sit 800 people. I did this day after day speaking to myself declaring what **God** had said to me.

Of course, then I had to act upon this declaration by doing the obvious. We checked with local construction companies to put up this building. Just to put up the exterior steel building and pour the concrete floor would cost us more than $800,000. I knew in my heart that this was not the way to go. There was a man in our congregation who represented Wedge Core a steel building company from South Dakota. We began to coordinate with them for the purchase of the steel we needed. They provided us with all the blueprints that were necessary for the foundation.

I located an architectural company in Hanover, Pennsylvania that was willing to work with us. I drew up a rough, simple schematic of what we were looking for, and with this drawing they were able to provide for us the simplest blueprint possible which would be approved by the state of Pennsylvania. We went through the proper process to get the right building permits from local, county, and state authorities. We had everything in hand to start the project. We had done everything we could do. Daily I was continuing to speak to myself in agreement with what **God** Had Quicken to my heart. This maintained and caused **Faith** to continue to operate within me.

Now what? We had no money. As I was in prayer, the Spirit of **God** quickened my heart to simply step out in **Faith** and do it. There was a man in our church who owned a backhoe. I approached Richard about what I wanted to do, and he said, "Let's do it." We went out to the property and staked out where the footers and foundation were going to be. Then he brought his son Carol up from Maryland to dig these footers. We ended up with a 100 x 150-foot ditch. We prayed every step of the way. As the Spirit of the Lord would quicken me, I would order the building materials.

On the day we were to lay the blocks that the metal building would sit on, it was pouring down rain. The men of the congregation wanted to cancel the Saturday work party. I told them that **God** was going to make it possible for us to lay the blocks on that day. As we were on the building site, we cried out to the Lord and immediately the rain stopped, and the sun came out! By the end of that day 500 feet of block had been laid.

My Life on the Line

The company that was providing the steel for our building called from South Dakota, telling us that the steel building was almost ready to be shipped. They said they could ship it by cash on delivery. When the building arrived, I would have to give them approximately $49,000. At the time, we only had $1,000 in our building account, with no other means of finances. The representative from the steel company also informed us they could store the building for about $1,200 a month, or they could ship it out within six to eight weeks.

As I was listening to the man over the phone, I heard the Spirit of the Lord say to me, tell them to send it! I became very still before the Lord because I wanted to make sure that I heard him correctly. The Spirit spoke to me again, tell them to send it! I told the gentlemen from the steel company to go ahead and send the building! He told me that would be fine and they would prepare it to be sent. On the other hand, he also informed me that we better be aware that if the building got there and I did not have the money, that I would be breaking interstate laws (I believe he said there were five of them) and that I would be going to jail, as I was the one who gave the approval for the building to come! I got very quiet before the Lord and asked Him.

What should I do? The Spirit once again reconfirmed, and quickened to my heart, to have them send it. Once again, I told the representative to go ahead and send it. He gave me a warning again.

The gift of **Faith** was operating in my heart, and I knew that it was done. After I got off the phone, a desire came into my heart to give away the $1,000 in our building account. I was not trying to bribe **God** to do something for us. The $1,000 we had was not going to do a thing for us, so why not give it away out of **Faith**? We took those thousand dollars and divided it up into ten different checks, sending it to ten different ministries. That Sunday, I went before the congregation and told them this story. I told them the steel was coming and if they wanted to, they could get involved. I also told them we had invested $1,000 into ten other ministries. I did inform them that if I was missing **God** in this regard, I was going to have a prison ministry. I had put my life on the line.

Amazingly, I had no fear or anxiety whatsoever during the six weeks leading up to the steel arriving. Without a shadow of a doubt, I knew the money would be there. I kept thanking **God** to myself and declaring that the money was there. The finances began to trickle in. To this day, I do not remember where it all came from. I did not beg, plead, or call anybody for money. I received a phone call approximately six weeks later from the representative of the steel company. They told me that they were loading this steel up on their big trucks and was I ready to receive it. At that point we were still $15,000.00 short of the finances we needed. I told them to go ahead and send it. Within three days the truck pulled onto our property.

I went and met the truck driver at the construction site. He handed me the paperwork. There were certain documents which I had to fill out. I started filling out the paperwork, knowing that I was still $15,000 short of the $49,000 I had to pay them in just a few short moments. As I was signing the papers, one of the men from our church pulled into the parking lot. He drove his car right up to me with his window rolled down. There was something in his right hand. He handed a check to me for $15,000! Thank you, **Jesus**!

One day as we were busy putting the steel sheeting on the roof of our new facility with a handful of volunteers, a violent windstorm blew in. It was coming over the top of the Allegheny Mountains, which are just two miles west from us. We could see very dark blue and purple clouds swirling violently and racing toward us. Lightning was striking everywhere in those clouds as echoes of thunder rolled across the valley. This was a fast-moving thunderstorm system. If that storm were to hit us with its fierce winds, we would be in big trouble. I was on the top of the building with all our volunteers. It seemed like all of us had stopped working at the same time. There were about fifteen of us there that day.

FAITH BASED OUTCOME INDEPENDENT

As I was looking at this storm, the Spirit of the Lord quickened me. **Faith** rose in my heart. Every supernatural work of **God** is from His Spirit. I told them all to stretch forth their hands toward the storm. I pointed my hand with the rest of the men towards the storm. I declared, "In the name of **Jesus Christ** of Nazareth I rebuke this storm. I command it to split in half and go around us in the name of **Jesus Christ** right now!" Whatever **God** quickened to my heart is what I spoke at that moment

When I knew it was done inside of me, I turned my back to the storm and went back to work. It seemed as if this same **Faith** also came upon the other men. As far as I know, we all turned our back to the storm and did not look back. Why? It was because we knew in our hearts that this storm had to obey. I kept on working with the men until I saw flashing and movement to my left and to my right. I stood up and looked, and this violent lightning storm was on the north and south side of us. The storm was behind us and in front of us. It had literally obeyed us. It had split right down the middle and had gone around us. When it reached the east side of us, it joined itself back together and went on its way. We just kept on with constructing our new facility that day.

Within five months of breaking ground, we had our dedication service. This first phase of construction was 15,000 square feet. The next year we added 7,500 more square feet for our Christian school. The day the steel came in for that edition we were still $5,000 short. Once again, a man from the church drove up and handed me a check for $5,000. At the time of this book being written, we have close to 40,000 square feet of building. To **God** be the glory!

Isaiah 54:17No weapon that is formed against thee shall prosper; and every tongue that shall rise against thee in judgment thou shalt condemn. This is the heritage of the servants of the Lord, and their righteousness is of me, saith the Lord.

If we had the time in this space, we could talk about many different men of **God** in the Bible. For instance, listen to what **God** said to Abraham in Genesis.

Genesis 17:3 And Abram fell on his face: and God talked with him, saying,:4 As for me, behold, my covenant is with thee, and thou shalt be a Father of many nations.:5 Neither shall thy name any more be called Abram, but thy name shall be Abraham; for a Father of many nations have I made thee.:6 And I will make thee exceeding fruitful, and I will make nations of thee, and kings shall come out of thee.

We could look at what **God** told Abraham about Sarah.

Genesis 17:15 And God said unto Abraham, As for Sarai thy wife, thou shalt not call her name Sarai, but Sarah shall her name be.

He has just told Abram to declare that he was Abraham which means **Father** of many nations. From that moment forward Abraham began to declare this to himself, and to others. Then **God** had Sarai change her name to Sarah. Because she was going to be a mother of many nations. As far as **God** was concerned it was done. But Abraham and Sarah had to get it into their hearts. For **Faith** to come and grow within our hearts, a **Faith** that will overcome the world, the flesh, and the devil, we must begin to say what **God** says about us to ourselves!

IF YOU DO NOT HAVE A FAITH THAT CRUCIFIES YOUR FLESH THEN YOU DO NOT HAVE A FAITH THAT WILL SAVE YOUR SOUL!

1 John 4:4 Ye are of God, little children, and have overcome them: because greater is he that is in you, than he that is in the world.

We could talk about **God** telling Joshua to march around the city of Jericho one time every day, and seven times on the seventh day. That when the children of Israel obeyed this direction **God** himself would cause the walls of Jericho to fall flat. If we could have been there on those seven days, I believe we would have heard the children of Israel talking about what was going to happen on the seventh day when they had completed their **God**-given task. **Faith** always requires you to agree with **God** and obey Him! People who are teaching that you do not have to do anything are extremely deceived, and never will really have many results!

When the Going Gets Tough the Tough Get Going

Remember spiritual leaders can only take you where they live. There is an old saying that declares: **when the going gets tough, the tough get going!** The Christian meaning of this declaration would be: when there are problems, spiritually strong people look to **God** and stand upon the word no matter the **Circumstance**. the Scripture declares that we are required to be faithful.

1 Corinthians 4:2 Moreover it is required in stewards, that a man be found faithful.

Practice what we preach!

Pastors have been leaving congregations so quickly Christians assume this is what pastors should do. Many people look at me in a strange way when I tell them I have been in the same church for going on 40 years.

It is amazing the number of pastors who criticize people for "church hopping, but all reality Church hopping describes what most pastors are doing.

If churches are going to help people grow in **Christ**, it's going to take a long time (a "long time" is more than four years incidentally). It requires stability, consistency, patience, time, and effort. If every four years a believer starts over with another pastor who has no idea who they are, how are they going to grow? In what way are pastors helping people grow if they are constantly leaving people?

Staying at a church for 20 years to prove a point is not what I am talking about. But four years is not enough time to really help people grow spiritually. Four years is here and gone in a nanosecond.

We then blame our lack of **Faith** on **God**'s calling. They will say: "I really feel as though **God** is leading me to another church," based upon their **Circumstances**. Pastors who have need to develop a **Faith That Is Outcome Independent**.

"But every pastor I know is constantly moving on to another church they might say". That is no justification. I guess the question you need to ask yourself is: did **God** really call me to this church? Did he even really call me to pastor? If you're trying to pastor a church without **God**'s divine call it is like a square peg in a round hole.

If **God** did not call you to pastor, or the pastor that church, then you need to repent, and move on. People pastor churches because of convenience, security or because of promised provisions. That is not a good reason the pastor a church. You should only pastor the church if **God** has called you to that church.

Now, if **God** has called you to a church, it does not mean it's going to go your way. Most likely it will be the greatest battle of your life to stay there. You have to stick it out and pay the price. Yes, there will be sacrifices, sufferings and hard times. I know what I'm talking about. For almost the first 36 years of pastoring the same church, it was tough going. Yes, there is times of refreshing's and blessings, but most times it was nothing but a battle. A spiritual fight to keep it open, to keep preaching, to keep believing, to be faithful.

Lack of Faith and Not of Money

FAITH BASED OUTCOME INDEPENDENT

I was walking the floor of our sanctuary one afternoon, crying out to **God** concerning the finances of the church. We had some overwhelming financial needs that were weighing heavily upon my heart. As I was letting my needs be known, I Heard in my heart **God** say to me:

Your problem is not money or lack of finances. Your problem is a lack of **Faith**! You do not need more money. You need more **Faith** in Me.

I took this to heart and asked **God** to forgive me for complaining and whining. Just a couple days after that I was sitting in my office with approximately twenty-four thousand dollars' worth of bills sitting in front of me. I had piled all the bills in one spot, laid my hands upon the needs, and confessed every bill paid according to **God**'s riches in glory.

As I was praying, there was a knock on my door. I told the person who was knocking to come on in. One of the men of the church came into my office. He was a very quiet man, and we had never really spoken very much to each other. He seemed to be just a very nice everyday person. Out of the blue, he asked me "Pastor, how much money do you need to bring all the bills up to date?"

I asked him, "You mean to bring the bills current?"

He responded, "Yes, to pay the bills up to date."

He pulled out a blank check and began to write on it. The thought entered my mind that he was going to make a small contribution towards the bills. I told him it would take twenty-four thousand dollars to bring the bills up to date. He handed me a check and I thanked him for it. Then I took a peek at it. I looked up at him, and back down to the check again.

He had handed me a check for twenty-four thousand dollars! In a thousand years, I would never have guessed this quiet man who seemed to have no money, would have that kind of wealth available. It took this man more **Faith** to give that money than it did for me to receive it. Thank **God** for obedient people that are willing to do what **God** says no matter what it costs them.

GOD's presence disappears.

This Little Teaching Could Save Your Life!

In our walk with **GOD**, there are many things that we absolutely must learn. I wish that we could instantly learn them just from reading the Bible, but this is not the case. I had to learn a very hard lesson early in my Christian walk that many who have walked with **GOD** for years still have not learned. I believe the reason I had to learn this lesson was because of the number of trials, tests, and hardships that I was about to experience throughout my lifetime. I had to learn how to not live by feelings or by the **Circumstances** that surrounded me.

I gave my heart to **CHRIST** on February 18th, 1975. The reality of **CHRIST** came rushing inside of me like a mighty ocean of life. My whole life before had been filled with pain, sorrow, depression, low self-esteem, physical disabilities, etc. You name it, and I had it. But when I gave my heart to **CHRIST**, the presence of **GOD** instantly overwhelmed me. It was like electricity going through my body 24 hours a day, seven days a week. This did not go away but continued upon me.

I instantly was set free from all addictions, as well as my emotional and mental problems. I was a brand-new creation in **CHRIST JESUS**. I fell in love with my Lord Head over heels. I immediately began devouring the Word of the Living **GOD**, specifically the four Gospels. I got filled with the Holy Ghost, healed, and preached my first sermon very shortly after I was saved. I think that I took the presence and the touch of **GOD** upon my life for granted at that time as if that was the normal everyday experience for every believer. I was soon to discover this was not true.

One morning I got up early to pray and to read my Bible as normal, but something was wrong. I had grown used to the very tangible presence and the manifestation of **GOD** but, to my shock and horror, it was gone. I mean to me personally; the presence of **GOD** was gone. Confusion suddenly clouded my heart and my mind. I cried out to **GOD**, "Lord, what's wrong. How have I offended you?" I did not hear any answer which was, to me, also very strange. The Lord was constantly speaking to my heart. I examined myself to see if there was something I was doing that was against the will of **GOD**. I could not find anything wrong.

I didn't know what else to do, and I didn't really have anyone that I could go to at that time who was mature enough to help me. So, I kept reading my bible, kept on praying, worshipping, praising, and sharing **CHRIST** as I went along. I went to bed that night with no sense of **GOD**'s presence.

The next morning, I got up early, hoping that His presence had come back, but to my shock and sadness, **GOD** was not there. Once again, I went through the torment of examining my heart, crying out to **JESUS**, and following my regular routine throughout the day. I went to bed that night in the same condition. Now, during this whole experience, I did not back off or give up but just kept pressing on.

This went on day after day after day. **GOD** just was not there in His tangible presence. Yes, I did get depressed, but I did not give up. I did not stop praying or reading my bible. I never ceased worshiping and praising **GOD**. I did not stop sharing my **FAITH** with others and telling them the wonderful things **JESUS** had done for me. I think approximately two weeks went by with me in this spiritual desert —a no man's land— a dark and dry place in my daily walk.

I did not know what was wrong, but there was nothing else I could do but to keep pressing in closer. After about two weeks, I went to bed one night praying and talking to **GOD** even though he was not answering me in the same way as He did before.

The next morning, I got up early once again and began to pray when, out of the blue, **GOD**'s presence came rushing in stronger than ever like a mighty wind. It was like a powerful tsunami, a forceful flood of His presence and His Spirit. **GOD**'s touch was upon me greatly. I began to laugh, to cry, and to shout. Oh, it was so good to have **GOD** with me again. I said to the Lord when I was finally able to talk, "Lord, where were you?"

There seemed to be a long pause, then He said to me with what seemed to be a bit of amusement in His voice, "I Was Here All along." You were, Lord? Yes, He replied. And then he said something that was to forever change my life. "I was teaching you how to live by **FAITH**." He then began to very specifically teach me out of the scriptures that man does not live by bread alone but by every word that comes out of the mouth of **GOD**.

I learned that our walk with Him does not depend upon our feelings, emotions, location, or **Circumstance** and that many of those who are believers are destroyed by the enemy because they do not understand nor believe this. Even the apostle Paul had to learn how to be content in **CHRIST** in whatever condition, trusting **GOD**, knowing that He is not a man that He should lie. **CHRIST** has said that he would never leave us nor forsake us. We may call upon **CHRIST** with a sincere heart, knowing that He will be there for us to answer us and to show us great and mighty things which we know not!

Over 45 years have come and gone since I learned this lesson. I now no longer allow the feelings of either His absence or His presence to affect me. Of course, I constantly examine my heart but if I can find nothing wrong, I simply realize that I am flying by instruments, no longer operating by visual flight rules (VFR).

Thank **GOD**, as the aviation industry would say, I am SFR

rated! There are two sets of regulations governing all aspects
of civilian aircraft operations: the first is Instrument flight
rules (IFR), and the second is visual flight rules (VFR) defined as
flying by sight and sensory input. All believers are to be rated as
(SFR) which would equate to **Spiritual Flight Rules**!

*Romans 4:18 Who against hope believed in hope, that he might
become the FATHER of many nations; according to that which
was spoken, So shall thy seed be.*

Tuck Going to Beat Me to a Pulp

I knew a big Texan in the Navy who rode bulls in rodeos at one
time. We called him Tuck; to this day, I don't know why. We also
called him TEX. After I gave my heart to **Jesus Christ**, as a 19-
year-old kid, I shared the gospel with him, his friends, and as many
as I could. The Spirit of the Lord had begun to move upon one of
Tuck's friends. Tuck was extremely irritated at me for causing this
man to come under conviction. Up until the time I had given my
heart to **Jesus**, tuck had been a good friend of mine. But now that I
was in love with **Christ**, he did not want anything to do with me.
Whenever he looked at me, it was with great disdain.

One-night, Tuck came into my room completely intoxicated with
alcohol. He woke me up banging on my door like a madman. I
went out to see what he wanted. When I entered the foyer, he
grabbed me by the neck with his large left hand. He picked me up
off the floor by my neck and slammed me against the wall.

 He clenched his right hand into a fist right in front of my face
pulling it back as if getting ready to hit me with all of his might. It
seemed as if his fist was as big as my face. He told me that he
would pulverize me if I did not promise to leave one of his
drinking buddies alone. The man he was speaking about had taken
an interest in the gospel.

In the natural, my heart should have been filled with great fear because, without a shadow of a doubt, he could easily beat me to death. I could see and feel the devil in him. His face was all red, and his steely blue eyes were bulging, but instead of fear, what rose in my heart was great compassion for his soul.

Right there on the spot, as I was hanging from my neck with his hand pinning me against the wall, I began to weep for him. I told him that he could do whatever he wanted to do to me, but I would never stop preaching and exalting **Jesus Christ**. I told him that I loved him, and he needed to get right with **God**.

He began to shake violently, like a leaf in a strong wind. His fist was moving back and forth in front of my face. His mouth was moving erratically, with foam coming between his teeth and hanging on his lips. During this time the other men in my barracks had heard the commotion and were all standing around watching this event unfold. After what seemed a long time, Tuck finally lowered his fist and put me down. He turned around without a word and walked away from me. From that moment until I left the Navy, he never spoke to me again.

Many years later, I was talking with Willie, the cowboy. Willie had become a master chief in the Navy, and his expertise was underwater demolition. I asked what had happened to Tuck. Right after that event with me, he said, Tuck lost his mind. He took his Colt 44 magnum pistol and walked up to our military base commander and put the gun against his head.

Thank **God** he did not shoot the man, but of course, he was arrested and court-martialed. Tuck ended up being an alcoholic, which caused him to lose his wife and family, and then he was diagnosed with cancer.

Up to this point, it would look like there is no hope talk at all. Oh, how wrong we can be. **God** is more than able to intervene when people stand in the gap. From the time that talk was going to beat me to a pulp until I heard about him years later, I never stopped lifting him before the Lord. Years later, when Willie contacted me and told me the rest of the story, my heart was filled with tremendous joy. The day will come when I meet Tuck on the other side.

Tucks Tragic Beginning - But a Glorious End

Now the story has a wonderful ending. Willie, the cowboy, told me that he was not right with **God** during his Navy time. But the spirit of **God** had arrested him, and he had gotten right with **Jesus**.

Willy the cowboy had stayed in contact with Tuck all of those years and eventually had a chance to speak to him about the Lord. Before Tuck died, Willie had the opportunity to lead Tuck to **Christ**, and he was gloriously born again. Shortly after that, Tuck died and went home to be with the Lord. Someday, Lord willing, I will see him again. Only this time, we will have sweet fellowship.

Not by works of righteousness which we have done, but according to his mercy he saved us, by the washing of regeneration, and renewing of the Holy Ghost (Titus 3:5).

I TELL MY BODY TO GET INLINE!

Times and I can tell you when I had been hit by sickness or disease, I boldly stood against it. In the natural it seemed like I should have run to the doctors, but instead I looked to the great physician. You see I was **Faith-Based Outcome Independent**. The reality of what **Christ** had done for me when he received 39 stripes upon his back created this **Faith** within my heart.

How I Was HEALED of a Broken Back

I share these stories, my personal experiences, hoping that they will give you an insight in how to receive healing, even in the most difficult situations. Now in the winter of 1978, I was working at the Belleville Feed & Grain Mill as a 21-year-old kid. My job was to pick up the corn, wheat, and oats from the farmers, and bring it to the mill. There it would be mixed and combined with other products for the farmers' livestock.

One cold, snowy day, the owner of the feed mill told me to deliver a load of cattle feed to an Amish farm. It was an extremely bad winter that year, with lots of snow. I was driving an International 1600 Lodestar. I backed up as far as I could to this Amish man's barn without getting stuck.

The Amish never had their lanes plowed in those days, and they most likely still do not. I was approximately seventy-five feet away from his barn, which meant that I had to carry the bags at least seventy-five feet. I think there were about eighty bags of feed, with each bag weighing approximately one hundred pounds. During those years I only weighed about 130 pounds.

I would carry one bag on each of my shoulders, stumbling and pushing my way through the heavy, deep snow to get up the steep incline into the barn. Then I would stack the bags in a dry location. As usual, nobody came out to help me. Many a time when delivering things to the farms, the Amish would watch me work without lending a helping hand.

About the third trip, something frightening happened to me as I was carrying two one-hundred-pound bags upon my shoulders. I felt the bones in my back snap. Something drastic just happened. I fell to the ground at that very moment almost completely crippled. I could barely move. I was filled with intense overwhelming pain.

I had been spending a lot of my time meditating in the Word of **God**. Every morning, I would get up about 5:00 a.m. to study. I had one of those little bread baskets with memorization scriptures in it. I believe you can still buy them to this day at a Christian bookstore. Every morning I would memorize from three to five of them. It would not take me very long, so all day long I would be meditating on these verses.

The very minute I fell, immediately I cried out to **Jesus**, asking him to forgive me for my pride, and for being so stupid in carrying two hundred pounds on my little frame. After I asked **Jesus** to forgive me, I commanded my back to be healed in the name of **Jesus Christ** of Nazareth.

Since I believed I was healed, I knew that I had to act now upon my **Faith**. Please understand that I was full of tremendous pain, but I had declared that I was healed by the stripes of **Jesus**. The Word of **God** came out of my mouth as I tried to get up and then fell back down.

Even though the pain was more intense than I can express, I kept getting back up speaking the name of **Jesus**, then I would fall back down again. I fell down more times than I can remember. After some time, I was able to take a couple steps, then I would fall again. This entire time I was saying, "In the name of **Jesus**, in the name of **Jesus**, in the name of **Jesus**."

I finally was able to get to the truck. I said to myself if I believe I'm healed then I will unload this truck in the name of **Jesus**. Of course, I did not have a cell phone in order to call for help and the Amish did not own any phones on their property. Now, even if they would have had a phone, I would not have called for help. I had already called upon my help, and His name was **Jesus Christ**. I knew in my heart that by the stripes of **Jesus** I was healed. I then pulled a bag off of the back of the truck, with it falling on top of me. I would drag it a couple feet, and then fall down.

Tears were running down my face as I spoke the Word of **God** over and over. By the time I was done with all of the bags, the sun had already gone down. Maybe six or seven hours had gone by. I painstakingly pulled myself up into that big old 1600 Lodestar. It took everything within me to shift gears, pushing in the clutch, and driving it. I had to sit straight like a board all the way.

I finally got back to the feed mill late in the evening. Everybody had left for home a long time ago with the building being locked up. I struggled out of the Lodestar and stumbled and staggered over to my Ford pickup. I got into my pickup and made it back to the converted chicken house. I went back to my cold, unheated, plywood floor room. It took everything in me to get my clothes off. It was a very rough and long night.

The next morning when I woke up, I was so stiff that I could not bend in the least. I was like a board. Of course, I was not going to miss work, because by the stripes of **Jesus** I was healed. In order to get out of bed, I had to literally roll off the bed, hitting the floor. Once I had hit the floor, it took everything for me to push myself back up into a sitting position.

The tears were rolling down my face as I put my clothes and shoes on, which in itself was a miracle. I did get to work on time, though every step was excruciatingly painful. Remember, I was only twenty-one at the time, but I knew what **Faith** was and what it wasn't. I knew that I was healed no matter how it looked, that by the stripes of **Jesus Christ** I was healed.

When I got to work, I did not tell my boss that I had been seriously hurt the day before. I walked into the office trying to keep the pain off of my face. For some reason he did not ask me what time I made it back to work. I did not tell him to change the time clock for me in order to be paid for all of the hours I was out on the job. They had me checked out at the normal quitting time. (The love of money is what causes a lot of people not to get healed.)

My boss gave me an order for feed that needed to be delivered to a local farmer. If you have ever been to a feed and grain mill, you know that there is a large shoot where the feed comes out. After it has been mixed, you must take your feed bag, and hold it up until it's filled. It creates tremendous strain on your arms and your back, even if you're healthy.

As I was filling the bag, it almost felt like I was going to pass out, because I was in tremendous pain. Now, I'm simply saying, "In the name of **Jesus**, in the name of **Jesus**, in the name of **Jesus**" under my breath. The second bag was even more difficult than the first bag, but I kept on saying, "In the name of **Jesus**."

I began on the third bag and as I was speaking the name of **Jesus**, the power of **God** hit my back and I was instantly and completely, totally healed from the top of my head, to the tip of my toes. I was healed as I went on my way. My place of employment never did know what had happened to me. That has been 38 years ago, and my back is still healed by the stripes of **Christ** to this day.

And from the days of John the Baptist until now the kingdom of heaven suffereth violence, and the violent take it by force (Matthew 11:12).

JESUS OPERATED IN FAITH BASED OUTCOME INDEPENDENCE

When he said: eat my flesh and drink my blood, he knew that his disciples would walk away from him. And when they did, he said to the 12 that were left, do you wish to go to? He never held anything back but spoke everything the **Father** told him to even though he knew the people to rise up against him.

Fourteen times it is revealed from Matthew to the gospel of John, they either tried to kill him or plotting to kill him. But he did not back off for one second from the will of the **Father**. He said his face like a flint all the way to the cross.

Isaiah 50:7For the Lord God will help me; therefore shall I not be confounded: therefore have I set my face like a flint, and I know that I shall not be ashamed.

Ezekiel 3:9As an adamant harder than flint have I made thy forehead: fear them not, neither be dismayed at their looks, though they be a rebellious house.

He was not moved by anything that was contrary to the will of his **Father**. We will go into much greater detail about the sufferings of **Christ**, and how he did not allow these sufferings to stop him from doing the **Father**'s will.

THE PATIENCE OF JOB

James 5:11 Behold, we count them happy which endure. Ye have heard of the patience of Job, and have seen the end of the Lord; that the Lord is very pitiful, and of tender mercy.

I really believe that **God** was happy with job because he did not curse **God** or give up on **God**. Yes, his theology was all messed up. (I've written a book about job, and the fact that there were 21 things he said about **God** that was not true. But he could not be held to blame because there was no one to teach him proper theology.)

 Even though his theology was all messed up guess what job did? Remember his wife told him, why don't you just curse **God** and die? And he said: you talk like one of the foolish women. And remember, that's what the devil said to **God**. The devil said, if you would just let me go after job and rob him of everything he has and even afflict his body with terrible afflictions, then he will curse you.

Well, guess what job did? Now, job was confused. He was messed up because he did not have the four Gospels of **Jesus Christ**. He did not have Matthew, Mark, Luke, and John, to reveal to him exactly how the heavenly **Father** operates, and what he does. Remember these life-changing words of **Jesus**:

John 10:10The thief cometh not, but for to steal, and to kill, and to destroy: I am come that they might have life, and that they might have it more abundantly.

 Job said: **though, he slays me yet, will I praise him?** That's being independent of outcome. You're being free. You're not being controlled. **God** has not given us a spirit of fear, but of power, love, and a sound mind. As we look at the church today, are they being moved by **Circumstances**? Are they being they being shifted? Are they being driven? The reason why the early church was so persecuted and prosecuted, imprisoned. They were abused and even murdered because they were outcome independent.

They were not allowing themselves to be controlled, to be manipulated, to be bullied, to be put under the thumb of the government. They were even told to not preach the name of **Jesus** anymore. You know what they said:

Acts 5:28 saying, Did not we straitly command you that ye should not teach in this name? and, behold, ye have filled Jerusalem with your doctrine, and intend to bring this man's blood upon us.29 Then Peter and the other apostles answered and said, We ought to obey God rather than men. 30 The God of our fathers raised up Jesus, whom ye slew and hanged on a tree.

ONE OF HE GREATEST NEEDS

We need people today in the body of **Christ**, in the church to arise and be **Faith Based Outcome Independent**. Duration says: I am going to obey **God** what the outcome is.

I will do what **God** tells me to do. I will not turn away from it to the left hand or to the right hand. I'm going all the way. That's what **Jesus** did. Remember. He was in the garden of Gethsemane when he said his soul was close to death. Walking and living and moving in **Faith**, in confidence in **God**, does not mean it's going to be easy peasy. It does not mean it's going to be cotton candy.

It does not mean it will be apple pie. It does not mean you are getting everything you want in this world. Matter of fact, the Bible says all that live righteously will be persecuted. Why would they be persecuted? Because people who live by **Faith-Based Outcome Independence**, cannot be controlled by the world, flesh, or the devil.

There is this place in **Faith** that keeps you right smack dab in the middle of the will of **God**. No matter what the **Circumstances** or the environment is. You might say that is a spiritual GPS system. This GPS system will take you where the flesh does not want to go. No matter what the condition of the road is, no matter what the weather is, no matter what is happening, this type of **Faith** does the same thing.

A good quality compass is going to give you true north, no matter what. That's what **Faith** does. **Faith** causes you to discover the will of **God**. How by the word of **God**, you find out what the will of **God** is. And if you're really walking by **Faith** you go in that direction. For instance:

Philippians 4:19 But my God shall supply all your need according to his riches in glory by Christ Jesus.

We agree with this declaration whether it looks like our needs are met or not. **Circumstances** cannot make **God** a liar. So, this type of **Faith** says let **God** be true, and everything else a lie. This type of **Faith** also declares:

1 Peter 2:24 who his own self bare our sins in his own body on the tree, that we, being dead to sins, should live unto righteousness: by whose stripes ye were healed.

God also declares: ***Hebrews 13:5 Let your conversation be***

FAITH BASED OUTCOME INDEPENDENT

*without covetousness; and be content with such things as ye
have: for he hath said, I will never leave thee, nor forsake thee.*
No matter what it looks like or how it feels or what's happening.
Circumstances cannot change the promises of **God**.

There are over 7000 promises within the Bible for the believer.
You see when we agree with **God** matter what the **Circumstance**,
this is **Outcome Independent**. I don't feel like **God** loves me. I
don't feel like **God** is with me. I don't feel like **God** is helping me,
but he is. He said: call on me and I will answer you and show you
greater mighty things, which, we do not know. **God** is an ever
present helping in the time of trouble. Do you believe that dear
Saint? That he is who he says he is? No matter how it looks, no
matter it seems, no matter what's going on.

This is **Faith-Based Outcome Independence.** Oh, how we need
that today in this modern-day church. Oh, how we've watched
people get moved out of the will of **God** because of their bodies,
because of their **Circumstances**, because of so-called experts'
opinions.

CHAPTER THREE
FAITH Comes by Hearing JESUS
CHRIST Preached And Exalted!

Romans 10:13-15 For whosoever shall call upon the name of the Lord shall be saved. 14 How then shall they call on <u>him</u> in whom they have not believed? and how shall they believe in <u>him</u> of whom they have not heard? and how shall they hear without a preacher? 15 And how shall they preach, except they be sent? as it is written, How beautiful are the feet of them that preach the gospel of peace, and bring glad tidings of good things!

GAVE IT ALL AWAY

All these years, we've been married, we always been givers. A lot of times it looked like we were being stupid. Many times, the Lord would have us to give in **Circumstances** that seemed to be completely insane. For, another words, we needed every penny we had plus a lot, lot, lot more, and we didn't have it. And the Lord would speak to me and tell us to empty our bank account and give it away. Isn't that crazy? No, it's the obedience of **Faith**. It's living by **Faith**. It's not easy. It's an audacious **Faith**. It's a **Faith** that says, you know what? All I know is what **God** it is telling us to do, and we are going to be obedient.

Not that I speak in respect of want: for I have learned, in whatsoever state I am, therewith to be content. I know both how to be abased, and I know how to abound: everywhere and in all things I am instructed both to be full and to be hungry, both to abound and to suffer need. I can do all things through CHRIST which strengtheneth me (Philippians 4:11-13).

LEFT THE PEA PATCH FOR THE LAST TIME

2 Samuel 23:11 And after him was Shammah the son of Agee the Hararite. And the Philistines were gathered together into a troop, where was a piece of ground full of XXXentils: and the people fled from the Philistines. 12 But he stood in the midst of the ground, and defended it, and slew the Philistines: and the Lord wrought a great victory.

Schamma was recorded as one of David's mighty men. Now Schamma had a pea patch that he farmed. Every year they would plant beans or lentils. And, and right during the time of harvest the Philistines would come and they would take away their hard worked harvest.

And every year, all the Israelites would run for their life. But finally, Schamma had had enough. He rose up in **Faith** and declared: enough it is enough. I'm not going anywhere. He was not a warrior. He was not a soldier. He said: I'm going to stand on this ground, and if I die, I die!

It wasn't pride. It wasn't arrogance. The Bible says, **God** gave him a mighty victory. Now stop and think about this. A mighty, mighty victory. **God** gave him a mighty, mighty victory. Why? Because he stood his ground. See, this is what we're talking about. **Faith-**

Based Outcome Independent. I am going to stand my ground.

That's what we've done for almost 40 years here at this church. **God** sent us to this area back in 1982. And we have stuck with it. We have stood and we are going to stand until the Lord tells us it's time to move on. We are going to be faithful. The Bible says:

Proverbs 25:19 Confidence in an unfaithful man in time of trouble is like a broken tooth, and a foot out of joint.

People will come and they will seem like they're drawing close to **God**, but the next thing you know, they're gone. I'm not assuming people are just going to leave, but they're just gone. Why? Because their **Faith** was not deep in **God**. See, I remember the, the song, I'm like a tree planted by their rivers of water. I shall not be, I shall not be moved. That's what we're talking about. We're talking about **Faith Based Outcome Independence**. We're talking about being obedient to **God**.

POWERFUL SCRIPTURES

I think one of the most powerful set of scriptures dealing with **Faith-based outcome independent is** in Habakkuk chapter three, beginning with verse. Listen to what this prophet said by the spirit of the Lord.

Habakkuk 3:17 Although the fig tree shall not blossom, neither shall fruit be in the vines; the labour of the olive shall fail, and the fields shall yield no meat; the flock shall be cut off from the fold, and there shall be no herd in the stalls: 18 yet I will rejoice in the Lord, I will joy in the God of my salvation.

I want you to listen to this Prophets attitude. This is what **Faith-Based Outcome Independent** looks like. This Psalmist, this writer of the book said: I'm going to stay with **God**'s even if it seems like everything is a disaster. I'm not giving up. I'm not quitting. You know, some people would have you to believe that if you're in the will of **God**, everything is going to be peaches and cream, hunky-dory. Many times, when you're smack dab in the middle of the will of **God** is when the devil hits you the hardest.

Truskowski Tries to Stab Me to Death

After being born again for a while, I perceived in my heart that I needed to reach out and witness to the gang I used to run with right outside of Chicago. We were not a gang in the sense that we had a name or any entrance rituals that we had to go through. We were just a group of young men who were constantly involved in corruption, drinking, fighting, using drugs, stripping cars, and doing other things too horrible that I will not mention. One day, I was sitting in a car between the two instigators of most of our shenanigans, Gary, and Claire. Both men were very large and quite muscular.

I had fervently shared **CHRIST** with them and the others to let them know how much **GOD** had changed me. They sat around drinking, using dope, and cussing while I shared the good news with them. I explained I was on a heavenly high that drugs and the world could never take them to. Most of them just stared at me, not knowing how to respond. They all had known the old Mike Yeager. The crazy and Ungodly stuff that I had done. They had seen me many times whacked out on drugs and alcohol. Now here I was a brand-new creation in **CHRIST** preaching **JESUS** with a deep and overwhelming zeal.

Now Gary who was one of the main leaders, was different in many negative ways than the other guys. He was like a stick of dynamite ready to explode at any moment. He had been up to the big house already and spent some time behind the bars of justice. He never did like me, but now there was an unspoken, seething hatred for me under the surface, which eventually exploded. We were coming out of Racine, Illinois, as Gary was driving the car we were in. Claire was sitting against the door on the right side in the front seat, with me in the middle. At that moment I did not realize why they had put me in the middle, but it became obvious.

Before I knew it, Gary reached up and grabbed a large knife from the dashboard of the car. I believe the vehicle was an old Impala that had the old-style steel dashboard. The heating and air conditioning were controlled by sliders in the dash. The knife had been shoved down into one of the slots. He pulled the knife out of the dashboard with his right hand, jabbed it high up into the air, and drove it down toward me very fast, trying to stab me in the gut with this knife. I saw him reach for the knife, and at that very moment, I entered the realm of the Spirit when time seems to come to a standstill. This has happened to me on numerous occasions in such dangerous situations.

When I enter this realm, time slows down while my speed or movement seems to increase. You could argue whether I speed up or time slows down. I really can't say, though; it just happens.

The knife came down toward my guts in slow motion, and I saw my hands reaching up towards the knife and grabbing Gary's wrist to prevent him from stabbing me through the gut. I could not prevent the knife from coming down, but I was able to cause it to plunge into the seat instead. His thrust had been so powerful that the knife literally pierced all the way down through the Springfield car seat. He immediately pulled it out of the car seat and tried to stab me again. He continued to try to stab me as he was driving down the road. Every time he tried to stab me, I was able to divert the stab just fractions of an inch away from my privates and for my legs.

During this entire event, the peace of **GOD** was upon me in an overwhelming way. I was not shaking or breathing hard in the least; neither was my heart beating fast. It sounds unbelievable, I know, but it felt as if I were in heaven. The presence and the peace of **GOD** were upon me in a powerful supernatural way. I know this might sound extremely strange and weird, but I was kind of enjoying myself as I was watching **GOD** deliver me from this madman.

During this entire time, it was like a slow-motion review of a movie. Up and down the knife came as he kept on trying to kill me. This large muscular man was not able to kill a small 5'8" skinny guy. I just love how **GOD** does supernatural miracles. There was not one thing in my life in which I knew I was out of **GOD**'s will. I believe if I had been out of the will of **GOD** most likely Gary would've succeeded in murdering me. He kept on trying to kill me until up ahead of us a police car came out from a side road. Gary's car window was open and when he saw the policeman, he threw the knife out the window.

Gary continued to drive down the road without ever saying a word about what had just happened. In this whole situation, Claire who I had thought was a friend of mine, did not in any way try to help me. No one said a word as we drove down the road, but the peace of **GOD** was upon me like I have the invisible blanket.

Thou wilt keep him in perfect peace, whose mind is stayed on thee: because he trusteth in thee. Trust ye in the LORD forever: for in the LORD JEHOVAH is everlasting strength (Isaiah 26:3-4).

Truskowski Shoots Me with a Shotgun

About two days later I had to go to Gary's house. I really shouldn't have gone there, because there was just something satanic and evil about him. Just the day before, he tried to stab me to death! When I pulled up in my sister's red Maverick, he was sitting on his porch. When he saw me get out of the car, he grabbed a shotgun (I think it was a twelve gauge) that had been leaning against his house on the porch.

I walked toward him, and he aimed it right at my stomach. What was there about my gut that he was so enamored by it? There was no fear in my heart in the least. I just kept walking toward him with Divine confidence and boldness. I was about twenty feet away from him when the barrel of the gun jerked slightly to the right as the gun went off.

The sound of the gun echoed through the valley. Nothing happened to me! As I think back to that day, I firmly believe an angel nudged that gun barrel with his little finger. If there was birdshot in the gun, no pellets hit me, and if there was a deer slug in it, I did not feel it go by.

I was not shaking or breathing hard in the least; neither was my heart beating fast. It sounds unbelievable, I know, but once again, it felt as if I was in heaven. I walked up the steps of the porch and walked up to Gary. I took the gun out of his hand and leaned it back against the house. Gary just stared at me without saying a word. That was the last time I ever saw Gary. I have no idea what happened to him.

No weapon that is formed against thee shall prosper; and every tongue that shall rise against thee in judgment thou shalt condemn. This is the heritage of the servants of the LORD, and their righteousness is of me, saith the LORD (Isaiah 54:17).

A Good Description of How FAITH In CHRIST Operates

I love this quote from Smith Wigglesworth Who was Mightily used of **GOD**:

"Natural" men see things only as they appear, but "spiritual" men see things completely differently. There is a divine, and inward violence called **FAITH** that refuses to agree with the devil. It refuses to call **GOD** a liar by disagreeing with Him. **No Matter What Men of FAITH** understand that **Change Will Not Come Without Confrontation**.

FAITH BASED OUTCOME INDEPENDENT

We must confront ourselves, our **Circumstances**, and the demonic world: without compromising our character, attitude, or personality.

I HAVE LEARNED TO NOT BE MOVED BY CIRCUMSTANCES

Paul the apostle reveals within the epistles that he wrote that he had learned how to live by **Faith – Based Outcome Independence!**

Philippians 4:11 Not that I speak in respect of want: for I have learned, in whatsoever state I am, therewith to be content. 12 I know both how to be abased, and I know how to abound: every where and in all things I am instructed both to be full and to be hungry, both to abound and to suffer need.

We're talking about **Faith** that is rooted and grounded, deep into **God**. A **Faith** that is not moved by the **Circumstances**. We will not allow ourselves to be driven out of the will of **God** by whatever problems confront us. A perfect example is the three Hebrew children, who refused to bow before the statue of Nebuchadnezzar.

Nebuchadnezzar had a dream that was of **God**, but it became perverted in his mind. The devil put a thought in his head that he needed to build a statue to himself covered in gold. And that everyone needed to bow down and worship this statue. We can pick the story up in chapter 3 of the book of Daniel.

Daniel 3:1Nebuchadnezzar the king made an image of gold, whose height was threescore cubits, and the breadth thereof six cubits: he set it up in the plain of Dura, in the province of Babylon. 2 Then Nebuchadnezzar the king sent to gather together the princes, the governors, and the captains, the judges, the treasurers, the counsellors, the sheriffs, and all the rulers of the provinces, to come to the dedication of the image which Nebuchadnezzar the king had set up. 3 Then the princes, the governors, and captains, the judges, the treasurers, the counsellors, the sheriffs, and all the rulers of the provinces, were gathered together unto the dedication of the image that Nebuchadnezzar the king had set up; and they stood before the image that Nebuchadnezzar had set up him.

As the story continues it is revealed to Nebuchadnezzar that three Hebrew children will not bow down and worship this false golden idol. Of course, Nebuchadnezzar is filled with great rage and has the furnace heated seven times hotter than it would normally it is. These three Hebrew children could not be intimidated by nebuchadnezzar.

13 Then Nebuchadnezzar in his rage and fury commanded to bring Shadrach, Meshach, and Abed-nego. Then they brought these men before the king. 14 Nebuchadnezzar spake and said unto them, Is it true, O Shadrach, Meshach, and Abed-nego, do not ye serve my gods, nor worship the golden image which I have set up? 15 Now if ye be ready that at what time ye hear the sound of the cornet, flute, harp, sackbut, psaltery, and dulcimer, and all kinds of musick, ye fall down and worship the image which I have made; well: but if ye worship not, ye shall be cast the same hour into the midst of a burning fiery furnace; and who is that God that shall deliver you out of my hands?

They dragged these men before the king. Of course, you know they were not too gentle when they pulled them before the king. The three Hebrew children declared that they were not careful in their answer to this situation. They were very bold in their declaration because they were not ashamed of their Lord and **God**. If you study this in Hebrew context, it means that they were not afraid or intimidated in any way by Facing death for what they believed.

They boldly declared we are not afraid. We're not intimidated. We are telling you to your face, Nebuchadnezzar no matter what you do to us, no matter what you say about us, no matter how you treat us, we're not doing this. That's all there is to it. We are not doing this.

I told him go for it

I reminds me some years ago when some people got upset because I was going through the proper channels of trying to turn our gymnasium into a homeless shelter for women and children. This was during the Obama years. There were so many homeless Women and children that it was in our heart to try to help them.

Now I was following the legal process. The next thing I know The Township was knocking at my door. They had sent the head of the Sewage Enforcement Company. Now why did they do that? I have no idea. What did he have to do with homeless people? They were demanding the right to go into our building to see if we had homeless people. I informed them that we did not. I also asked him if they had gone to the local architect to find out that I had spoken to him. This man told me that they had not. But a found out later that they were lying to me.

It was late one night when suddenly there was a tremendous banging at my door. Here was the sewage enforcement officer demanding to get into our building. He was huffing and puffing and very upset. It was so comical to me that I began to laugh at him. Well, maybe I wasn't really laughing at him. I was just laughing.

 I informed him, very straightforward, that he was not going to get into our building. He said they were going to take me to court. I said let's go for it. He kept yelling at me for a while, but then eventually he left. I did eventually let them into the building, but it just proved to them that we did not have any homeless in the building.

16 Shadrach, Meshach, and Abed-nego, answered and said to the king, O Nebuchadnezzar, we are not careful to answer thee in this matter. 17 If it be so, our God whom we serve is able to deliver us from the burning fiery furnace, and he will deliver us out of thine hand, O king. 18 But if not, be it known unto thee, O king, that we will not serve thy gods, nor worship the golden image which thou hast set up.

19 Then was Nebuchadnezzar full of fury, and the form of his visage was changed against Shadrach, Meshach, and Abed-nego: therefore he spake, and commanded that they should heat the furnace one seven times more than it was wont to be heated.

Remember they told the disciples that they could not preaching the name of **Jesus**. Now, they had already been in prison because of this. They boldly declared that we will obey **God** and not man. The whole book of acts is filled with men and women that were bold in **Jesus** and did not give into the intimidation of the political leaders and religious leaders of their day.

Philippians 1:28 and in nothing terrified by your adversaries: which is to them an evident token of perdition, but to you of salvation, and that of God.

I love how the Bible says this: and do not [for a moment] be frightened or intimidated in anything by your opponents and adversaries, for such [constancy and fearlessness] will be a clear sign (proof and seal) to them of [their impending] destruction, but [a sure token and evidence] of your deliverance and salvation, and that from **God**.

Notice what the three Hebrew children said in verse 17: if it be so our **God** whom we serve can deliver us from the burning fiery furnace, but if he doesn't, were okay. That is what I call **Faith Based Outcome Independent**. That's **Faith**. Yes. Praise the Lord. We're not going to bow down to you king. We're not going to bend our knees. We're not going to compromise. Notice once again verse *18: But if not, if our God doesn't deliver us, be it known unto you Nebuchadnezzar that we will not serve your God's nor worship the golden image, which you have set up.* We're not budging a nanosecond.

I can tell you right now that **God** was extremely pleased with these three Hebrew children.

FAITH BASED OUTCOME INDEPENDENT

They're operating in **Faith-Based Outcome Independence**. They said: we are not bowing down. Nebuchadnezzar got extremely angry. He heated that furnace up seven times hotter than normal. Then it says in verse:*20 And he commanded the most mighty men that were in his army to bind Shadrach, Meshach, and Abed-nego, and to cast them into the burning fiery furnace.*

Of course, we know what happened then. Those mighty men from the army of Nebuchadnezzar were burned to death. Those three Hebrew children fell into the burning fiery furnace. When they did something supernatural took place. The ropes that were binding him burned off them. Then they began to dance and shout and praise the Lord amid those flames. Suddenly, a heavenly being was there with them. Nebuchadnezzar said he look like the son of **God**.

25 He answered and said, Lo, I see four men loose, walking in the midst of the fire, and they have no hurt; and the form of the fourth is like the Son of God.

26 Then Nebuchadnezzar came near to the mouth of the burning fiery furnace, and spake, and said, Shadrach, Meshach, and Abed-nego, ye servants of the most high God, come forth, and come hither. Then Shadrach, Meshach, and Abed-nego, came forth of the midst of the fire. 27 And the princes, governors, and captains, and the king's counsellors, being gathered together, saw these men, upon whose bodies the fire had no power, nor was an hair of their head singed, neither were their coats changed, nor the smell of fire had passed on them.

28 Then Nebuchadnezzar spake, and said, Blessed be the God of Shadrach, Meshach, and Abed-nego, who hath sent his angel, and delivered his servants that trusted in him, and have changed the king's word, and yielded their bodies, that they might not serve nor worship any God, except their own God. 29 Therefore I make a decree, That every people, nation, and language, which speak any thing amiss against the God of Shadrach, Meshach, and Abed-nego, shall be cut in pieces, and their houses shall be made a dunghill: because there is no other God that can deliver after this sort. 30 Then the king promoted Shadrach, Meshach, and Abed-nego, in the province of Babylon.

Faith-Based Outcome Independent

God will be with us in the trial. **God** will be with us in the test. There are many amazing stories throughout the Scriptures about those who stood upon **God**'s word. They were not moved by the **Circumstances**, the opposition, or the dangers that were confronting them. May **God** give us people like that today in this 21st-century. **Faith-Based Outcome Independent**, people who can boldly declare I do not care what it looks like.

I do not care what persecution comes. I do not care what affliction comes. I do not care what my body says. I do not care what my head says. I do not care what my **Circumstances** say. I do not care what the politicians say. I do not care what other preachers say. I do not care what a congregation says. I am going to obey **God**. I am going to do his will. This is what I call **Faith-Based Outcome Independent**.

Completely Engulfed in a Consuming Fire

Back in 1980 I began to memorize and meditate on Scriptures declaring that fire could not consume me.

Isaiah 43:2, "When thou passest through the waters, I will be with thee; and through the rivers, they shall not overflow thee: when thou walkest through the fire, thou shalt not be burned ; neither shall the flame kindle upon thee."

I meditated on the scriptures because I kept burning myself with our woodstove. Through the years, I have maintained these scriptures in my heart. In the summer of 2011, I had an amazing experience when **GOD** used these scriptures to come to my rescue; otherwise, I would have been burned to death.

This morning, I woke up lost, totally DRUNK in the Holy Ghost. I mean, my mind and my heart was so caught up in **GOD**, that I was totally **intoxicated** in the spirit. I was so heavenly minded at the time that you could even say I was not much earthly good. In this condition, I decided it was a good day to burn the large pile of brush that we had on our property.

This very large brush pile, which was way over my head, and needed to be burned. It was a very, very hot day. I am sure it was over 90° outside! I took a 2-gallon plastic gas container to this pile of brush with the full intention of lighting the brush on fire. When I took the cap off this container, the container was so hot you could see the visible fumes pouring of the gasoline in the air. I had with me one of those long-stemmed lighters that you can pick up at any hardware store.

I stepped into this pile of very dry brush which was higher than my head by about ten feet. I took the gas container and began to spread gasoline over the pile by splashing it out of the container all over the brush and woodpile. The liquid gasoline was up to the edge of my feet. Realize I am completely drunk in the Spirit.

At the time I was not at all thinking about what I was doing, I was simply meditating on the WORD of **GOD** Lost in the Holy Ghost. My son Daniel had come out of our house and was walking toward me. He saw me put the gas container in my left hand, with long stem Lighter in my right hand. The fumes were visible as they were radiating out of this container. I took the long stem lighter in my right hand and reached down to light the gas.

My son Daniel saw what I was about to do and started yelling at the top of his lungs, **DAD DONT**! I only heard him partly because I was so lost in the spirit, drunk, intoxicated. I pulled the trigger of the long-stemmed lighter and instantly there was an explosion of fire all around me and I was totally engulfed in the flames of this explosion of fire. I was surrounded by fire. My son Daniel said that he could not see me because the fire had swallowed me up. Daniel thought was burning to death, and there was nothing he could do about it! The FIRE was so hot he could not reach me to pull me out!

I remember being in the flames of this fire and it seemed as if there was this shimmering invisible force field around me, and the heat and the flames could not penetrate this invisible force field. This force field sparkled like glistening fog. Its color was light blue, silver, gold, and glistening white!

I remember standing being surrounded completely by fire thinking **WOW; this is Awesome**. And immediately at the same time, something clicked in my head: You're in the **fire dummy**! You need to get out of this fire!

Immediately, I began to backtrack away from the fire walking backward through the flames with the gas container still in my right hand! When I was out of the fire about 30 feet, I looked down at my body and my clothes and not a flame had kindled upon me. The gas container in my left hand alone should have exploded, because of the fumes that were coming out of it. I can truly say that not once did I feel the heat!

Once again **GOD** had miraculously delivered me from my stupidity. My son Daniel can attest to this story for he saw the whole thing. We rejoiced in **GOD** for His great mercy! Of course, my son Daniel was extremely upset with me and was in a state of shock and amazement because he saw me engulfed in the fire.

He thought surely, I was a dead man! He also was traumatized because he could not get anywhere near the flames to rescue me. I told him years later that there was nothing he could have done. At the time it happened he did not realize that **GOD** was shielding me from the flames and **1500°-degree heat!**

FAITH BASED OUTCOME INDEPENDENT

The most commonly known flammable liquid is gasoline. It has a flash point of about -50° F (-65° C). The ignition temperature is about 495° E (232° C), a comparatively low figure. Burning gasoline has a temperature above 1500° E (945° C)

Totally Engulfed in a Gasoline Tar Fire!

Everything around me exploded into fire! (Tears are filling my eyes as I share this incredible story of **GOD**'s protection in the midst of my stupidity.) It all began as I was stirring gasoline into a five-gallon bucket of black tar, thinning it to be spread on our Churches Steal roof! We had a thirty-gallon galvanized garbage can with an LP torch under this container melting the tar! The fumes ignited and this massive wave of fire came rushing from about 20 feet away completely engulfing me.

I mean I am completely swallowed up in this gasoline and black tar fire. The two buckets of gasoline are burning at my feet. The bucket of tar and gasoline I was stirring is on fire. I myself had been using an excessive amount of gas to keep my hands, arms and face free from tar. Gasoline is the only thing that would clean the black tar off me. My clothes are completely saturated with gasoline, as well as my hands, arms, and face. I'm standing there in the midst of all of this fire with no fear in my heart. Just utter peace, but still knowing that I was in big trouble.

Back in 1980 I began to memorize and meditate on Scriptures declaring that fire cannot consume me.

Isaiah 43:2, "When thou passest through the waters, I will be with thee; and through the rivers, they shall not overflow thee: when thou walkest through the fire, thou shalt not be burned ; neither shall the flame kindle upon thee."

I meditated on the scriptures because I kept burning myself with our woodstove. Through the years, I have maintained these scriptures in my heart. In the summer of 2011, I had an amazing experience when GOD used these scriptures to come to my rescue, otherwise I would have been burned to death.

I can honestly tell you that I did not feel the heat, flames or the fire upon me. I grabbed a metal canister and put it over the top of the one bucket of gas that was burning. I quickly found another canister that I could put over the other bucket. During this time, I'm literally running in and out of the fire.

I'm not thinking, I'm just moving knowing that our gymnasium and our whole church could go up in flames at any moment. We are right up against the gymnasium with a house trailer right there. The apartment and the stairs to the apartment above our gymnasium were right there. I had to get the fire out, and I mean fast! Everything was on fire, including the ground where we had spilled tar and gas.

The whole place is nothing but infernal. During this time, Jesse had made his way around the flames nurturing his burnt arm, which he had received standing outside of the flames! He was trying to find a water hose we had laying there to water a small garden. I'm still running in and out of the flames trying to put out this raging fire. Jesse had been through a terrible fire in the past, being seriously hurt. I could see that he was in the midst of some shock from the fire and the heat.

Right before my very eyes, the bucket that was filled with tar and gasoline had melted at my feet to less than 8 inches high. Now the flames were getting worse, they were reaching high into the sky. The men who have been spreading the mixture of tar and Gasoline come running seeing the flames on top of our Church Sanctuary. The whole thing was nothing but a massive blaze. During this time, brother Mark, who lives in the apartment up above, comes running out onto the deck of his apartment. He sees everything that is happening.

Brother Jesse is wrestling with the water hose, trying to disconnect it from another hose in order that we can use it to fight the fire. I ran over and began to help him. And then I took the hoses from him, heading back into the fire. Praise **GOD** the water did the job even with gasoline and burning tar everywhere. We were able to douse the flames. Praise **GOD**, praise **GOD**, praise **GOD** the fire was out.

Things happened so fast at the time that I did not even realize exactly the events that had transpired. But **GOD** in His grace and in His mercy once again protected me from my own massive stupidity. Jesse did receive burns on his right forearm. Amazingly, I did not receive one burn, not one singed hair or even the smell of smoke on me. All of the gas that was on me, my hands, my face, and my clothes never ignited. **GOD** is so good! His Mercy Endures Forever!

HAVING THE MIND OF CHRIST

Philippians 2: 5 Let this mind be in you, which was also in Christ Jesus: 6 who, being in the form of God, thought it not robbery to be equal with God: 7 but made himself of no reputation, and took upon him the form of a servant, and was made in the likeness of men: 8 and being found in fashion as a man, he humbled himself, and became obedient unto death, even the death of the cross. 9 Wherefore God also hath highly exalted him, and given him a name which is above every name:

Faith-Based Outcome Independent will take you to places that your flesh does not want to go. Many Christians are being taught that **Faith** is given to you simply to get what you want or even what you need, but it's way beyond that. True biblical **Faith** is going to take you where natural man will not go. True saving

Faith, follows, loves obeys, serves **God. Jesus** it is our Supreme example when it comes to being outcome independent. Here is the truth that most will not want to hear. True **Faith** will bring suffering. Listen to me now, true **Faith** in **Christ** will bring suffering. The apostle Paul, said:

Acts 14:21 And when they had preached the gospel to that city, and had taught many, they returned again to Lystra, and to Iconium, and Antioch, 22 confirming the souls of the disciples, and exhorting them to continue in the Faith, and that we must through much tribulation enter into the kingdom of God.

Now this is New Testament Christianity. This is not American Christianity because American Christianity teachers that pay for taking down the path of least resistance. Actually, the opposite is true. **Faith** that pleases **God** take you down the most difficult, problematic, challenging path who have walked. Paul throughout his writings talks about the difficulties that they had.

2 Corinthians 1:8 For we would not, brethren, have you ignorant of our trouble which came to us in Asia, that we were pressed out of measure, above strength, insomuch that we despaired even of life:

There is an aspect of **Faith** that will rise up in your heart and help you to deny your flesh. This is the **Faith** that overcomes the world, the flesh, and the devil. **Faith Based Outcome-Independent** means that I do not care about the **Circumstance**. I do not care about the situation. I do not really care about the problem. I do not care about the results. All I care about is the Lord.

Now, the Bible's full of testimonies of those who walked in this realm of **Faith**. Those who said: I'm not surrendering to this. I'm not yielding to this. But I am yielding to **God**. I am obeying **God**. I am following **God**, no matter what it costs. This is **Faith Based Outcome-Independent**. For, another words, you're independent of the threats. You're not moved by the intimidation, by the fear, by what could happen.

FAITH BASED OUTCOME INDEPENDENT

Daniel when he was confronted with the threat of being thrown to the lions, he kept praying and worshiping towards Jerusalem. Everybody who knew down all new that he would bow down and worship towards Jerusalem three times a day. He did not allow the kings edict to stop his routine. Even though in the natural it meant his death by a gruesome method.

Of course, his enemies turned him in. When they deceived the king into making this edict, they knew that Daniel was a man who would not quit praying. They used his faithfulness and his love for **God** against him. Yet we know what the ultimate outcome was.

Daniel 6:20And when he came to the den, he cried with a lamentable voice unto Daniel: and the king spake and said to Daniel, O Daniel, servant of the living God, is thy God, whom thou servest continually, able to deliver thee from the lions?

Daniel 6:22My God hath sent his angel, and hath shut the lions' mouths, that they have not hurt me: forasmuch as before him innocency was found in me; and also before thee, O king, have I done no hurt.

Daniel 6:24And the king commanded, and they brought those men which had accused Daniel, and they cast them into the den of lions, them, their children, and their wives; and the lions had the mastery of them, and brake all their bones in pieces or ever they came at the bottom of the den.

Dan's attitude was, hey, if I live, I live, If I die, I die. And he was thrown into the lion den. Then now how many? **God** spared him. But in Hebrews 11, it talks about those who weren't spared.

Hebrews 11:36 and others had trial of cruel mockings and scourgings, yea, moreover of bonds and imprisonment: 37 they were stoned, they were sawn asunder, were tempted, were slain with the sword: they wandered about in sheepskins and goatskins; being destitute, afflicted, tormented; 38 (of whom the world was not worthy:) they wandered in deserts, and in mountains, and in dens and caves of the earth.

THE LAMB SLAINED BEFORE FOUNDATION OF THE WORLD

How many of you ever experienced suffering because of your commitment to **Christ**? How many have ever been suffered because you decided to obey **God**? It could be that you were fired from your job. I know if you look at the life of **Jesus**, he suffered greatly for us.

Revelation 13:8 And all that dwell upon the earth shall worship him, whose names are not written in the book of life of the Lamb slain from the foundation of the world.

God the WORD himself said: I will become the lamb that will shed its blood for the redemption of humanity. What does that mean? That means that **God** had decided, the triunity, the **Father**, Son, and Holy Ghost had decided, it was necessary to suffer for the human race! The word was going to be made flesh to suffer and die so that we could live with him forever. Amen.

John 1:14And the Word was made flesh, and dwelt among us, (and we beheld his glory, the glory as of the only begotten of the Father,) full of grace and truth.

Thank you, Lord. Hallelujah.

We as believers should count it as a great honor to suffer for our Lord and Savior! That mindset is not in the American church. It's in other churches that are in Muslim nations and communist nations, where those who have named the name of **Christ** knew when they accepted **Christ**, they were going to be persecuted, prosecuted, afflicted, tortured, murdered and in prisoned. Matter of fact, they say the greatest slaughter of Christians is happening right now in the world.

FAITH BASED OUTCOME INDEPENDENT

Christians have a little bit of trouble, a little bit of problems, a little bit of difficulties, a little bit of hardship, and then they fall apart. They crumble like dry cookies because they don't really understand that Christianity is not a guarantee that you'll never suffer. That you'll never be afflicted. You'll never have a problem. Now, of course, most of our problems as American Christians, it's not because of our **Faith**. It's because of our wrong choices.

THE CAUSE OF MANY PROBLEMS

A lot of our physical problems are because were not eating right. We're not treating our bodies the way we should. A lot of our financial problems are because we are not handling our finances the way we should. A lot of the problems we are experiencing is because we're not walking in the character and nature of **God** in our relationships. A lot of our problems in America is not because of **Faith**, but it's because of unbelief.

I believe in the blessings. But also, I know many are the afflictions of the righteous, but the Lord delivers them out of them all. Think about Joseph. He was a godly and holy man who would not compromise with his master's wife. It is this **Faith** that said no to the devil and yes to **God**, they got them into prison. The book of Revelation declares that many of **God**'s people will be thrown into prison because of their **Faith**. They had a **Faith Based Outcome Independent** attitude.

Revelation 2:10Fear none of those things which thou shalt suffer: behold, the devil shall cast some of you into prison, that ye may be tried; and ye shall have tribulation ten days: be thou faithful *unto death, and I will give thee a crown of life.*

Joseph had **Faith** that was independent of the outcome. He said: I don't care what the outcome's going to be. I'm going to obey **God**. I'm going to trust **God**. I'm going to believe **God**. Of course, we know the end of the story that after an approximately three years in prison, **God** in one day put them over the most powerful nation in the world, the nation of Egypt.

But it wasn't for his prosperity. It was for the sake of his people. Realize that there will be suffering when it comes to obeying **God**. I went through the four gospels, Matthew Mark, Luke, and John and I found that there were 14 times when the religious leaders were conniving, manipulating, or trying to kill **Jesus**. Remember **Jesus** was the promised Messiah. Why would they try to destroy **Jesus**? Because he was walking in **Faith** with the **Father**. He only said, did, lived according to the **Father**'s will. He said, I am going to obey my **Father**. The threat of them killing him and doing him harm did not stop him. It did not shut him up.

Tried to Steam Me Alive

At the time that I was with the Yupik Indians, (1975) as a 19-year-old missionary, it did not seem as if I had any results. However, the Word of **GOD** never returns void. I have been told by reliable sources that one of the young men I shared **JESUS** with is now an Assemblies of **GOD** pastor in the Dillingham area. When I was there, there was no Christian testimony in the community. But now there is an Assembly of **GOD** church right outside of Dillingham, Alaska. Now to the story of how I was almost steamed to death.

Steam baths were introduced to Yupik Indians by Russian fur traders and missionaries. The steam baths I experienced in the Bristol Bay area consisted of a dressing room, a combination cooling room, and a hot room with very low ceilings that were only about four feet high. They were covered over with tundra to keep the steam and heat from escaping. These hot rooms were called a maqili or McQay.

FAITH BASED OUTCOME INDEPENDENT

The wood stove heater was an oil drum on its side with a chimney. Rocks were piled on top of the oil drum. There was half of a steel barrel full of water in the corner of the room next to the exit. They had about a four-and-a-half-foot long piece of wood with a kitchen pan attached so they could scoop water out of the barrel, stretch the pan over the top of the oil barrel stove and dump it on the rocks. This sent forth a tremendous amount of heat and steam. They packed the barrel full of wood for a steam bath. Steam baths seem to be an area of great pride for the Yupik men.

They told stories about how they would pass out, trying to outdo each other. They were known to have fallen on the rocks and burned to death. They stayed in the steam bath as long as they could and then go outside and roll in the snow or jump in the river. They also had a bench right outside where we would sit with nothing but a washcloth covering our loins.

One day they invited me to take a steam bath with them. On that day, there were three young Yupik Indians and an older man who looked like a walrus. The Spirit of the Lord spoke to my heart and told me not to be fearful. They were going to try to steam me out of the maqili /McQay. **GOD** said not to be concerned because He was going to reveal Himself to them through this test. When we were all in the McQay and had closed the door, they all stared at me, speaking in their native tongue to one another and laughing. Then they dumped water on the red-hot rocks.

The older gentleman had control of the scoop. As he continued to splash water on the rocks, it began to get extremely hot. I had a wet rag which they had given me, along with a pan of water at my feet. I dipped the cloth into the water and put it against my face and nostrils. I bowed my head and prayed quietly in tongues. I could hear the water hissing as more and more water was thrown on the red-hot rocks. I could feel their eyes staring at me. The heat was almost unbearable.

The minute I stopped thinking about **JESUS** and praying, it would feel like I was being steamed alive. Finally, I heard the door of the McQay open and closed three times. At this point, I looked up, and there was only the old Yupik Indian and myself. He smiled at me with a toothless grin. I bowed my head once again and continued to pray, knowing this was going to get extremely difficult.

I knew this was a fight for their souls. I wanted the Spirit of **GOD** to reveal Himself to them. They needed to understand this was not a white man's religion, but **JESUS** is the living **GOD** and Savior of all men. All at once, I heard a huge splash. The old Yupik Indian threw a whole scoop of water upon the rocks and ran out the door of the McQay.

I panicked. It felt like my flesh was being melted from off my bones. I ran for the door to open it, but either it was locked, or they were holding it shut from the outside. I pounded on the door, and at that instant, the Spirit of the Lord arrested me and told me to go back into prayer.

I fell on my face directly on the wood plank floor and began to speak in tongues. The Spirit of **GOD** sent a cool breeze where there was no wind. A cold wind blew over the top of me. After what seemed to be a long time, they let me out. I am sure they never understood how I could have beaten them at their native hobby, or how I survived such tremendous heat. They never did ask me. They stared at me when I came out.

James 1:2 My brethren, count it all joy when ye fall into divers temptations; 3 knowing this, that the trying of your FAITH worketh patience. 4 But let patience have her perfect work, that ye may be perfect and entire, wanting nothing.

And as ye go, preach, saying, The kingdom of heaven is at hand. Heal the sick, cleanse the lepers, raise the dead, cast out devils: freely ye have received, freely give (Matthew 10:7-8)!

CHAPTER FOUR
ARE WE WILLING TO SUFFER FOR JESUS?

We have precious brothers and sisters in **Christ** around the world that are suffering in prisons. Most of these believers are in prisons simply because they refused to obey the government when it was contrary to **God**'s word. They were told that they could not gather, that they could not share their **Faith**, and that they could not preach **Jesus Christ**. The prisons of China are filled with these precious brothers and sisters who refused to compromise their **Faith**.

But we as Americans who confess to know **Christ** and to love them gave into the tyrannical government. Even though large box stores, liquor stores and marijuana distribution stores were allowed to stay open. The government declared who was necessary and who was not necessary. Most of the 400,000 churches in America simply gave in to the demands of an ungodly edict.

There is a famous book written by a man who lived in Romania and was prosecuted because of his obedience to **Christ**. The name of this book is: **Tortured for Christ**

 the author of this book is Richard Wurmbrand, also known as Nicolai Ionescu (24 March 1909 – 17 February 2001). He was a Romanian Evangelical Lutheran priest, and professor of Jewish descent. In 1948, having become a Christian ten years before, he publicly said Communism and Christianity were incompatible. Wurmbrand preached at bomb shelters and rescued Jews during

World War II.[1] As a result, he experienced imprisonment and torture by the then-Communist regime of Romania, which maintained a policy of state atheism.

After serving a total of fourteen years, he was ransomed for $10,000. His colleagues in Romania urged him to leave the country and work for religious freedom from a location less personally dangerous. After spending time in Norway and England, he and his wife Sabina, who had also been imprisoned, emigrated to America and dedicated the rest of their lives to publicizing and helping Christians who are persecuted for their beliefs.

He wrote more than 18 books, the most widely known being Tortured for **Christ** and Answer to Moscow's (Atheist) Bible. Variations of his works have been translated into more than 65 languages. His son Michael operates the official Richard Wurmbrand Foundation, an Interconfessional Christian Missionary Organization, which offers his fathers books for free.

PILGRIMS PROGRESS

Another famous book that came about because of a man who was willing to suffer for what he believed in. His name was John Bunyan. While he was imprisoned for 12 years because he refused to stop preaching, he wrote this amazing and powerful book full of truth. It is the second most read book in the world.

John Bunyan (30 November 1628 – 31 August 1688) was an English writer and Puritan preacher best remembered as the author of the Christian allegory The Pilgrim's Progress, which also became an influential literary model. In addition to The Pilgrim's Progress, Bunyan wrote nearly sixty titles, many of them expanded sermons.

Bunyan came from the village of Elstow, near Bedford. He had some schooling and at the age of sixteen joined the Parliamentary Army during the first stage of the English Civil War. After three years in the army he returned to Elstow and took up the trade of tinker, which he had learned from his **Father**. He became interested in religion after his marriage, attending first the parish church and then joining the Bedford Meeting, a nonconformist group in Bedford, and becoming a preacher.

After the restoration of the monarch, when the freedom of nonconformists was curtailed, Bunyan was arrested because those in government told him he could not preach. He spent the next twelve years in jail as he refused to give up preaching. During this time, he wrote a spiritual autobiography, Grace Abounding to the Chief of Sinners, and began work on his most famous book, The Pilgrim's Progress, which was not published until some years after his release.

Bunyan's later years, despite another shorter term of imprisonment, were spent in relative comfort as a popular author and preacher, and pastor of the Bedford Meeting. He died aged 59 after falling ill on a journey to London and is buried in Bunhill Fields. The Pilgrim's Progress became one of the most published books in the English language; 1,300 editions having been printed by 1938, 250 years after the author's death.

LET'S TELL THE TRUTH

I gave my heart to **Jesus Christ** back in 1975 on my 19th birthday. From that day unto this present moment, I could count on one hand the number of times I heard ministers talk about what it means to suffer for **Christ**. We are not talking about sickness, disease, poverty. We are talking about a believer who must choose between obeying **God** and the world. Many believers around the world are experiencing terrible situations because they have a **Faith** that declares I will obey **God** no matter what the outcome is.

Personally, there has been at least five times where my life was in great jeopardy because of my commitment to **Christ**. These were times when people literally were trying to kill me. I remember one time when the Lord asked me if I was willing to die for him?

GOD Asked Me: Will you die for me?

I heard the voice of **GOD** asking me: are you willing to die for me? It was as I was getting ready to leave for the Philippines. I had been to the Philippines on numerous occasions. I had been going into an area of the Philippines where the NPA were extremely active. NPA is the abbreviation for the new People's Army, which are part of a communist movement.

At that time, they were very active, and they were extremely brutal and dangerous. Godly men who I have worked with in the Philippines had been murdered by them. I heard the Lord continue to say to me: if I can use your spilled blood like a seed planted into the ground to bring about a wonderful harvest, are you willing to die? When I heard the Lord say this to me, I took it very seriously. With deep sorrow in my heart and tears rolling down my face, I said yes Lord!

It was not that I was not willing to die for **CHRIST**, because I had been in many dangerous situations since I had been born again in 1975. I have had numerous encounters with people threatening and trying to kill me. A gang I used to run without of Chicago tried to kill me twice.

Some Yupik Indians in Alaska had tried to kill me. A demon-possessed woman had stabbed me multiple times in the face and yet the knife could not penetrate my skin. A Gang leader in Chicago tried stabbing me to death, and shot me with a shotgun, (the gun went off as he aimed for my belly, but nothing happened to me) A radical Muslim kept on wanting to shoot me, as he yelled and screamed in my face, with his finger ready to pull the trigger which would have sent me off into eternity, but the Holy Ghost restrained him.

Yes, I was more than willing to die, but in truth, I did not want to. I had a lovely wife, 3 sons and a beautiful little girl. But I said yes Lord if this is your will! I still remember that morning as I was getting ready to drive myself to the BWI Airport to catch a plane to the Philippines.

I hugged my precious wife very tight and my four beautiful children as if it was like the last time, I would ever hold them or hug them again on this side of heaven. As I looked at my little girl Stephanie, she was sucking on her 2 fingers, and I had lovingly nicknamed her two fingers Stephanie. My 2nd son Daniel, I had nicknamed him the watermelon kid because he loved watermelon so much. I hugged my oldest son goodbye who we had nicknamed Mick which is short for Michael. my 3rd son Steven could never give enough hugs even to this day.

As I backed out of my driveway leaving my family standing on the front porch tears were rolling down my face. I said Lord you died for me, you gave everything for me, so the least I can do is to be willing to give up everything you've given me, if I can be a seed of revival for others to be born again. As I was driving towards the airport on the main highway, I was weeping so hard that I could barely see where I was going.

I was thanking **GOD** for the years that he had given me with my lovely wife Kathleen. I was thanking **GOD** for my 3 sons and my daughter. I was thanking **GOD** for all the opportunities he had given to me to minister the word and help others. I was also reflecting upon the fact of how many times I should have been dead before I gave my heart to **Christ** like many of my former buddies who were now dead. As far as I know most of them died without **Jesus**.

I thought back on the times before I was born again when I had overdosed, drank way too much booze, played chicken with oncoming trains, driving on the other side of the road headed right towards others. When I had been in a gunfight with a crazy man. Oh, how many times **GOD** had spared me, and yet most of my worldly friends were now dead.

All those times when **GOD** spared my life, he could've allowed me to die and go to hell. But **GOD** had rescued me, and now it was my turn to die for him, how could I say no? I remember landing in the Philippines. I was completely free from fear. In my heart of hearts, I was already a martyr for **CHRIST**.

I was scheduled be in the Philippines for three weeks. For two weeks I preached like a house on fire not knowing exactly how the enemy was going to snuff out my life. It could be that it would be a sniper, or the communist would capture me and torture me to my death. Every day was my last day on this side of heaven as far as I was concerned. We saw many saved, healed and delivered. With my fellow Filipino ministers, we were starting churches everywhere we went.

Now to my wonderful amazement and my great surprise after about two weeks of ministering, **GOD** spoke to my heart while I was over there in the communist infested area. In my time of prayer heard the Lord say: **son you're not going to die!** I said what Lord? **He spoke to me again: you're not going to die!** I remember crying with joy, I said why Lord?

He said I needed to have you prove your love for me. He said I needed to have you to know that I was number 1 in your life. Even as Abraham offered up Isaac, and I gave him back, so in a sense, you have offered up your wife and your children, and I give them back to you.

That has been over 30 years ago when the Lord spared my life. I'm still going to areas at times that are extremely dangerous, but I have no fear because I know that **GOD** is with me. What if he ever asked me to offer up my life again as a seed with the shedding of my blood? All I can say is that if it ever happens again, by **GOD**'s grace I'll say, yes Lord! You gave your life for me, it's the least I can do.

Revelation 12:11And they overcame him by the blood of the Lamb, and by the word of their testimony; and they loved not their lives unto the death.

THROUGH OUT THE BIBLE

Suffering for **Christ** is throughout the Bible throughout the New Testament. But I have not heard very many ministers minister on this subject. Yet this is throughout the whole Bible. There are many scriptures dealing with this subject. Here are some of the Scriptures where it reveals that suffering for **Christ** is a part of the Christian experience.

SUFFER New Testament (117)

Acts 17:2 and Paul, as his manner was, went in unto them, and three sabbath days reasoned with them out of the scriptures, 3 opening and alleging, that Christ must needs have suffered, and risen again from the dead; and that this Jesus, whom I preach unto you, is Christ.

____

*Suffering was a normal part of Christianity in the early church. They were suffering because of their **Faith**, trust, confidence and reliance upon **JESUS**.

____

Acts 5:41 And they departed from the presence of the council, rejoicing that they were counted worthy to suffer shame for his name.

____

Acts 9:15 But the Lord said unto him, Go thy way: for he is a chosen vessel unto me, to bear my name before the Gentiles, and kings, and the children of Israel: 16 for I will shew him how great things he must suffer for my name's sake.

____

Romans 8:17and if children, then heirs; heirs of God, and

joint-heirs with Christ; if so be that we suffer with him, that we may be also glorified together.

Romans 8:18For I reckon that the sufferings of this present time are not worthy to be compared with the glory which shall be revealed in us.

---

1 Corinthians 13:4Charity suffereth long, and is kind; charity envieth not; charity vaunteth not itself, is not puffed up,

---

2 Corinthians 1:5For as the sufferings of Christ abound in us, so our consolation also aboundeth by Christ.

---

2 Corinthians 1:6And whether we be afflicted, it is for your consolation and salvation, which is effectual in the enduring of the same sufferings which we also suffer: or whether we be comforted, it is for your consolation and salvation.

---

2 Corinthians 1:7And our hope of you is stedfast, knowing, that as ye are partakers of the sufferings, so shall ye be also of the consolation.

Galatians 3:4Have ye suffered so many things in vain? if it be yet in vain.

Galatians 5:11And I, brethren, if I yet preach circumcision, why do I yet suffer persecution? then is the offence of the cross ceased.

FAITH BASED OUTCOME INDEPENDENT

Galatians 6:12As many as desire to make a fair shew in the flesh, they constrain you to be circumcised; only lest they should suffer persecution for the cross of Christ.

Philippians 1:29For unto you it is given in the behalf of Christ, not only to believe on him, but also to suffer for his sake;

Philippians 3:8Yea doubtless, and I count all things but loss for the excellency of the knowledge of Christ Jesus my Lord: for whom I have suffered the loss of all things, and do count them but dung, that I may win Christ,

Philippians 3:10that I may know him, and the power of his resurrection, and the fellowship of his sufferings, being made conformable unto his death;

Philippians 4:12I know both how to be abased, and I know how to abound: every where and in all things I am instructed both to be full and to be hungry, both to abound and to suffer need.

Colossians 1:24who now rejoice in my sufferings for you, and fill up that which is behind of the afflictions of Christ in my flesh for his body's sake, which is the church:

1 Thessalonians 2:2but even after that we had suffered before, and were shamefully entreated, as ye know, at Philippi, we were bold in our God to speak unto you the gospel of God with much contention.

1 Thessalonians 2:14 For ye, brethren, became followers of the churches of God which in Judæa are in Christ Jesus: for ye also have suffered like things of your own countrymen, even as they have of the Jews:

1 Thessalonians 3:4 For verily, when we were with you, we told you before that we should suffer tribulation; even as it came to pass, and ye know.

2 Thessalonians 1:5which is a manifest token of the righteous judgment of God, that ye may be counted worthy of the kingdom of God, for which ye also suffer:

1 Timothy 4:10 For therefore we both labour and suffer reproach, because we trust in the living God, who is the Saviour of all men, specially of those that believe.

2 Timothy 1:12 For the which cause I also suffer these things: nevertheless I am not ashamed: for I know whom I have believed, and am persuaded that he is able to keep that which I have committed unto him against that day.

2 Timothy 2:9wherein I suffer trouble, as an evil doer, even unto bonds; but the word of God is not bound.

2 Timothy 2:12if we suffer, we shall also reign with him: if we deny him, he also will deny us:

2 Timothy 3:12 Yea, and all that will live godly in Christ Jesus shall suffer persecution.

Hebrews 2:9 But we see Jesus, who was made a little lower than

FAITH BASED OUTCOME INDEPENDENT

the angels for the suffering of death, crowned with glory and honour; that he by the grace of God should taste death for every man.:10For it became him, for whom are all things, and by whom are all things, in bringing many sons unto glory, to make the captain of their salvation perfect through sufferings.

Hebrews 2:18For in that he himself hath suffered being tempted, he is able to succour them that are tempted.

Hebrews 5:8though he were a Son, yet learned he obedience by the things which he suffered;

Hebrews 9:26for then must he often have suffered since the foundation of the world: but now once in the end of the world hath he appeared to put away sin by the sacrifice of himself.

Hebrews 11:25choosing rather to suffer affliction with the people of God, than to enjoy the pleasures of sin for a season;

Hebrews 13:3Remember them that are in bonds, as bound with them; and them which suffer adversity, as being yourselves also in the body.

Hebrews 13:12Wherefore Jesus also, that he might sanctify the people with his own blood, suffered without the gate.

James 5:10Take, my brethren, the prophets, who have spoken in the name of the Lord, for an example of suffering affliction, and of patience.

1 1Peter 1:11searching what, or what manner of time the Spirit of Christ which was in them did signify, when it testified beforehand the sufferings of Christ, and the glory that should follow.

1 Peter 2:19For this is thankworthy, if a man for conscience toward God endure grief, suffering wrongfully.

1 Peter 2:20For what glory is it, if, when ye be buffeted for your faults, ye shall take it patiently? but if, when ye do well, and suffer for it, ye take it patiently, this is acceptable with God.

1 Peter 2:21For even hereunto were ye called: because Christ also suffered for us, leaving us an example, that ye should follow his steps:

1 Peter 2:23who, when he was reviled, reviled not again; when he suffered, he threatened not; but committed himself to him that judgeth righteously:

1 Peter 3:14But and if ye suffer for righteousness' sake, happy are ye: and be not afraid of their terror, neither be troubled;

1 Peter 3:17For it is better, if the will of God be so, that ye suffer for well doing, than for evil doing.

1 Peter 3:18For Christ also hath once suffered for sins, the just for the unjust, that he might bring us to God, being put to death in the flesh, but quickened by the Spirit:

1 Peter 4:1Forasmuch then as Christ hath suffered for us in the flesh, arm yourselves likewise with the same mind: for he that hath suffered in the flesh hath ceased from sin;

1 Peter 4:13but rejoice, inasmuch as ye are partakers of Christ's sufferings; that, when his glory shall be revealed, ye

may be glad also with exceeding joy.

---

1 Peter 4:16Yet if any man suffer as a Christian, **let him not be ashamed; but let him glorify God on this behalf.**

---

1 Peter 4:19Wherefore let them that suffer according to the will of God commit the keeping of their souls to him in well doing, as unto a faithful **Creator.**

---

1 Peter 5:1The elders which are among you I exhort, who am also an elder, and a witness of the sufferings of Christ, and also a partaker of the glory that shall be revealed:

---

1 Peter 5:10But the God of all grace, who hath called us unto his eternal glory by Christ Jesus, after that ye have suffered a while, make you perfect, stablish, strengthen, settle you.

Revelation 2:10Fear none of those things which thou shalt suffer: behold, the devil shall cast some of you into prison, that ye may be tried; and ye shall have tribulation ten days: be thou faithful **unto death, and I will give thee a crown of life.**

WRONG WESTERN THEOLOGY

We need to ask why we do not hear very many messages on sufferings in the Western church? I think it is because we've got a theology or philosophy that it is extremely twisted and perverted. Let's just be honest, many Western Christians are afraid of suffering. Even though **God** has not given us a spirit of fear, they are operating in fear. I do not say this lightly because I have been in situations where it looked like I was going to be killed because of my walk with **Christ**. **God** does not lead us with the spirit of fear but of spirit of **Faith**.

2 Timothy 1:7 For God hath not given us the spirit of fear; but of power, and of love, and of a sound mind.

When Adam and his wife committed sin in the garden, a spirit of fear took possession of them. From that moment forward the whole human race has been under the fear of death. Now, **Jesus** came to set us free from the fear of death. He said those who believe on him would never die. He came to deliver us from the fear of death, and yet you see it operating in many Christians.

Hebrews 2:14 Forasmuch then as the children are partakers of flesh and blood, he also himself likewise took part of the same; that through death he might destroy him that had the power of death, that is, the devil; 15 and deliver them who through fear of death were all their lifetime subject to bondage. 16 For verily he took not on him the nature of angels; but he took on him the seed of Abraham.

The just shall are to live by the spirit of **Faith**. We're talking about a **Faith** that is independent of the outcome. It declares to the world, the flesh, and the devil do your worst, but I am going to trust **God**, obey **God**, follow **God**, serve **God**. And I found out that there was 14 times that the Jewish people tried to kill **Jesus** are plotted to kill him. The very first sermon that **Jesus** preached in his very hometown synagogue caused the people to revolt against him, and to try to kill him.

Luke 4:16And he came to Nazareth, where he had been brought up: and, as his custom was, he went into the synagogue on the sabbath day, and stood up for to read.

Luke 4:20And he closed the book, and he gave it again to the minister, and sat down. And the eyes of all them that were in the synagogue were fastened on him.

Luke 4:28And all they in the synagogue, when they heard these things, were filled with wrath,29 and rose up, and thrust him out of the city, and led him unto the brow of the hill whereon their city was built, that they might cast him down headlong.

Jesus said today, this scripture is fulfilled. The Scripture was speaking about the Messiah. Now, supposedly they say in every synagogue there was a chair that was reserved for nobody, but the Messiah. And supposedly **Jesus** sat down in that chair. **Jesus** knew how they would respond to him the minute he did this. But because he had **Faith-Based Outcome Independence** he did as the **Father** let him. He knew they were going to try to kill him, but it was okay. He was in a perfect will of the **Father** at that time.

ARRESTED FOR PREACHING JESUS!

I knew as a 19-year-old baby Christian when I stood up in that old movie theater and I preached my heart out to those Navy men, that they were going to call the MPS and take me away. But I was so moved with compassion for those guys on that military base in my heart that I said I don't care.

   *I had a supernatural experience of going to hell. After my experience of going to Hell, the compassion of **GOD** was flowing in me like a mighty river. It was so strong that an overwhelming desire came upon me to reach as many people as I could at one time. The idea came to me that I could reach more men on that military base if I went to the movie theater we had on the island.

I remember going to the very front row of this movie theater. I sat down, shaking, and waiting, wondering if what I was about to do was right. I looked at my watch and knew the movie would begin any minute. Just before they started the movie, I stood upon the ledge where the movie screen was attached to the floor.

I stood there shaking for a while, trying to get up enough nerve to open my mouth. The men in the theater began to yell for me to get off the stage and sit down. Instead, I opened my mouth and began to preach. As I preached, I could see the Holy Spirit was beginning to move upon the hearts of the audience.

It wasn't long before the military police showed up to arrest me. It was amazing that they did not take me by force but instead waited for me to finish. When I finished what the Lord had told me to say, the police told me to come off the stage. The two of them grabbed my arms and dragged me out of the theater.

They arrested me, put me in their military vehicle, and took me to jail. They asked what I was trying to do in the theater. I took the opportunity to share with them how **JESUS** had radically changed my life by saving my soul. I told them **JESUS** wanted to do the same for them. They released me without pressing charges. I think it is because they knew that nobody would get any sleep if I was left in the prison to preach **Jesus** to all the inmates.

Where Is the Most Dangerous Place?

I have been in the Philippines multiple times. When I go, I work directly with a Filipino Bible college in the province of Samar. I have been told that this is one of the most poverty-stricken parts of the Philippines and one of the most dangerous. Missionaries very rarely go there because of this.

It is far away from all the modern conveniences of Manila. It is also inhabited by the New People's Army which is a Communist movement. The NPA are extremely dangerous. I have personally known Philippine pastors who I had preached with who have been killed by them. On one of my missionary endeavors, I was just finishing three weeks worst of outreach when the Spirit of **GOD** quickened my heart to ask them a strange question.

I said to them: Where it is the most dangerous place to go to in this province? They told me it was an island called Laoang. I asked him why? They told me that two American missionaries had gone to the island of Laoang, and had not come out alive. The NPA had slit their throats as they were there. There had been no missionary endeavor there for at least 10 years.As they told me this story, I heard myself say out of the blue: that I needed to go and take this place for **JESUS**. As I declared this bold statement to them, there was an amazing peace within my heart!

I informed them that the next time that I came back to the Philippines, that I needed to go to that island and preach the gospel. They asked me if I was serious. I said absolutely! I told them I would give them the money that they needed to make the flyers and posters to spread the word that we were coming.

COMMUNIST WERE WAITING TO KILL US

About six months later, I arrived back in the Philippines with one of the men from my church who is now a pastor in the Phoenix, Arizona area. When we arrived in the province of Samar, the brethren informed us that the Communists were aware of us coming and were going to be waiting for us. I did not ask them to explain to me what they meant.

I absolutely had no fear in my heart. It is hard to explain to people what it is like when you are operating in a gift of **FAITH**. It is not a normal **FAITH**. It is **FAITH** that makes you know that in **CHRIST** you cannot be defeated. In the operation of this **FAITH**, there is always overwhelming peace. It is the peace of **GOD** that passes all understanding. The minute you lose your peace, you need to stop and asked the **FATHER** what is wrong. This is a major way in which **GOD** leads and guides us is by his peace.

Isaiah 55:12 For ye shall go out with joy, and be led forth with peace: the mountains and the hills shall break forth before you into singing, and all the trees of the field shall clap their hands.

To get to this island, we were first going to have to go by land on a worn-out concrete road that had been built right after World War II. We had to travel from Catbalogan City to the town of Catarman. Then from Catarman, we continued our journey another 40 miles to reach the canoes that were going to take us to the island. Altogether the journey was a hundred and 14 miles.

Now, this may not sound like a long-distance when it comes to traveling in America, but that is a long way on a rough Filipino road. We finally reached a river called the Pambujan River.

To our dismay, the bridge was out. They were putting in a brand-new bridge that they had only begun to build. So we had to take a longer alternative route to reach another bridge to get across this river. This river was over 300 feet wide. (I only mention this because it's an important part of my journey on the motorcycle) We stayed on this road until it ran into the Philippine Ocean. From there we took two large canoes. Each canoe had an outboard motor on the back of them. We would have to traverse on the ocean over a mile to reach Laoang.

After all our equipment and the people were loaded into the first canoe, I found myself up front at the very tip of the vessel. During this time there was great excitement and peace in my heart to see what **GOD** was about to do. I was optimistic of **GOD** manifesting himself on this island that had been shut off from the gospel for many years.

I knew that **GOD** was going to have to perform miracles to keep us alive, and yet there was absolutely no fear within my heart, nothing but overflowing peace. As we were coming closer to the island, I could see that there were men lined up along the beach waiting for us.

There was absolutely no fear in my heart as we approach the island. There were approximately 30 men who were standing there with guns and machetes in their hands. The Filipino brothers who were navigating the canoes kept the engines of the canoes running fast enough so the canoes would drive themselves up a little bit onto the dry shore.

As we approached the shore, I was so excited that I stood up to my feet, getting ready to leap out of this canoe towards these communists. It had to be the spirit of **GOD** within me because no sane man would leap to his death.

I almost felt like George Washington's famous painting of him crossing the Delaware River. The moment we hit the beach, I was up and out of that canoe. The Communists were standing there waiting to kill us.

The Spirit of **GOD**, the gift of **FAITH**, the peace of **GOD** was possessing me as I began to walk towards them very rapidly. I headed right for the center of this crowd of gun toting and machete-wielding communist.

As I reached them, something supernatural happened. It was like the Lord splitting the Red Sea, but instead of water, it was men who had murder in their hearts. They separated from left to right and allowed our team of men to walk right through the midst of

Them.

The Blind See & the Deaf Hear

That night we held a crusade right in the middle of the village. As our worship team was singing, the Communists and pagan religious people were marching through our meeting. We simply ignored them and kept on with the meeting. There seemed to be a very large crowd that night, probably because they wanted to see a white man.

It was very seldom when Americans or Europeans came into this area. The tourists flock to Manila and Mindanao. It had been 10 years since anybody had dared come to this island to preach Christianity. The last missionaries they had murdered. Now here I was about to preach the gospel of **JESUS CHRIST** that saves, heals, and delivers just like it did in the days when **JESUS** walked in his earthly ministry.

After singing, it was my opportunity to preach. It literally felt like the spirit of **GOD** was flowing through me like a mighty river of electricity and power. I preached under the unction of the Holy Ghost, to a great extent not thinking at all what to say, but letting the spirit have his way.

When I was done preaching, there was barely enough light to make out the crowd in front of us. They had lit some torches around the meeting area, trying to bring as much light as possible. Because I could not get down into the crowd to pray for them, I had to speak the word of healing over them. I began to command their bodies to be healed in the name of **JESUS CHRIST** of Nazareth. Every time I would speak something in the name of **JESUS**, the interpreter would copy me in their language.

Miracles began to happen. One old lady who had been blind in one eye could now see. A little boy who had been deaf could now hear. It was too dark out for us to tell how many miracles happened that night, but to this day I have been told there is a thriving church there because of this meeting.

Surrounded by the NPA

The precious brothers we worked with had arranged for us to be put into a two-story house. We would be on the second floor, while they were going to be on the first floor. I know why they did this! They were going to make the Communists have to kill them before they would let the NPA get to us. These were the kind of men that would give their lives without hesitation for the sake of the gospel.

It was late by the time we went to bed. They gave my friend and I some type of straw mats to lie on. We threw these mats on the wooden floor and tried to go to sleep. During the night we could hear the Communists outside making a racket. The communist had surrounded our house with groups of men, had started little bonfires around the house where we were staying. As I went to sleep, I saw two large angels like pillars of fire in a dream with swords drawn standing over the top of the house we were in. When we woke up in the morning, it was very peaceful. And the Communists were gone.

The Spirit of the Lord is upon me, because he hath anointed me to preach the gospel to the poor; he hath sent me to heal the brokenhearted, to preach deliverance to the captives, and recovering of sight to the blind, to set at liberty them that are bruised, to preach the acceptable year of the Lord (Luke 4:18-19).

I had no guarantee. I wasn't concerned about the outcome. I was independent from it. Now, listen, because this is a key to **God** manifesting himself in your life. A lot of American Christians have got it in their heads that when they pray and believe to receive, that instantly they will feel or see a change. Yes, this does happen at times, but most times it does not. This would include any and every area where you are believing **God**, including your finances. Then people make the major mistake of getting their eyes on the manifestation. They get their eyes on their finances. Many times, I have had to be Outcome independent.

FAITH IS THE DOOR BY WHICH GOD LEADS & GUIDES

A person who does not learn how to live, walk, move, think, and operate by **Faith** will not be led of the Holy Ghost. They can't be led by **Jesus**. Why? Because **God** leads us and guides us through his word. Paul tells us:

let this mind be in you that was also in Christ Jesus, who being in a form of God thought or not robbed to be equal with God, but made himself of no reputation and took upon him the form of a servant and was made in the likeness of men.

Why did **Jesus** do that? Because the **Father** told him to. Can you imagine leaving the splendor of heaven into this pool of sin and darkness, this earth dominated by demonic powers, evil, asnd unbelief. And here comes **God** himself.

1 Timothy 3:16And without controversy great is the mystery of godliness: God was manifest in the flesh, justified in the Spirit, seen of angels, preached unto the Gentiles, believed on in the world, received up into glory.

John 1:14And the Word was made flesh, and dwelt among us, (and we beheld his glory, the glory as of the only begotten of the Father,) full of grace and truth.

It is hard to imagine the suffering that **Jesus** went through. His sufferings were not just upon the cross. It was spiritual, emotional, and physical. When **Jesus** walked among humanity, among his disciples, he was so grieved at times he said: how long will I have to be with you? He was so grieved in his heart because of their sins remember the Bible says that lot was grieved because of the sins of Sodom and Gomorrah.

2 Peter 2:6 and turning the cities of Sodom and Gomorrha into ashes condemned them with an overthrow, making them an ensample unto those that after should live ungodly; 7 and delivered just Lot, vexed with the filthy conversation of the wicked: 8 (for that righteous man dwelling among them, in seeing and hearing, vexed his righteous soul from day to day with their unlawful deeds;)

If lot was vexed, then how much more was **Jesus** vexed because of the immorality that surrounded him. I would not live in the city. I wouldn't live there. How we used to go down to the streets of Baltimore. I went into an area of Baltimore that white people wouldn't go into.

Why would I do that? It was **Faith Based Outcome-Independent**. I heard the Lord say, go down there and share the gospel and feed those drug addicts. So, we would go down there and sure enough, they threatened our lives. They were going to kill us.

Radical Muslim Going to Kill Me

A Radical Muslim was going to kill my son, so I took his place!(2001)

I had my family with some members of the church ministering on the streets of Baltimore. We were at one of my favorite fishing holes, the Lexington market. We had finished feeding the people. My wife and daughter had sung some songs. And now my son Michael was preaching a compassionate message on salvation and giving one's heart to **JESUS**. It was getting pretty late in the day so we were preparing to leave.

About a block away from us there were some radical Muslims preaching a message of hate and racial bigotry. We always left them alone, never attacking their philosophy but simply preaching **JESUS CHRIST** is the only answer for the sin-sickened soul. As my son Michael was finishing up his message, an African American Muslim came charging at him. He got right into my son's face screaming and yelling, cursing, and swearing, getting ready to do him bodily harm.

I immediately saw what was happening and intervened. I stepped between my son and this screaming madman. I turned my face away from the Muslim, telling my son to pack up the equipment and get everybody into the van. Then I turned back to face this man who was full of the devil.

My heart was filled with love for him and those who have been deceived along with him. Now that my son was out of the picture, this man's total focus was on me. He had his right hand in his pocket gripping onto something. I could see that it was in the shape of a gun pressing against the cloth of his jacket. The barrel of this gun was aimed right at my belly from all appearances.

There was absolutely no fear in my heart whatsoever as I spoke softly to him. I just kept on speaking about **JESUS** as he kept yelling at me. He seemed to get more infuriated that I was not intimidated. He purposely began to spit in my face as he was yelling and screaming. There were many people out on the street that day. It seemed like everything had stopped as they were watching and waiting to see what would happen. I could sense the spirit of murder and death was permeating the air.

I truly believe that people were waiting for him to gun me down. There was absolutely no fear in my heart but a sense of great sadness that I would leave behind my wife and my children. I'm sure that tears roll down my face along with his spittle as I prepared myself in my heart to die. My wife and children and those of the church had cleared away from the area. I could see them out of the corner of my eye loading into the van. My heart was filled with peace knowing they were safe.

This man would scream and yell and spit, then walk away just to come running back to me again. This continued, it seemed, for at least 15 minutes if not longer. I just was speaking to this Muslim softly about **JESUS CHRIST** when suddenly, he just simply walked away. I stood there watching him leave when an African American lady walked up to me. She looked me straight in the eyes and said this to me. I have never in my whole life seen anything like that. You just stood there as he screamed and spit on you. We could all see there was no fear or anger in your heart. You just kept responding with kindness and gentleness.

That was my opportunity to share **JESUS CHRIST** with her, telling her that it was not me but **JESUS** inside of me. The Lord had spared me once again to live another day to preach the glorious gospel of **JESUS CHRIST**. You see I was operating in **Faith Based Outcome Independence.**

John 15:13 Greater love hath no man than this, that a man lay down his life for his friends.

GETTYSBURG PENNSYLVANIA

I came into this area of Pennsylvania back in 1982. We join two churches together, one in Gettysburg and one from Chambersburg. I have been in the same church for 40 years. I'm still here because I heard the Lord say to me, go to Gettysburg and start a church. Oh, I wish he wouldn't have said that. Oh, I didn't want to be here for anything. Matter of fact, I knew I was called to preach the moment I gave my heart to **Christ**, but I did not ever want to be a pastor. But then **God** called me to pastor.

I've had people come to me through the years and say: I don't really believe that **God** has called you to be a pastor, brother, Mike. I said: will you please tell him? I've been telling him that for years. But I'm here because **God** told me to be here, and I am going to stay until the day he tells me to move on. If I had to be here another 40 years and so, be it. All I know is that I need to be faithful to **God**. I must live **Faith-Based Outcome Independent.** This is where **Jesus** lived 24 seven when he was on the earth. He obeyed the **Father** in every area. Not for one second did he ever step out of the **Father**'s perfect will for his life.

Jesus went through tremendous and horrific suffering for us. In the garden the night he was betrayed it says the pressure was so heavy on him that he declared his soul was nigh unto death.

Jesus was **Faith-Based Outcome Independent** before the foundation of the world. He was called the lamb of **God**. He knew that he was going to end up going to the cross, being made, sin, suffering, experiencing more pain then any human being had ever experienced. With all that he went through he should have died before he ever got to the cross, but he refused to offer up his life until everything was finished.

Luke 22:39 And he came out, and went, as he was wont, to the mount of Olives; and his disciples also followed him. 40 And when he was at the place, he said unto them, Pray that ye enter not into temptation. 41 And he was withdrawn from them about a stone's cast, and kneeled down, and prayed, 42 saying, Father, if thou be willing, remove this cup from me: nevertheless not my will, but thine, be done.43 And there appeared an angel unto him from heaven, strengthening him. 44 And being in an agony he prayed more earnestly: and his sweat was as it were great drops of blood falling down to the ground. 45 And when he rose up from prayer, and was come to his disciples, he found them sleeping for sorrow,

There are many Scriptures that declare the sufferings of **Christ** from Genesis to Revelation. Here is just a small handful of them.

SMITH WIGGLESWORTH

O this blessed **Jesus**, the Son of **God**, who loved me and gave Himself for me. This blessed, blessed Son of **God**. I want you to see that we receive son ship because of His obedience; because of His loyalty; and do not forget what the Scripture says: "He learned obedience through the things he suffered."

If you turn to the Scripture you will discover (as incredible as this may sound) that his whole kindred, His mother, brothers, sisters, and the rest of his kindred came and said, "He is possessed by Beelzebub the devil, and is doing his works."

See how **Jesus** suffered. They reviled Him and they tried to kill Him by throwing Him over the cliff, but **Jesus** passed through the midst of the whole crowd, and as soon as He was escaped, He saw a blind man and healed him as He was going on his Fathers way.

O it is lovely. He is **God**'s example of what can be, and I want to tell you all the attributes and the divine positions and the beatitudes that **Jesus** had. He was in the world, but not of it. O it is lovely; it is divinely glorious; and this power of the new creation, this birth unto righteousness by **Faith** in the atonement, can so transform and change you that you can be just like **Jesus Christ**. You can know without a shadow of a doubt that it is **God**'s power dominating, controlling, and filling you and making you like **Jesus**! Understand that though you are still in the body you can be governed by the Spirit.

 What a holy life! What a zeal! What a passion! 0, to live in all the beauties of all the glory and magnificent of the Holy Ghost! **Jesus** was truly the first fruits for us. O, the fascination of the **Christ** of **God** makes me realize there is nothing in this world worth grasping, worth having compared to him. O Lord, reveal yourself unto your people. I could never believe it was possible for any man to stand here and preach as I have preached if it was not real to me. I would be ashamed of myself if I did so. But it is not possible.

 Beloved, it is the reality of **Christ** that constrains us. There is a constraining power in this blessed **Jesus Christ** of **God** which makes us know that there is something in it that is different from anything in the whole world. It is called in the Scriptures an "unfeigned love." It is a tremendously deep word: "unfeigned love and **Faith**." Whatever is it?

SUFFERINGS OF CHRIST

Matthew 16:21From that time forth began Jesus to shew unto his disciples, how that he must go unto Jerusalem, and suffer many things of the elders and chief priests and scribes, and be killed, and be raised again the third day.

Luke 24:26ought not Christ to have suffered these things, and to enter into his glory?

Luke 24:46and said unto them, Thus it is written, and thus it behoved Christ to suffer, and to rise from the dead the third day:

Acts 3:18But those things, which God before had shewed by the mouth of all his prophets, that Christ should suffer, he hath so fulfilled.

Acts 17:3opening and alleging, that Christ must needs have suffered, and risen again from the dead; and that this Jesus, whom I preach unto you, is Christ.

Acts 26:23that Christ should suffer, and that he should be the first that should rise from the dead, and should shew light unto the people, and to the Gentiles.

Romans 8:17and if children, then heirs; heirs of God, and joint-heirs with Christ; if so be that we suffer with him, that we may be also glorified together.

2 Corinthians 1:5For as the sufferings of Christ abound in us, so our consolation also aboundeth by Christ.

Colossians 1:24who now rejoice in my sufferings for you, and fill up that which is behind of the afflictions of Christ in my flesh for his body's sake, which is the church:

Hebrews 2:9But we see Jesus, who was made a little lower than the angels for the suffering of death, crowned with glory and honour; that he by the grace of God should taste death for every man.

Hebrews 13:12Wherefore Jesus also, that he might sanctify the people with his own blood, suffered without the gate.

FAITH BASED OUTCOME INDEPENDENT

1 Peter 1:11searching what, or what manner of time the Spirit of Christ which was in them did signify, when it testified beforehand the sufferings of Christ, and the glory that should follow.

1 Peter 2:21For even hereunto were ye called: because Christ also suffered for us, leaving us an example, that ye should follow his steps:

1 Peter 3:18For Christ also hath once suffered for sins, the just for the unjust, that he might bring us to God, being put to death in the flesh, but quickened by the Spirit:

1 Peter 4:1Forasmuch then as Christ hath suffered for us in the flesh, arm yourselves likewise with the same mind: for he that hath suffered in the flesh hath ceased from sin;

1 Peter 5:1The elders which are among you I exhort, who am also an elder, and a witness of the sufferings of Christ, and also a partaker of the glory that shall be revealed:

Jesus knew that all the people were going to reject him. He told his disciples that they needed to Eat his flesh and drink his blood. That only by doing this could they have life and have it more abundantly. And they all were walked away but 12 of them. He said to those 12, do you want to leave to? He was **Faith-Based Outcome Independent**.

God himself in the flesh was going to be made sin for us. That we might be made the righteousness of **God** in **Christ**. All of heaven stood in shock as the Lamb of **God** was crucified upon the cross for us. These things had been hid from the angelic realm. These were the deep mysteries that were hid from the foundation of the world, but now in these last days is made manifest.

Who would ever think that the creator himself would be willing to take our place, our punishment, our separation from **God** the **Father** in order to redeem us. I can honestly say that since I gave my heart to **Christ** in 1975 as a 19-year-old kid, I have never once doubted **God**'s love for me. I have never doubted his love for humanity. He proved his love when he became a man, took our place, was made sin, suffered, crucified, and resurrected.

 I really cannot comprehend even one, one thousandeth of what **Jesus** went through for me. But notice where **Faith** took him. **Faith** took him into the midst of the deepest, darkest sufferings and miseries that a human mind cannot even comprehend. He was separated from the **Father**.

Psalm 22:1My God, my God, why hast thou forsaken me? why art thou so far from helping me, and from the words of my roaring?

Matthew 27:46And about the ninth hour Jesus cried with a loud voice, saying, Eli, Eli, lama sabachthani? that is to say, My God, my God, why hast thou forsaken me?

Now this could be a little bit confusing because **God** has basically promised that if we walk up rightly, he will bless us. **Jesus** walked uprightly his whole life. So, **Jesus**, he could have said, I don't deserve this. This shouldn't be happening to me. Nobody ought to treat me like this. But **Faith** kept him out of bitterness. **Faith** kept him out of accusing the **Father**.

Faith kept him from complaining. Yes. **Faith** kept him out of that realm. **Faith** kept him out of the flesh. **Faith** took him to the cross and giving his life as the sacrificial lamb. It took **Faith** people. It takes **Faith** to be committed. I'm talking about being independent of **Circumstances**. We do not hear this in the modern-day church. **Jesus** paid the ultimate price, and **God** blessed him accordingly!

FAITH BASED OUTCOME INDEPENDENT

Hebrews 2:7 Thou madest him a little lower than the angels; thou crownedst him with glory and honour, and didst set him over the works of thy hands:8 Thou hast put all things in subjection under his feet. For in that he put all in subjection under him, he left nothing that is not put under him. But now we see not yet all things put under him.9 But we see Jesus, who was made a little lower than the angels for the suffering of death, crowned with glory and honour; that he by the grace of God should taste death for every man.

The reason why all authority was put under the feet of **Jesus** is because he walked in this realm of **Faith**-based outcome independence. He said, I don't care about what my enemies, or the devil can do to me. I'm just going to obey my **Father**. You do what you must do. I'm going to obey my **Father**. Whatever happens, happens. I'm going to do the will of my **Father**.

Personally, I have found great blessings when I have been amid a trial or a test or an affliction, when I said, you know what? I don't care. I'm going to obey **God**. And when I got through that terrible time, when the devil was attacking my mind, and my emotions, my body, I said, I'm going to obey **God**. If nobody else obeys, I'm going to obey **God**. I have decided I am going to follow **Jesus**. If none go with me yet I will follow **Jesus**. No turning back, no turning back. Now you can't just decide, "I'm going to do this" without putting **God**'s word in your heart. That's like trying to drive a car with no gasoline.

Faith operates upon truth. If you don't have the truth in your heart, you will not be able to operate in this kind of **Faith**! It's not a decision of the mind. It's **Faith** in **God**. It's trust in **God**. We see **Jesus** who has made a little lower than the angels for the sufferings of death. Notice it goes back to the sufferings of **Christ**. You know, there's all kinds of suffering. There's not just physical suffering. There's self-denial. **Faith** says, I could have that, but I'm not because I don't need it. I could do that, but I'm not going to do that because it is against **God**'s will.

I'm telling you, there are times when I could have had good things, but I heard the Lord say, no, you don't need that. Story, after story, when I, by **Faith** said, you know what? I'm just going to trust **God**. I'm just going to believe **God**. **Jesus** by the grace of **God** should taste death for every man. **Faith** becomes strong, mature, and developed through suffering caused by **Faith**. Now you may not want to go to the place I'm talking about, but really you got one or two choices.

When the enemy comes in, whatever way he comes either, you're going to be driven with the wind and you're just going to go along to get along. Or you must decide, I'm going to begin to trust **God**. I'm going to begin to believe **God**. I'm going to begin to build my **Faith**. I am going to go on with the Lord. This is a **Faith** that takes you out of sin. You need to get a spiritual backbone and obey **God**.

CHAPTER FIVE

The No Matter What Take It By FORCE!

(2013)

Back in 2013, I was lying in bed when I heard the **audible voice** of **GOD**. **HE** said to me: "**The No Matter What take it by force!**" For a while now, this has been marinating in my soul. Sometimes when **GOD** speaks to me, it takes time for it to become a reality. It could be four years later, or maybe even decades later, as the spirit of **GOD** is at work on my insides. You could say it is rather like a pregnant woman: life is growing inside of her womb. **FAITH** begins as a seed and must grow within us, in our hearts. We have a lot to do with that **FAITH** growing, expanding, enlarging, and becoming mature.

Please understand, everybody has **FAITH**. Everyone was born with a measure, a proportion of **FAITH.** When **JESUS** shared the parable of the ten virgins who were asleep, He said they all woke up when the trumpet sounded; but there were five foolish virgins and five wise virgins. It was only the five wise virgins that had enough oil to take them to the arrival of their Husband to be. I believe that one of the realities of the oil **JESUS** was speaking of is the **oil of FAITH.** I believe it is **FAITH** in **GOD** and **FAITH** in **JESUS CHRIST**.

People who do not have sufficient **FAITH,** in this time, are going to have it rough. They are going to try to find somebody that does have **FAITH**, but it will be too late.

Then there are those who do have **FAITH**, but it has been in hibernation. **FAITH** can be lying dormant inside of you for many years. Then suddenly, something supernatural happens, and it begins to come forth, like a bear coming out of hibernation!

Hebrews 11:32-34 And what shall I more say? for the time would fail me to tell of Gedeon, and of Barak, and of Samson, and of Jephthae; of David also, and Samuel, and of the prophets: 33 Who through FAITH subdued kingdoms, wrought righteousness, obtained promises, stopped the mouths of lions, 34 Quenched the violence of fire, escaped the edge of the sword, out of weakness were made strong, waxed valiant in fight, turned to flight the armies of the aliens.

GOD Said: You Better Not Lie or You'll Die!

One day (1981), I picked up a book by a well-known author. The book was highly recommended by one of my favorite preachers at that time; the topic was angelic visitations. This was something I was interested in because of my many experiences with the supernatural.

I began to read the book and noticed immediately there were experiences he said he'd had, which did not seem to line up with the Scriptures. I did not want to judge his heart, but we do have the responsibility to examine everything considering **GOD**'s Word. If it does not line up with the Word of **GOD**, then we must reject it - no matter who wrote it.

FAITH BASED OUTCOME INDEPENDENT

As I was pondering the stories in the book, the Spirit of the Lord spoke to my heart very strongly. It was as if He was standing right there next to me, speaking audibly. What He said to me was rather shocking! The Lord told me that the writer of the book would be dead in three months from a heart attack! I asked the Lord why He was telling me this; He said the stories in the man's book were exaggerated, and that judgment was coming. That he had opened the door for the devil to take him out.

The Lord warned me that day that if I were ever to do the same thing, judgment would come to me too. I did not realize, back then, that the Lord would later have me writing many books - many of them filled with my own personal experiences. Now I know why He spoke this to me, telling me that I better not exaggerate my experiences!

When the Spirit of the Lord spoke to me, I turned and told my wife. I held the book up trembling, and in a very quiet, whispering, trembling, wavering voice, I said: "Honey, the man who wrote this book will be dead in three months from a heart attack!" I went on to explain to her why the Lord had told me this. I wish I had been wrong. Exactly three months later, the man died from a heart attack. **GOD** can speak to us through the positive and the negative **Circumstances** of life. We better take heed to what He is saying!

Revelation 12:11 And they overcame him by the blood of the Lamb, and by the word of their testimony; and they loved not their lives unto the death.

PASTOR MIKE: WHY DO YOU GET ATTACKED SO MUCH BY THE DEVIL? You see, I have been HEALED of at least **Twenty** major ailments! Without the use of medicine or doctors!!

#1   Healed of major allergies
#2   Healed of loss of the sense of smell
#3   Healed of birth defects in the bones of my ears
#4   Healed of a speech impediment
#5   Healed of a broken back
#6   Healed of burned-out vocal cords
#7   I was raised from the dead by my wife
#8   Healed of painful tumors in my abdomen
#9   Healed of a serious hernia
#10 Healed of a broken and crushed kneecap
#11 Healed of a dangerous attack of conjunctivitis
#12 Healed of arthritis
#13 Healed instantly of a broken foot
#14 My son was Healed from rabies
#15 Healed from prostate cancer
#16 Healed from life-threatening colon cancer
#17 Healed instantly of a broken, twisted index finger
#18 Healed overnight of second-degree burns
#19 Healed of gushing bright red blood
#20 And many Healings, daily since February 18, 1975.

PLEASE UNDERSTAND I AM BRAGGING ON **JESUS**!

I have experienced the enemy trying to Kill Me - and my loved ones - over **Sixty** times! In all those dangerous situations (many times it looked like I was a goner!), **GOD** miraculously stepped in and delivered me. You might ask: **But How Pastor Mike?** I would tell you that it was a **No Matter What I Will Not Be Moved by the Circumstances Type of FAITH in CHRIST** that preserved me, and My Loved Ones.

*In the natural, I should have been dead when the gang leader tried to stab me to death.

FAITH BASED OUTCOME INDEPENDENT

*When the same man shot me with a 12-gauge shotgun.
*I should have been dead when the Yupik Indians tried to steam me to death.
*I should have been dead when I fell into the Bering Sea in rough weather.
*I should have been dead when my motorcycle flipped out underneath me, on black ice, on the main Highway.
*I should have been dead when the demon-possessed woman kept stabbing me in the face with a knife etc.....

I COULD TELL YOU STORY AFTER STORY!
(Well over 2000 to date)

I asked the Lord: **"FATHER**, why in the world have I gone through so much?" He spoke to my heart and said: **"I Will Use You as an Example of What I Can Do in a Person's Life - If They Will Have FAITH in Me!"** But, I said Lord: "Why Me?" And He answered: **"I Use the Foolish to Confound the Wise!"**

*1 Corinthians 1:27 But **GOD** hath chosen the foolish things of the world to confound the wise; and **GOD** hath chosen the weak things of the world to confound the things which are mighty;*

Do Not Think for a moment that I am bragging on Mike Yeager. I wrote a book called: **"I Need GOD Because I'm Stupid."**

That book was written for the total purpose of causing people to realize that Mike Yeager is nobody. It is **JESUS CHRIST** that we put our complete confidence and hope in. If **GOD** can use Mike Yeager: I can guarantee that He can use anybody! It is our **FAITH** in **CHRIST** that gives us the victory.

*1 John 5:4-5 For whatsoever is born of **GOD** overcometh the world: and this is the victory that overcometh the world, even our* **FAITH**. *5 Who is he that overcometh the world, but he that believeth that **JESUS** is the Son of **GOD**?*

I Pray with All My Heart That as You Continue to Read This Book that **FAITH** will come exploding into your inner being. And that **FAITH** in **CHRIST** will bring you into a place Of Amazing Victory!

HOW TO BE FAITH-BASED OUTCOME INDEPENDENT

BECOME OBSESSED WITH A DEEP HUNGER TO KNOW GOD AND HIS WORD!

I remember giving my heart to **JESUS CHRIST** on February 18, 1975. As I got up from the floor, born again, saved, and delivered, I was a brand-new person. Immediately a **Hunger And Thirst for the Word of GOD** took hold of me. I began to devour the Gospels of Matthew, Mark, Luke, and John.

I just could not get enough of the Word of **GOD**, because of my love for **JESUS CHRIST** and His **FATHER**. **JESUS** became my hero in every area of my thoughts and daily life. He became my reason for getting up, going to work, eating, sleeping, and living. I discovered that everything I did was based on the desire of wanting to please Him.

I carried my little green military Bible with me wherever I went. Whenever I had an opportunity, I would open it up and study it. It wasn't very long before I believed for a larger Bible. This larger Bible gave me much more room to make notes, highlight and circle certain Scriptures. The more I fed on the Scriptures: the greater my hunger became for them.

FAITH BASED OUTCOME INDEPENDENT

I probably wasn't even saved for two months before I was asked to speak, for the first time, at a small Pentecostal church. I believe it was called "Adak Full Gospel Church." As far as I know, it was the only Pentecostal church on the military base situated on an Aleutian Island, in Alaska. Since 1975 I have never lost my hunger or my thirst for **GOD**'s Word. I can even truly say what the psalmist said:

Psalm 104:34 My meditation of him shall be sweet: I will be glad in the Lord.

The hunger for **GOD**'s Word has caused me to memorize over one-third of the New Testament. I am not bragging or boasting; I'm just simply saying that **GOD**'s Word is the joy and rejoicing of my heart. There are People Who Love to Swim, People Who Love to Work out, People Who Love to Do Push-Ups and Chin-Ups and Lift Weights - but we need people who love **GOD**'s Word!

Psalm 16:3 But to the saints that are in the earth, and to the excellent, in whom is all my delight.

Psalm 37:4 Delight thyself also in the LORD: and he shall give thee the desires of thine heart.

Psalm 37:23 The steps of a good man are ordered by the LORD: and he delighteth in his way.

---

*Psalm 40:8 I delight to do thy will, O my **GOD**: yea, thy law is within my heart.*

Psalm 112:1 Praise ye the LORD. Blessed is the man that feareth the LORD, that delighteth greatly in his commandments.

Psalm 119:16 I will delight myself in thy statutes: I will not forget thy word.

Psalm 119:24 Thy testimonies also are my delight and my counselors.

Psalm 119:35 Make me to go in the path of thy commandments; for therein do I delight.

Psalm 119:47 And I will delight myself in thy commandments, which I have loved.

Psalm 119:70 ......but I delight in thy law.

Psalm 119:77 Let thy tender mercies come unto me, that I may live: for thy law is my delight.

Psalm 119:92 Unless thy law had been my delights, I should then have perished in mine affliction.

Psalm 119:143 Trouble and anguish have taken hold on me: yet thy commandments are my delights.

Psalm 119:174 I have longed for thy salvation, O LORD; and thy law is my delight.

Psalm 104:34 My meditation of him shall be sweet: I will be glad in the LORD.

GOD Healed Me of Being Tongue-Tied

FAITH BASED OUTCOME INDEPENDENT

One day I was reading my Bible and discovered where **JESUS** said that it was necessary for him to leave. That because when he would go back to the **FATHER**, he would send the promise of the **Holy Ghost** to make us a witness. Furthermore, I learned it was His will for me to be filled to overflowing with the **Holy Ghost** and that the **Holy Ghost** would empower and equip me to be a witness an ambassador for **GOD**. The **Holy Ghost** would also lead me and guide me into all truth.

With all my heart, I desperately wanted to reach the lost for **JESUS CHRIST**, for they could experience the same love and freedom that I was now walking in. I searched the Scriptures to confirm this experience. In the book of Joel, in the old covenant, the four Gospels and especially in the book of acts, I discovered the will of **GOD** when it comes to this baptism. I perceived in my heart that I needed to receive this baptism the same way that I had received salvation.

I had to look to **CHRIST** and trust by **FAITH** that he would give to me this baptism of the Spirit. It declared in the book of acts that after they had been baptized in the **Holy Ghost**, they all began to speak in a heavenly language. I had not been around what we would call Pentecostal people, so I had never heard anybody else speak in this heavenly language. But that did not matter to me because it was within the Scriptures.

*Acts 2:39 For the promise is unto you, and to your children, and to all that are afar off, even as many as the Lord our **GOD** shall call.*

I remember getting on my knees next to my bunk bed where I cried out and asked **GOD** to fill me with the **Holy Ghost** so I could be a witness. As I was crying out to **GOD**, something began to happen on the inside of me. It felt like hot buckets of oil was beginning to be poured upon me and within me. Something then began to rise out of my innermost being. Before I knew what I was doing, a new language came out bubbling of my mouth, which I had never heard before or been taught to speak. I began to speak in a heavenly tongue.

Now up to this time, I had a terrible speech impediment. You see I had been born tongue-tied. Yes, they had operated on me, and I had gone to speech therapy, and yet most people could not understand what I was saying. I could not even pronounce my last name YEAGER properly. My tongue simply refused to move in a way in which I could pronounce my Rs.

After I was done praying in this new language, I discovered to my absolute surprise that my speech impediment was instantly and completely gone! From that time on, I have never stopped preaching **JESUS CHRIST**. For almost 40 years, I have proclaimed the truth of **JESUS CHRIST** to as many as I can.

I have written a Book on the Why of Tongues!

Saw CHRIST upon the Whipping Post

Why **GOD** heals me Time

While reading my Bible as a brand-new believer, I discovered that **JESUS CHRIST** went about healing **ALL** who were sick and oppressed of the devil. I began to search the Scriptures on this particular subject, and as I studied, I discovered many Scriptures that support this:

*Surely he hath borne our griefs, and carried our sorrows: yet we did esteem him stricken, smitten of **GOD**, and afflicted. But he was wounded for our transgressions, he was bruised for our iniquities: the chastisement of our peace was upon him; and with his stripes we are healed (Isaiah 53:4-5).*

FAITH BASED OUTCOME INDEPENDENT

Who his own self bare our sins in his own body on the tree, that we, being dead to sins, should live unto righteousness: by whose stripes ye were healed.1 Peter 2:24

When the even was come, they brought unto him many that were possessed with devils: and he cast out the spirits with his word, and healed all that were sick: That it might be fulfilled which was spoken by Esaias the prophet, saying, Himself took our infirmities, and bare our sicknesses. Matthew 8:16-17

As I read and meditated upon these Scriptures, something wonderful happened within my heart. Great, overwhelming sorrow took hold of me as I saw the pain and the agony that **JESUS** went through for my healing. In my heart and in my mind, I saw that **JESUS** had taken my sicknesses and my diseases. I then experienced great love for the son of **GOD** and recognize the price he paid for my healing.

When **GOD** gave me this revelation, revealed to me by the Scriptures, I experienced a great overwhelming love for the son of **GOD**, recognizing the price he had paid for my healing. It was like an open vision in which I saw my precious **Lord and Savior** tied to the whipping post. I saw the Roman soldiers striking, beating, and whipping the back of **JESUS** with the cat of nine tails.

This was a Roman whip that had nine long strands, coated with oil, and covered with glass, metal shards, and sharp objects. In this vision, I saw the flesh and the blood of my precious Savior splashing everything within a 10-foot radius, with each terrible stroke of the Romans soldier's whip hitting his body.

As I saw this open vision (as I was on my knees in prayer) I wept because I knew that this horrendous beating, he was enduring was for my healing and my deliverance. To this day, even after 40 years, whenever I retell this story, great love, and sorrow still fills my heart for what **CHRIST** had to endure for me. This is the reason why I am so aggressive in my fight to receive healing.

Still, I have great joy, wonderful peace, and enthusiasm in this battle, because I know that by the **stripes of JESUS CHRIST, I am healed**. This amazing price that he paid (**GOD** in the flesh) was not only for me but for every believer who has received **CHRIST** as their Lord and Savior.

In this moment of this vision, something exploded within my heart; an amazing **FAITH** possessed me with the knowledge that I no longer must be sick. In the name of **JESUS** for over 40 years, I have refused to allow what my precious Lord went through to be for nothing. I have refused to allow sickness and disease to dwell in my body, which is the temple of the **Holy Ghost**.

JESUS has taken my sicknesses and my diseases. No, if, an, or butts, no matter what it looks like or how I feel, I know within my heart **JESUS CHRIST** has set me free from sicknesses and diseases. Now of this revelation great anger, yes great anger, rose up in my heart against the enemy of my Lord. The demonic world has no right to afflict me or any other believer because **JESUS** took our sicknesses and bore our diseases.

Healed of Three Infirmities

Now I had been born with terrible physical infirmities, but now I found myself speaking out loud with authority to my ears, commanding them to be open and to be normal in the name of **JESUS CHRIST** of Nazareth. Then I spoke to my lungs and commanded them to be healed in the name of **JESUS CHRIST** of Nazareth. Next, I commanded my sinuses to be delivered, so I could smell normal scents in the name of **JESUS CHRIST** of Nazareth.

FAITH BASED OUTCOME INDEPENDENT

The minute I spoke the Word of **GOD** to my physical man, my ears popped completely open. Up to this moment, I had a significant hearing loss, but now as I was listening to **Christian** music playing softly (at least I thought it was), the music became so loud that I had to turn it down. My lungs were clear, and I haven't experienced any lung congestion since in 40 years.

I used to be so allergic to dust that my mother had to work extra hard to keep our house dust-free. I would literally end up in an oxygen tent in the hospital. From that moment to now, dust, allergies, mold, or any such thing have never come back to torment me or cause me problems. Instantly my sense of smell returned! I had broken my nose about four times due to fights, accidents, and rough activities. I could barely smell anything.

Suddenly, I could smell a terrible odor. I tried to find out where it was coming from, and then I looked at my feet and wondered if it could be them. I put my foot on a nightstand and bent over toward it. I took a big sniff and nearly fell over. Man, did my feet stink! I went straight over to the bathroom and washed them in the sink.

The very 1st thing we must do to build a solid foundation for our lives is to let go of all our traditions, philosophies, doctrines, and experiences that contradict what is revealed to us through **JESUS CHRIST**. We must go back to Matthew, Mark, Luke, and John rediscovering who **JESUS CHRIST** really is. Whatever **JESUS** said and did is what we agree with wholeheartedly. Any voice or teaching that contradicts **CHRIST** and his redemptive work I immediately reject.

*How **GOD** anointed **JESUS** of Nazareth with the **Holy Ghost** and with power: who went about doing good, and healing all that were oppressed of the devil; for **GOD** was with him (Acts 10:38).*

***I have written up to this date three books on Divine Healing**

For 40 years, I have aggressively, violently, persistently, taken hold of my healing. I refuse to let the devil rob me of what **JESUS** so painfully purchased. It is mine, and the devil cannot have it. The thought has never even entered my mind to go see a doctor when physical sickness attacks my body, for I already have a doctor, his name is **JESUS CHRIST** of Nazareth . He is the great physician, and he has already healed me with his stripes.

Yes, there have been times when the manifestation of my healing seemed like it would never come, but I know that I know that I know by his stripes I am healed. Strong **FAITH** never considers the **Circumstances**.

*Romans 4:18-20, Who against hope believed in hope, that he might become the **FATHER** of many nations, according to that which was spoken, So shall thy seed be. And being not weak in **FAITH**, he considered not his own body now dead, when he was about an hundred years old, neither yet the deadness of Sarah's womb: He staggered not at the promise of **GOD** through unbelief; but was strong in **FAITH**, giving glory to **GOD**;*

One of my most common declarations is: if I were, then I was, and if I was, then I am, if I am, then I is. I is healed!

HAVING THE MIND OF CHRIST

Philippians 2: 5 Let this mind be in you, which was also in Christ Jesus: 6 who, being in the form of God, thought it not robbery to be equal with God: 7 but made himself of no reputation, and took upon him the form of a servant, and was made in the likeness of men: 8 and being found in fashion as a man, he humbled himself, and became obedient unto death, even the death of the cross. 9 Wherefore God also hath highly exalted him, and given him a name which is above every name:

FAITH BASED OUTCOME INDEPENDENT

Faith-Based Outcome Independent will take you to places that your flesh does not want to go. Many Christians are being taught that **Faith** is given to you simply to get what you want or even what you need, but it's way beyond that. True biblical **Faith** is going to take you where natural man will not go. True saving **Faith**, follows, loves obeys, serves **God**. **Jesus** it is our Supreme example when it comes to being outcome independent. Here is the truth that most will not want to hear. True **Faith** will bring suffering. Listen to me now, true **Faith** in **Christ** will bring suffering. The apostle Paul, said:

Acts 14:21 And when they had preached the gospel to that city, and had taught many, they returned again to Lystra, and to Iconium, and Antioch, 22 confirming the souls of the disciples, and exhorting them to continue in the Faith, and that we must through much tribulation enter into the kingdom of God.

Now this is New Testament Christianity. This is not American Christianity because American Christianity teachers that pay for taking down the path of least resistance. Actually, the opposite is true. **Faith** that pleases **God** take you down the most difficult, problematic, challenging path who have walked. Paul throughout his writings talks about the difficulties that they had.

2 Corinthians 1:8 For we would not, brethren, have you ignorant of our trouble which came to us in Asia, that we were pressed out of measure, above strength, insomuch that we despaired even of life:

There is an aspect of **Faith** that will rise up in your heart and help you to deny your flesh. This is the **Faith** that overcomes the world, the flesh, and the devil. **Faith Based Outcome-Independent** means that I do not care about the **Circumstance**. I do not care about the situation. I do not really care about the problem. I do not care about the results. All I care about is the Lord.

 Now, the Bible's full of testimonies of those who walked in this realm of **Faith**. Those who said: I'm not surrendering to this. I'm not yielding to this. But I am yielding to **God**. I am obeying **God**. I am following **God**, no matter what it costs. This is **Faith Based Outcome-Independent**. For, another words, you're independent of the threats. You're not moved by the intimidation, by the fear, by what could happen.

Daniel when he was confronted with the threat of being thrown to the lions, he kept praying and worshiping towards Jerusalem. Everybody who knew down all new that he would bow down and worship towards Jerusalem three times a day. He did not allow the kings edict to stop his routine. Even though in the natural it meant his death by a gruesome method.

Of course, his enemies turned him in. When they deceived the king into making this edict, they knew that Daniel was a man who would not quit praying. They used his faithfulness and his love for **God** against him. Yet we know what the ultimate outcome was.

Daniel 6:20And when he came to the den, he cried with a lamentable voice unto Daniel: and the king spake and said to Daniel, O Daniel, servant of the living God, is thy God, whom thou servest continually, able to deliver thee from the lions?

Daniel 6:22My God hath sent his angel, and hath shut the lions' mouths, that they have not hurt me: forasmuch as before him innocency was found in me; and also before thee, O king, have I done no hurt.

Daniel 6:24And the king commanded, and they brought those men which had accused Daniel, and they cast them into the den of lions, them, their children, and their wives; and the lions had the mastery of them, and brake all their bones in pieces or ever they came at the bottom of the den.

Dan's attitude was, hey, if I live, I live, If I die, I die. And he was thrown into the lion den. Then now how many? **God** spared him. But in Hebrews 11, it talks about those who weren't spared.

Hebrews 11:36 and others had trial of cruel mockings and scourgings, yea, moreover of bonds and imprisonment: 37 they were stoned, they were sawn asunder, were tempted, were slain with the sword: they wandered about in sheepskins and goatskins; being destitute, afflicted, tormented; 38 (of whom the world was not worthy:) they wandered in deserts, and in mountains, and in dens and caves of the earth.

Exodus 14:21-22 KJV And Moses stretched out his hand over the sea; and the LORD caused the sea to go back by a strong east

wind all that night, and made the sea dry land, and the waters were divided. And the children of Israel went into the midst of the sea upon the dry ground: and the waters were a wall unto them on their right hand, and on their left

Bought Five Tents with No Money

Doc Yeager: Eventually, we ended up purchasing an old church bus. With all the scrap material I could find, we turned that bus into living quarters. Once I had everything installed, Kathee, young Michael, and I moved into our new home. The idea that had come to me was that we would go to different fairs and carnivals to hold tent meetings. Kathleen was in complete agreement with me, but we had one little problem. We did not own a tent, PA equipment, chairs, lights, or anything else to do with a tent ministry! I was not going to ask anyone to help us with this equipment, **GOD** was our source.

Not only did we not have anything we needed to have a tent ministry, but we also did not have two pennies to rub together. In other words, we were flat broke. (As I think back to this time in our lives, I must laugh. **GOD** is so good. He has such a wonderful sense of humor. All we must do is look to Him).

Well, I needed a tent to start with, so I went to prayer with supplication and thanksgiving. The Spirit of **GOD** quickened to my heart to get the tents from the brethren denomination, where I had rented my last tent for the Huntington County Fair. I began to pray seriously what the Lord would have me to do. This is what came into my heart, call up the brother and Campground telling them that you want to buy tents.

I called up the Roxbury campgrounds and told them that I would like to purchase some of their tents if they had any for sale. They said that they would get back in touch with me. We had our old bus parked at Kathee's grandma's house during this time. Not long afterward, I received a phone call from them on grandma's phone, informing me they had some tents they would like to sell us.

I set up a time when I could come down and pick these tents up. Kathleen had a nephew whose name was Gary. Gary's mother was a pastor and evangelist. Gary was about nineteen years old at that time (I was an old man of twenty-six, myself). I called Gary up and asked him if he wanted to go into the tent ministry with us. He said he would pray about it and get back in touch with me.

Gary called back that same day and said he was interested. I told him that I had to go to Roxbury to pick up our tents and asked him if he would like to go along with me. Kathee's grandma had a neighbor who owned a gas station and had a tire business. This gentleman possessed a large steel truck that he transported tires in. I asked if I could rent his truck. He said he would not rent it to me, but that I could use it.

On the day we were to meet with the personnel at Roxbury, Gary met me at Kathee's grandma's house. We both got into the big truck and were on our way. As we were driving and discussing spiritual matters, I told him there was something he needed to know.

I told him when we get to Roxbury, I did not want him to say anything about us not having any money to these people that we were purchasing the tents from.

He looked over at me kind of strange and asked what I meant. I told him I did not have a penny to my name.

With great surprise, he said, **"What?"**
I told him once again, "I don't have any money to my name."
He asked what we were going to do then.
I said, "They don't know it yet, but they are going to give us these tents." PS: this was quickened in my heart as I was praying.

FAITH BASED OUTCOME INDEPENDENT

He said, **"They're going to do what?"**

I repeated my statement again, operating in the gift of **FAITH** and the word of wisdom. It was not just hoping, wishing, guessing, making a good confession, or coveting their tents.

It was the gift of **FAITH** at work in my heart with the word of wisdom. I emphasized to him that he needed to be quiet about the finances no matter what.

We got to the campgrounds in Roxbury where they were waiting for us. They had gathered a group of men to help pull the tents and all that went with them out of storage. I think there were about a dozen men. They opened the large doors on one of their storage buildings. Then the men would sweat and groan as they pulled a big canvas bag out of the storage barn. In those days all the tents were made of canvas and they were not easy to handle or put up. The tie-down stakes and side poles were all brought out into the light.

Next came the center poles, which were made of heavy steel. They were extremely heavy and difficult to handle. Of course, then you had all of the side curtains. I'm just emphasizing this because there was a lot of work involved in bringing these tents out of the barn and loading them up.

They would pull a tent out of one of their buildings and spread it out, asking me if I wanted to buy that tent. Each time I would say yes! By the time they were done, there were five tents on our truck. I wish you could have seen Gary's face; he was very nervous. When the men had finished uploading all the tents on our truck, I asked them how much I owed.

The truck itself was squatting because it was so full, and the tents were almost bulging over the side. When I asked him how much I owed them, one of the men said they had not yet discussed the cost per tent. I said OKAY, I would wait for them to let me know. These men went off together in a circle. After much discussion, they came back to me and told me that they had prayed about it and felt in their hearts they should give me these tents for free.

Hallelujah! There was one other tent that was out in the field being used. It was a very large tent and some of the sections of that tent, for some reason, were loaded on our truck. They told me if I wanted the rest of that tent that it would cost me $250. Praise **GOD**, the Lord provided for that later, and we were also able to pick it up later.

How GOD Healed Me of Kidney Stones

My Step-by-Step Process That I went through Dealing with Kidney Stones!

(Warning this will be a long article, but I believe it'll be worth the time for you to read)

Many have read my stories after the fact of how **GOD** healed me. It came into my heart to share with you the fight, the struggle, and the wrestling that I'm going through right now at this moment: until I see a manifestation of my healing over these kidney stones.

Yes, thousand times yes by **FAITH** I received my healing the moment I take hold of **GOD**. I still must deal with the symptoms, pain, and associated situations with this attack. But this is that time in which patients, endurance, longsuffering, Trusting in **GOD** must prevail. Speaking, Exercising **FAITH**, standing on **GOD**'s word, Thanksgiving and praise must be the order of the day.

Now, in July I had seen a miracle for another brother who had prayed for who had kidney stones. He informed me that immediately all pain left his body, and then he passed the kidney stone the next morning with absolutely no pain. Hallelujah, thank you, **JESUS**.

FAITH BASED OUTCOME INDEPENDENT

I wish I could say that was the case for me, but it's not. Even as I dictate this article, my body is extremely protesting, filled with pain. But Pastor Mike, why aren't you healed? And why are you going through tremendous pain? This is maybe where I'm different from most people that I know. I'm not moved by the **Circumstances**.

Smith Wigglesworth said: Any Man Who Considers the **Circumstances**, Is Not a Man Who Is Walking in the Spirit or by **FAITH**! I can truly testify that this statement is true. This article might be a little bit hit and miss right now because when the urge to head for the bathroom hits me, I better get up and get there quick.

I'm not writing this article to cause anybody to feel sorry for me. Plus, I'm not really wanting anybody to give me suggestions, not that I'm not teachable. But I'm standing upon **GOD**'s Word as I have done for over 40 years. This too shall pass! I have gone through much greater tests and trials for what this is. In 2005 I had a bout with colon cancer. I had this confirmed by a medical expert, who might even respond to this post.

I did not use medical help or the physicians of this world. It did not even enter my mind. I cried out to Dr. **JESUS**. Three long, grueling, painstaking months I stood upon **GOD**'s word. Sometimes walking in the sanctuary of our church almost all day just barely hanging onto life. But after three months, I went to bed one night, and glory to **GOD**, I got up the next morning, and it was all gone. That was over 12 years ago. You see my **FAITH** is not in ME! My wisdom, spirituality, maturity, or even knowledge of the Word it's all established and founded upon **GOD**'s Word.

Now, if people encourage me to go to the doctors, I am not offended. Yes, if the spirit of **GOD** Quicken to my heart and told me that I needed to go, I would! There have been times when I told people to go because I knew they were not going to make it if they did not. Many times, people convince themselves are walking by **FAITH**, but the words, actions, and emotions revealed that there are not. If you are squalling and bowling in fear, asking **GOD** why he won't hear will you, I can guarantee you're not in **FAITH**. You Better Get Help Now!

HOW THIS BATTLE BEGAN!

On Friday, August 5, 2017, I had a rough evening sleeping. My body just did not seem to be right. Yes-I just simply Speak in a word, agreeing with **GOD**. Then Saturday, August 6 my wife and I went to her 40th school anniversary. Even though I wasn't feeling good, I never allow myself to be bedridden. If I believe I'm healed (and I know I am) I just keep going. On the way home from that reunion at about 9 o'clock at night, it really hit me. I began to get the chills. My wife was hot, but I was cold! Lol - I just took hold of **GOD**'s word and bound the spirit of infirmity. All night I had a keep on wrestling, not getting any sleep. Sunday morning, I think I rolled out of bed early to go pray and get my heart ready for the message.

Yes-I preached that morning and that night. A yes-my body was full of pain with backaches, chills, slight fever. I didn't tell anyone, except my wife. I was not trying to hide it, I was just standing on **GOD**'s word. I did notice that I was not able to hold my water like normal. For the last couple of months every time my hands got wet, I had a run for the bathroom. That should've told me something wasn't normal. On Sunday it began to get painful to make water. I thought to myself: Come on, Now What? I took authority over these problems.

My head began to hurt, my back, my kidneys, my drawings. Yes-I am going to be very graphic. If you're squeamish at all, it's time for you to stop reading. But I want to give to you in detail this battle. No-I's not glorifying the devil. I'm just telling you how it is. How I Fight This Fight of **FAITH**! Sometimes the manifestation of my healing is immediate. Sometimes it's in a matter of hours, or days, or weeks, or even months. I just won't let go because I Know That **GOD** Cannot Lie! I do not command **GOD** to do anything because I know I am dealing with demonic powers.

Acts 10:38 How **GOD** anointed **JESUS** of Nazareth with the Holy Ghost and with power: who went about doing good and healing all that were oppressed of the devil; for **GOD** was with him.

Ephesians 6:12 For we wrestle not against flesh and blood, but against principalities, against powers, against the rulers of the darkness of this world, against spiritual wickedness in high places.

Maybe through my battle, you can learn some things. On August 7, I woke up feeling even worse. We were supposed to head out for an RMAI conference in Lancaster. There isn't no way I was going to cancel because of my body screaming, pouting, yelling for my attention. I Told the Body to Shut up. Yes, shut up and be healed. Well, we made it to the conference, and I sat there trying to be a good boy with a smile on my face all the time being full of pain and terrible symptoms. Thank **GOD,** I made it through that day.

All night long I kept struggling again and getting up to have to make water it seemed every half-hour. I let my precious wife sleep, just speaking the word over my body. At about 8 o'clock in the morning as I was standing over the toilet, and extreme overwhelming pain hit me. It was not fire shut up in my bones either.

 I had to grab ahold of the toilet and hold on for a rough ride. Something was coming out of me. Before I knew it blood, and an ugly slimy lump came forth. The pain did not subside. I just kept on thanking **JESUS** that I was healed. I made my way back to bed without flushing the toilet. I just laid there, and every time an urge came to go to the bathroom, away I went.

I'm Giving Details for Your Benefit!

When my wife finally awoke, I told her what had happened. We decided to investigate online. From all, we could discover it absolutely was kidney stones. I guess it must be like that of when a woman goes into travel and getting close to delivery. My family and I have researched on the Internet all the symptoms I had, I have and am going through. Without a shadow of a doubt, it is kidney stones. So now that I know what I'm dealing with, I'm taking natural and spiritual steps to deal with it. (Second time I've had a stop with his article, to run for the bathroom)

Symptoms of Kidney stones
Severe pain in the side and back, below the ribs
Pain that radiates to the lower abdomen and groin
Pain that comes in waves and fluctuates in intensity
Pain on urination
Pink, red or brown urine
Cloudy or foul-smelling urine
Nausea and vomiting
Persistent need to urinate
Urinating more often than usual
Fever and chills if an infection is present
Urinating small amounts

YUP that about sums up what I've been going through! One thing I did not mention that I've been going through during fight is Extremely Terrible Headaches! They seem to be nonstop, but my focus is on **JESUS CHRIST!**

Kidney stone facts

A kidney stone is a hard, crystalline mineral material formed within the kidney or urinary tract. One in every 20 people develop kidney stones at some point in their life.

Kidney stones form when there is a decrease in urine volume and/or an excess of stone-forming substances in the urine. Symptoms of a kidney stone include flank pain (the pain can be quite severe) and blood in the urine (hematuria).

So what did I do? I spoke to my body; kidneys be healed In **JESUS** Name! Kidney stones be dissolved In **JESUS** Name! Pain leave now In **JESUS** Name! Thank you, **JESUS**, I'm healed right now. Thank you by the stripes of **CHRIST** I am made whole.

FAITH BASED OUTCOME INDEPENDENT

Thank you, **JESUS**! On, and on, and on as it is permissible. For another word I don't do this in public.

WE WENT TO THE MEETING

Yes-I went to the meeting. Ate a light breakfast. Put a smile on my face and try to talk to people. As the meeting proceeded, there were times I had to make myself hang onto **GOD** because I could not get up to go to the restroom, not wanting to disturb the meeting. My wife and I were sitting all the way up front. Finally, lunch came. I ran for the bathroom, and I would go into the toilet stall and grit my teeth for I would not moan, or cry out as I was making water. In my heart I was saying: I Am Healed, I Am Healed, in **JESUS**'s name, I Am Healed!

I came out of the restroom and when I got a light meal, basically a salad. After ate once again I had to run to the bathroom and go through the whole process again. To be honest, the pain was so intense, I began to cry some with the difficulty of dealing with the pain. But **GOD** and his Word is greater than the pain or the symptoms.

 If I would've been a wimp all these years, I would've been dead more times than I can count. Lol amazingly sometimes when the enemy attacks my body with symptoms, is quickened in my heart to slam and hit my body. I know this sounds abusive, but not when the Holy Ghost is in it. Every time it's quickened in my heart to do this I'm almost always instantly healed. This has not yet happened to me in this situation.

ON TO SIGHT AND SOUND!

It was a good message from the guest speaker, brother Tony, but was I having to fight the fight of **FAITH**. After the meeting was dismissed, many of us headed to sight and sound to watch Jonah and the Whale! It was a wonderful presentation of the gospel, but that I must fight pain. I had to sit there for I think over two hours, to wait for the intermission. Somehow by **GOD**'s grace and only by **GOD**'s grace, I was able to do this. Thank **GOD** the second half wasn't near as long.

My wife and I made it out to our car and headed back to the hotel for a brief rest before that night's gathering. To say the least, I was having to go through this whole process by looking to **GOD**. Now I'm going to be a little bit descriptive of what I've been doing to stand upon **GOD**'s word. When the urge hits me to make water, a run to the bathroom, and position myself over the toilet.

Here comes the pain, if I'm in a public restroom I just grit my teeth and hang on for dear life. But if I'm somewhere nobody can hear me or just my family, this is what comes out of my mouth as I'm making water. **IN JESUS NAME, IN JESUS NAME, IN JESUS NAME, IN JESUS NAME,---OH -- OH-- OH --- AH -- AH -- AH, THANK YOU JESUS, THANK YOU JESUS!** Over and over until I'm done at the toilet. I'm just being blunt and honest with you in this battle.

You see, the thought doesn't even come to my head about going to a natural doctor because I know, that I know, that I know, that By the Stripes of **JESUS** I Am Healed!

After that night's meeting (long painful meeting because of what I was going through) we headed back to the hotel. The thought came into my head about canceling the little vacation my wife and I were going to take right after this meeting on Wednesday.

We were going to go to Ocean City because my wife likes the water. Maybe walk the boardwalk a little bit and go out to eat. On August 19 it will be our 39th wedding anniversary. Oh-what a wonderful life I have! But **FAITH** rose in my heart, and I determined that we were going to go no matter what because no man that walks by **FAITH** considers the **Circumstances**.

Wednesday morning came around, with a long struggle through the night. We made it to the morning session. Before the meeting began, I pulled a good brother aside for he could pray with me because I know he's a man of **FAITH**. Gary Bailey agreed with me in prayer that in **JESUS**'s name I was healed, I am healed, and I is healed. At the end of the service, the wonderful apostolic gift that **GOD** had put over this ministry encouraged us to come to him at any time if we needed prayer or help for anything.

His name is Sam Smucker who started the worship center in Lancaster over 40 years ago. After many people had left the meeting, I walked up to him. Asked him to step aside with me. He agreed. I informed them what I was going through and asking him if he would stand on the word with me, and pray, believe for the complete manifestation of my healing. He did not pray any real long religious prayer, but simply spoke the word of **FAITH** over my body. Then my wife and I got in her Toyota Prius and left the meeting.

HEADED TO OCEAN CITY

Away we went headed for Maryland. A 3-hour drive to get to the hotel. What a journey. It got so bad at one time, I had to pull off the road, with my wife's side facing woods. She opened her door for I could, squat to make water. Moaning, groaning, speaking the name of **JESUS**. On Tuesday night I had a dream where I was driving a vehicle during the day. In this dream, my wife was with me.

I was extremely nauseated, tired, and my head wasn't working. I kept finding myself wanting to fall asleep. In this dream, I saw my foot hit the gas and put it to the metal without thinking at a very sharp corner. We came up off the ground off this corner headed right for a large barn. Then in this dream, everything went completely dark. I woke up at that moment and perceived this was a warning of **GOD**.

So here we are on our way to Ocean City when all of a sudden, I began to feel all of the symptoms I experienced in this dream. Immediately I pulled into the nearest gas station, informing my wife that she was going to have to drive. Thank **GOD** for supernatural warnings of the Holy Ghost. I am convinced that if I had not had that dream, my wife and I would've been in a terrible car accident.

I won't bore you with all the details, but we finally got to Ocean City. We walked the boardwalk for a little bit. Went out to eat. I told her I would take her out onto the beach when the moon was high in the sky. Away we went, speaking **GOD**'s word in my heart, hanging on for my dear life and my dear wife. Made it through another rough night.

Now it's August 10, Thursday, and we laid in bed a little bit longer than normal. Then we had to do a little bit of shopping. Ate a light meal on the boardwalk. She wanted to walk all the way down to the Museum. My body was screaming, lay down and get into a fetus position and scream. In my heart of hearts, I told her to shut up. I did not listen to it one iota. We finally made it to the museum and made our way through it. No complaining. No moaning out loud. No speaking death over my life. Simply agreeing with the Bible in **JESUS**'s name. (I just had a run for the bathroom again)

We headed back to our hotel for a much-needed rest. Later that night she wanted to go out and have a fish meal, and so did I. We went to Jonah and The Whale, no kidding. After I must admit we ate too much, we headed to the beach. This restaurant is right on the boardwalk. We really liked it here because there was hardly anybody. I think this is about 7 o'clock or maybe earlier. We laid down our sheet and towels.

INTO THE OCEAN

We did not have swimming suits on, just simply our shorts and shirts. I laid down on the blanket as He made her way into the water. Just crying out to **JESUS** under my breath. And then it was quickened in my heart that I needed to join my wife no matter what. She was being pushed around by white Waves. Her back was to me, so I made my way through the cold water up behind her. Right as a big way was about to hit her, I grabbed her from behind and hugged her tight.

FAITH BASED OUTCOME INDEPENDENT

The wave washed over us, taking us away. For about the next 45 minutes we just held onto each other being hit with salty wave after salty wave. My wife was extremely surprised because she knows I hate getting into the water. She also knows I don't really like the beach that much. I had enough of the ocean when I was in the Navy and whatnot was a fisherman in the Bering Sea up in Alaska, and off the coast of the state of Washington. We were both tired after that time in the ocean together.

HEADED BACK HOME

On our way to the hotel, my wife said: Honey let's go home tonight. I asked her, really? She usually does not like to drive late at night. She said yes, we need to go home. It had been a long day, but I told her if she could be ready by 9 PM with me helping her, we would go. Well, amazingly she was ready. Thank **GOD** we left Thursday night at 9 AM instead of waiting until Friday morning.

We had come to Ocean City by the Northern route, but now we were going to be heading towards the bay bridge and around Baltimore city Maryland. What a mess! Everywhere we went there was construction. Maryland, Delaware, Bray bridge, Baltimore, even throughout Pennsylvania. What took us about 4 1/2 hours would've taken probably eight hours. **GOD** is so good!

I fell on the bed completely exhausted, just thanking **GOD** that by his stripes I am healed! I woke up early Friday morning talking to the Lord. I didn't let my body be pampered but I rolled out of bed. I came over to the church, into my office to pray, and the cry out to **GOD**. This is what I've been endeavoring to do all day long!

I fell on the bed completely exhausted, just thanking **GOD** that by his stripes I am healed! I woke up early Friday morning talking to the Lord. I didn't let my body be pampered but I rolled out of bed. I came over to the church, into my office to pray, and the cry out to **GOD**. This is what I've been endeavoring to do all day long!

This whole test began on Friday, August 4. I had a rough night, and then Saturday night was extremely painful. My whole body hurt from head to toe. Of course, by Tuesday I passed a kidney stone while attending a ministers' conference. From that time up to Sunday, the 13th was extremely difficult. Yes, yes, yes, I drink lots of water. Yes, I did change my diet and have done so permanently. I do realize that we need to take care of our bodies. Sometimes we can abuse our physical man not realizing that we will pay the consequences.

Now, let me tell you what happened on Sunday, August 13th. I woke up extremely early and came over to the church to pray. I just kept thanking **GOD** and walking out my healing by **FAITH**. The 10 AM church service began, and I made myself worship **GOD**, preparing my heart to preach the word no matter how I felt.

My wife, daughter and other worship leader finished the worship service. I went to the pulpit and exhorted the people to keep worshiping and thanking **GOD** for the miracles that were about to happen. When it finally came time to minister the word, I just began to simply preach by **FAITH** with my mind and nothing but **GOD**'s will at that time. As I was preaching the spirit of **GOD** began to move mightily. Probably after approximately 20 minutes of preaching all the symptoms of the kidney stones were gone.

I have experienced this many times in over 40 years of ministry. I would say 99.9% of the time as I am preaching the Word of **GOD**, and then ministering to the people afterward, all symptoms of whatever has been attacking me has stopped. I can only remember one time that I did not preach because I was hit with an illness. I should've preached because it wasn't that bad. I had simply wimped out on that day. I felt so bad about wimping out, that I determine from that day forward I would never do it again. The Bible says a man must be found Faithful.

I shared with the congregation that Sunday morning that all the symptoms were gone as I was preaching. Of course, the congregation erupted in applause and praise to **GOD**. After that morning service, some of the symptoms did try to come back, but I knew that they were nothing but lies. In a very short matter of time, all the symptoms had disappeared.

Today is Tuesday, 22 August at 9 o'clock in the morning. I waited all of this time to share this testimony because I did not want to exaggerate in any way form or fashion this miracle. Sometimes the miracles that **GOD** does for us are not explosive, thunder or lightning. They are simply progressive. They must be walked out by **FAITH**.

In the gospel of Mark, it tells them that believe shall lay hands on the sick. Notice: and they shall recover. Many times, my healing, or I should say the manifestation of it has been progressive. And during this whole process I just simply keep thanking and praising **GOD** that it is done by **FAITH**. I keep getting up, going to work, staying in the word, and doing what I must do.

I think it's wonderful if you can live a life without any challenges to your physical man. I've heard people share testimonies of living nothing but healthy lives. This is indeed marvelous. But, and that's a big but: if you are attacked by the enemy, you must take a hold of **GOD**'s promises, speak to the problem, stand upon **GOD**'s word, walk it out through action, praise, worship, and Thanksgiving.

Habakkuk 3:17 Although the fig tree shall not blossom, neither shall fruit be in the vines; the labour of the olive shall fail, and the fields shall yield no meat; the flock shall be cut off from the fold, and there shall be no herd in the stalls:18 Yet I will rejoice in the Lord, I will joy in the GOD of my salvation.

CHAPTER SIX
The No Matter What Take HEALING

This statement may seem presumptuous or inaccurate but believe me - it is the truth. It is built on the biblical principles of **FAITH** and obedience to the will of **GOD**.

Most Bible believing **Christian**'s will acknowledge that all that ever needed to be done, was accomplished when **CHRIST** went to the cross, died and rose again. The Scriptures declare we were healed by the stripes upon the back of **JESUS**.

This is not just pertaining to spiritual healing, but absolutely also implies physical healing. **GOD** took me to the Scriptures within the first month that I was saved (in 1975) pertaining to the subject of healing. There are many Scriptures that deal with this, but more specifically: Isaiah 53, Matthew 8:17, and first Peter 2:24. After I studied and meditated upon the Scriptures, **FAITH** rose in my heart, and I literally took the Word of **GOD**, aggressively, for my own healing. I was healed from lifelong illnesses and generational curses.

Yet, still today many believers - in spite of the Scriptures declaring that **JESUS** paid the ultimate price for our physical healing - are having a difficult time receiving their healing. There are reasons for this.

TRUSTING IN THE ARM OF THE FLESH

The Lord said to me in prayer one morning something very shocking. It brought tears to my eyes and trembling in my heart. He said: **my people have forsaken me as their HEALER.** I could hear great sorrow and sadness in the voice of the Lord. Then the Scripture he gave me shook me even more. He said to me:

Jeremiah 2:13For my people have committed two evils; they have forsaken me the fountain of living waters, and hewed them out cisterns, broken cisterns, that can hold no water.

They have chosen to believe the devil who has told them that I who am their **God** and Savior (**JESUS CHRIST**) lied when I said: By My Stripes, You Are Healed.

When the Lord spoke this last part to me this morning it was like thunder in my soul. As I write this article I am shaking in the very depths of my being. Yes, a very small portion of the ministers of the gospel still preach healing, but yet themselves to a great extent look to man instead of going to **God**.

I sensed great sorrow and sadness in the heart of the Lord as HE spoke this to my heart this morning. The price that HE paid when HE received those 39 lashes upon HIS body was for HIS bride could be healed of not just physical, but emotional, psychological, and spiritual healing. But the enemy has deceived the church of **Jesus**, that what **Jesus** did for them was not enough. That they would have to go to man, and then mix a little bit of **God** in the midst of their affliction.

Why is there such a lack of **Faith**, trust, and confidence in what **Christ** has done for us? I truly believe it is because we have not hidden the truth within our hearts. We do not believe 1Peter 2: 24, Isaiah 53:4,5, Matthew 8: 17

There would be those who would rise up and say what I am saying is condemnation, but in all reality, the problem is not me, but those who would attack this simply have not really seen **Jesus Christ** as their healer. Our healing as believers was already purchased over 2000 years ago because of the stripes on the back of **Jesus**!

In 1975 as a 19-year-old baby Christian when I read the previously mentioned Scriptures, I had an open vision. I saw **Jesus** receiving the stripes on his back when he was on the whipping post. My heart broke with great sorrow and saw the sufferings HE went through for my healing. Up to that moment, I had been very sickly in my life. Many times going to the Doctors, being admitted to Hospitals. But at that very moment,(when I saw the sufferings of **Christ**) I declared with all the fiber of my being that I would not allow what **Jesus** did for me and HIS bride to be in vain!

For over 45 years anytime the enemy has attacked me physically I have aggressively taken hold of **God** with all of my heart. **God** has never failed me even though at times it looked like my healing was not going to manifest. Broken bones, burns, tumors, cancer, hernia, busted kneecap, gushing blood, kidney stones, dimming eyesight, and many other healings, too many to mention **Jesus Christ** has HEALED me from.

It is time for the body of **Christ** to arise, to truly once again come back to **Jesus Christ** the great physician. The price has been paid, take your healing. Stop believing the devil who is calling **Jesus Christ** a liar by saying what he did upon the whipping post by receiving those 39 lashes was not enough for your healing.

But how Pastor Mike? I have written extensively on how you can receive your healing. To this date, I have published numerous books on the subject of healing. Plus, numerous books on how you can take what **God** has already given to you with an aggressive and violent **Faith**. I have provided a link to my one book called: **God** healed me; he will heal you.

PS: What truly is dumbfounding me is that believers will spend thousands of dollars a year going to the medical world, and yet they will not spend a little bit of money to get the directions they need for their healing. May **Jesus** help us!

WHY I GET HEALED EVERY TIME

Not too long ago, I was in the sanctuary of the church I pastor. I was simply in prayer, crying out to **GOD** for His will to be done: in every area of my life and in others' lives. As I was in prayer, I heard the Lord, in my heart, say: **"Do You Know Why I Always Heal You?"**

Pastor Mike: How do you know this is **GOD** speaking to you? Because over 90% of the time, He always asks me questions about nothing that I am presently praying or thinking about. I know this is not a trick of my mind because I'm not even meditating upon what He says to me at the time. Plus, it does not contradict His Will, His Word, or His Personality.

I responded to the Lord with my own question. I said: "Lord, what do you mean?" He asked me again: **"Do You Know Why I Always Heal You?"** My mind was blank at this question, so I said: "How Come, Lord?"

He said this to me: **"Because You Are Not Afraid to Die!"** The moment He said this, I knew that it was true. It is not that I want to die, because I know the Lord has so many more things that He still wants me to do. But I am not afraid to die **Believing His Word!**

As I stood there, on that day, my mind ran through many occasions when, in the natural, I should have gone to the arm of the flesh.

Something in my heart, though, wouldn't allow me to. It's what we call **No Matter What FAITH!** It is not a thing of pride or arrogance. It's simply that, in my heart, for me to run to the world for my physical needs is literally to call **GOD** a liar.

For over forty years, I have simply stood upon **GOD**'s Word. Even though for months at times, I have endured pain-filled days, all-night wrestling's with tears and groanings, yet I have stood upon **GOD**'s Word. **GOD**, in every **Circumstance**, has always brought to me Supernatural Deliverance!

Living on the mudflats

Doc Yeager: (1976) Right outside the town of Dillingham, there is what was commonly called "The Mud Flats." It is an area that many natives would set their tents up to live and work from during the salmon season. At that time, I was living in a makeshift shack right outside of town on these mudflats. It was traditionally only a summertime place for those who were fishing to set up a temporary residence. Everybody had left it a long time before except for me.

I had nowhere else to stay. The winter had come before I knew it. After summer, with some help, I covered a tent with plywood on the outside and with thin insulation and plywood on the inside. We had found a big old bay window with only single-paned glass and installed it in the back portion of the tent. This window faced the Nushagak River upon which Dillingham was built next to. This is where all the boat docks were located, close to an old cannery.

I got myself an old 55-gallon barrel and put a wood stove pipe on one end and a door on the other where I could insert wood. To support myself during the wintertime, I applied for a job at one of the only gas stations at that time. They hired me to pump gas, change tires, and do grunt work as required.

FAITH BASED OUTCOME INDEPENDENT

Before I knew what happened, winter came with her full Arctic vengeance. I'm telling you it was one cold and snowy winter. In my plywood covered tent, the wind would shake it as it blew across the mudflats. It was over 50° below outside, not counting the wind-chill factor. My bed was nothing but a wooden frame with a piece of plywood. I would crawl into my sleeping bag, praying, and believing **GOD** that I would not freeze during the night. I would get up the next morning to walk 5 miles to work.

Over 90% of the time, I would never get a ride. My heart was content; however, as I would cry out to **JESUS**, I would ask Him for the opportunity to share the good news with anyone I met or who would listen to me. My heart yearned to win souls and to be more like **JESUS** every day. This cry has never left me. Here was an environment that would try the hearts and test the **FAITH** of any **God**ly man. I want you to know that **GOD** was with me in a powerful way in this situation.

Saved a Man from Bleeding to Death

In the late fall of 1975 (I was 19 years old at the time) I ended up working at a gas station in Dillingham, Alaska. This was the fishing village of Gov. Sarah and Todd Palin. Primarily, my job was to repair tires, fill people's vehicles with gas, clean up, help the mechanics, and do whatever was necessary. Previously when I was 16 years old, I had worked at a gas station in my hometown of Mukwonago, Wisconsin.

Now, this was the only gas station at that time that was available in Dillingham, Alaska. One of the main roads that ran through that area from the airport to the small-town Dillingham was still nothing but a dirt road. The name of the road was called Kanakanak that led to a hospital about 6 miles from the gas station. The main mechanics name was George, who was a Seventh-day Adventist. He had become a good friend of mine. Previously I purchased a 250 Kawasaki dirt motorcycle, and an old four-wheel-drive Ford Bronco.

This gas station was pretty much a rundown facility, with lots of old junk vehicles parked and stacked along one side of the mechanic shop. The gas pumps probably should've been replaced 20 years ago. One day as I was repairing tires in the shop, George, the mechanic was backing up the tow truck with a vehicle connected out of one of the bays onto the main road. The next thing I know, I heard a collision. Being busy with the repair of a tire, I just kept working.

A couple of minutes after the sound of this collision, George, the mechanic, came running into the shop telling everybody that there had just been a terrible accident. A young native Alaskan had come speeding around the corner on a motorcycle while George had the vehicle backed out onto the main dirt road. This young native with his motorcycle had slammed right into the car that was connected to George's tow truck. When this young Yupic Indian slammed into the vehicle with his motorcycle, he had gone flying high through the air over the top of the car George was towing.

The spirit of **GOD** quickened in me with an overwhelming urgency. I knew in my heart at that very moment I had to get to this young man because his life was in danger. I cannot explain it to people who have never moved in the **Holy Ghost**, but I knew by a word of knowledge he was bleeding to death. Immediately I jumped away from the big semi-trailer tire that I had been working on. I yelled to George: "Where is he right now," with great urgency in my heart?" He said to me, "He flew through the air, and he's in the middle of all the junk vehicles." I ran out through the large garage doors and headed over to the Junkers. I saw his crumpled-up motorcycle, but I did not immediately see him because he had fallen between two vehicles.

I came around the corner and began to look among the scrapped junked vehicles. I saw him lying on his back amidst a bunch of jagged steel. I ran over to him, noticing immediately that there was blood everywhere. I jumped down into the midst of the scrap metal, examining what was going on. The young man had already gone into shock. I began to examine his body, trying to find out where all the blood was coming from. I noticed immediately that it was from the calf of his right leg.

When he had hit the vehicle with his motorcycle, he had flown through the air and had come down amid some very sharp metal. His left leg had hit some sharp steel from an old vehicle, slicing his leg calf muscles to his bare bone. He must have cut the main artery because blood was gushing from this wound. Immediately I tore away the remainder of the leg of his pants that had been torn. I quickly pulled off my outer long sleeve shirt, and made a makeshift tourniquet, making it as tight as I could, using the long sleeves of the shirt as a turn a tourniquet.

During this whole time, I was not even thinking; I was moving under the power of the Holy Spirit. I knew within my heart what I had to do at that very moment, with total peace, boldness, and a divine urgency. He had already lost a lot of blood, and I began to speak life over him in the name of **JESUS CHRIST** of Nazareth. I boldly declared he would live and not die. Once I was able to get the blood to stop flowing, I began to yell for someone to come and help me.

** If the main femoral artery is severed, one could bleed to death within minutes. If you happen to cut completely through (like if you cut your foot off), you will bleed out considerably slower. The muscle's natural sponginess and your body's natural response to this kind of wound to some extent plug the gap, slowing the bleeding. You will still bleed to death if left unattended, but if pressure is applied and you're not in water, you can survive for about a half an hour. But if the cut is to the bone then is very bad. The body has no way to stop this kind of wound since the defensive mechanism of the body (narrow the artery to lower blood flow) does not work in this kind of a situation.*

I do not know why, but during this whole time, nobody had come out of the mechanic shop to see if everything was okay with the young man. I think I was moving so supernatural fast to where everything seemed to have slowed down. I've experienced this on numerous occasions where everything seems to come to a standstill, and time itself seems to cease to exist. It might've been only a matter of minutes since the accident happened, but it felt like a long time to me. George heard my yelling and came around the corner. I told him we needed to get him to the hospital right now! The only hospital around was Kanakanak Hospital.

Somehow all by myself, I was able to get this young man up as George was bringing his old Jeep Wagoneer around to the front of the gas station. Now, this Native American was taller and bigger than me. He looked to be right around the same age as I was. I picked him up and put him into the car unto the back seat of this old Jeep Wagoneer. As George was driving us to the hospital, I examined this man's leg more closely. It was ripped down the middle like an overcooked hotdog in the microwave.

You could see all the veins and muscles right down to the bone. In the natural, I should have been shaking and trembling because I do not like the sight of blood and mangled muscles. As we bounced along on the dirt road, I was simply speaking life and healing, praying in the name of **JESUS** for this young man. He was completely gone, lost amid the shock and the trauma he was experiencing.

We finally arrived at the hospital. I was able to get him out (it had to be **GOD**) of the Jeep and into the emergency room. For some strange reason, there was hardly any personnel there. Back in those days, the hospital was not very large, and it was very old and rustic. I started yelling out loud for help. Finally, a young man who was training to be a doctor came to see what the fuss was all about.

When he examined the wound, he became extremely concerned. Because there was no one else there to help him, he asked if I would be willing to remain and be his assistant. There was a complete calmness and yet a divine boldness about me. I told him I would be more than willing. We got him over to a room where there was a surgical table. Then together, this young doctor and I were able to get him up onto this operating table. The young physician began to cut away the rest of the scraps of his pants. There was an overhead operating light that he turned down and turned on to examine more carefully the damage to this man's leg.

I noticed immediately that this young physician began to shake and tremble. I know this will be hard to believe, but here I am an inexperienced 19-year-old kid by the spirit of **GOD** who began to speak calmness to this young physician. I began to tell him by the Spirit of **GOD** what he needed to do. I had no medical knowledge whatsoever, and yet at that moment, I knew what needed to be done. I had to push together this man's leg, and its cloven separated parts, for it to be sewed back together.

The physician's hands were shaking like leaves in the wind as he was handling the large needle and thread. My hands were covered in blood, and yet there was not one bit of tremble in my hands. I pressed his sliced and wounded flesh together. There was no fear or anxiety in my heart.

I cannot tell you exactly how long this operation took, but when it was done, this young man's leg was put back together. During this whole time, I was praying and speaking very quietly. You do not have to get loud and boisterous when you're walking and moving by **FAITH** in the **Holy Ghost**. I left that young man in the hands and the care of the hospital. I do not think that I ever saw him again, but I still pray and hope the **Holy Ghost**, the residue of the spirit of the Lord that I imparted as I laid my hands upon him, is still working in him mightily.

Do not allow the devil, Circumstances, or any other situation, to Rob you of what JESUS did when He received those thirty-nine lashes upon His precious

back. In the Name of JESUS CHRIST of Nazareth, I Command You to Be Healed.

Looking at the sufferings of Jesus

Before **God** ever created the world, the tri-unity came up with an amazing plan. In the book of revelation, **Jesus** is called the lamb, slain before the foundation of the world.

Revelation 13:8And all that dwell upon the earth shall worship him, whose names are not written in the book of life of the Lamb slain from the foundation of the world.

We all have emotions: The 27 major emotions are: admiration, adoration, aesthetic appreciation, amusement, anger, anxiety, awe, awkwardness, boredom, calmness, confusion, craving, disgust, empathic pain, entrancement, excitement, fear, horror, interest, joy, nostalgia, relief, romance, sadness, satisfaction, sexual desire, surprise, sorrow, grief. These all rage in the human heart, but did you know that **God** has emotions also. Now, how many have ever had the emotion called regret? Do you know, **God** has regrets. When he created man in the days of Noah, the Bible literally says that **God** wished he would've never made man.

Gen6:6 And it repented the LORD that he had made man on the earth, and it grieved him at his heart.

God has sorrow. **God** would have all men to repent and to come into the knowledge of salvation. **God** did not make hell for humanity. He made it for the angel for Lucifer and his angels. **God**'s heart is broken over the choices men make. Matter of fact, did you know when **God**'s people were suffering in the old covenant because of disobedience, he said in all of their afflictions, he was afflicted with them.

Isaiah 63:9 In all their affliction he was afflicted, and the angel of his presence saved them: in his love and in his pity he redeemed them; and he bare them, and carried them all the days of old.

The Bible tells us to weep with them, who weep, and rejoice with those who rejoice. But one thing I think we're really missing from the modern church in the Western world is the reality of what it really means to suffer for **Jesus**.

If you look at the New Testament over a hundred times, it talks about suffering. A lot of those sufferings are dealing with what **Christ** went through, what **Christ** experienced, what **Christ** partook of. **Jesus** partook of our sufferings. We're not just talking about a man who was sinless. We're talking about the word made flesh. We're talking about **God** himself becoming a man.

1 Timothy 3:16 And without controversy great is the mystery of godliness: God was manifest in the flesh, justified in the Spirit, seen of angels, preached unto the Gentiles, believed on in the world, received up into glory.

Now it's one thing for us to say **Jesus** spoke all things into existence. And without him was nothing made that was made. **Jesus** came to this earth. **Christ** came to this earth. The word became flesh for one main reason to suffer a tremendous unimaginable sorrow grief, pain. When he was in the garden, he said to his disciples: *Matthew 26:38Then saith he unto them, My soul is exceeding sorrowful, even unto death: tarry ye here, and watch with me.*

He was being overwhelmed with sorrow. He was made sin for us, who knew no sin. **God** himself became human flesh, then made sin. **Jesus** never sinned, but he was made sin. That we might be made the righteousness of **God** in **Christ**. That's why the Bible says, no, you're not that your body is not your own, but you have been bought with a price, therefore glorify **God** in your body and your spirit, which are gods.

We have been bought by the blood of **Jesus**, but **Jesus** experienced tremendous pain and suffering for us. He went through tremendous agony. And it says when he was in the garden, the night, he was betrayed, he prayed earnestly, and it was as great drops of blood came from his head. Now it's medically recorded that there have been people who were under so much mental, emotional, psychological pressure that blood vessels literally broke in their face. And that blood would literally come from their heads. I cannot imagine that kind of pressure, but **Jesus** was under such pressure because he knew that the **Father** was going to have to turn His back on him for us.

Matthew 27:46 And about the ninth hour Jesus cried with a loud voice, saying, Eli, Eli, lama sabachthani? that is to say, My God, my God, why hast thou forsaken me?

There are specific scriptures in the old covenant where it prophetically reveals the sufferings of **Jesus**

Psalm 22:1 My God, my God, why hast thou forsaken me? why art thou so far from helping me, and from the words of my roaring?

Isaiah 53:10 Yet it pleased the Lord to bruise him; he hath put him to grief: when thou shalt make his soul an offering for sin, he shall see his seed, he shall prolong his days, and the pleasure of the Lord shall prosper in his hand.

Lamentations 1:12 Is it nothing to you, all ye that pass by? behold, and see if there be any sorrow like unto my sorrow, which is done unto me, wherewith the Lord hath afflicted me in the day of his fierce anger.

Psalm 71:11 Saying, God hath forsaken him: persecute and take him; for there is none to deliver him.

FAITH BASED OUTCOME INDEPENDENT

I really think that we as American Christians, to a great extent, do not understand that **God** wants us to have a **Faith**, a trust, a confidence in him that literally is going to bring us into a place of suffering. Well, what do you mean? Bring us into a place of suffering? The Bible even says that when you and I say no to sin, by **Faith** that is a form of suffering. This is revealed to us in Hebrews 12.

Hebrews 12:1 Wherefore seeing we also are compassed about with so great a cloud of witnesses, let us lay aside every weight, and the sin which doth so easily beset us, and let us run with patience the race that is set before us,2 Looking unto Jesus the author and finisher of our Faith; who for the joy that was set before him endured the cross, despising the shame, and is set down at the right hand of the throne of God.3 For consider him that endured such contradiction of sinners against himself, lest ye be wearied and faint in your minds.4 Ye have not yet resisted unto blood, striving against sin.

We see this in Joseph, when he was presented the opportunity to sin with his master's wife! She was after Joseph to seduce him. Finally, she got him all alone and he said: I'll not sin against **God**, and I'll not sin against your husband. I'm not doing this. And she grabbed his cloak and pulled it off as he ran away from her. She lied about him, and he ended up in prison. He suffered for righteousness's sake. I think a lot of Americans are afraid to suffer for **Christ**. I really think that's the reason why the pharmaceutical world is so filthy rich, because so many Americans pop pain pills because they cannot handle pain! They're afraid of a little bit of pain, a little bit of agony, a little bit of a little bit something that hurts. See, I'm talking about a **Faith** that says, you know what, I'm going to believe the word of **God**. And who cares about the pain?

Slamming My Broken Foot Down the

5th Time, God Instantly Healed It!

One day I had to climb our 250-foot AM radio tower to change the light bulb on the main beacon. However, to climb the tower, I had to first find the keys, which I never did. Since I could not find the keys to get the fence open, I did the next best thing - I simply climbed over the fence.

This turned out not to be such a wonderful idea after all! With all of my climbing gear hanging from my waist, I climbed the fence to the very top. At this point, my rope gear became entangled in the fencing. As I tried to get free, I lost my balance and fell backward off the fence. Trying to break my fall, I got my right foot down underneath me. I hit the ground with my foot being turned on its side and I felt something snap in my ankle. I knew instantly I had a broken foot, my ankle.

Most normal people would have climbed back over the fence, set up a doctor's appointment, had their foot x-rayed, and then placed into a cast. But I am not a normal-thinking person, at least according to the standards of the modern-day church. When I broke my foot, I followed my routine of confessing my stupidity to **God** and asked Him to forgive me for my stupidity. Moreover, then I spoke to my foot and commanded it to be healed in the name of **Jesus Christ** of Nazareth. When I had finished speaking to my foot, commanding it to be healed, and then praised and thanked **God** for the healing, there seemed to be no change whatsoever in its condition.

The scripture that came to my heart was when **Jesus** declared: **"The kingdom of heaven suffereth violence, and the violent take it by force!"** Based completely upon this scripture, I decided to climb the tower, by **Faith**, with a broken foot mind you! Please do not misunderstand, my foot hurt so bad I could hardly stand it. And yet, I had declared that I believed I was healed.

There were three men watching me as I took the Word of **God** by **Faith**. I told them what I was about to do, and they looked at me as if I had lost my mind. I began to climb the 250-foot tower, one painful step at a time. My foot hurt so bad that I was hyperventilating within just twenty-to-thirty-feet up the tower. It literally felt like I was going to pass out from shock at any moment. Whenever I got to the point of fainting, I would connect my climbing ropes to the tower, stop and take a breather, crying out to **Jesus** to help me. It seemed to take me forever to get to the top.

Even so, I finally did reach the very top of the tower and replaced the light bulb that had gone out. Usually, I can come down that tower within ten minutes, because I would press my feet against the tower rods, and then slide down: using my hands and arms to lower myself at a very fast pace. However, in this situation, my foot could not handle the pressure of being pushed up against the steel. Consequently, I had to work my way down very slowly. After I was down, I slowly climbed over the fence one more time. I hobbled my way over to my vehicle and drove up to the church office. The men who had been watching this unfold were right behind me.

I hobbled my way into the front office, which is directly across the street from the radio tower. I informed the personnel that I had broken my foot and showed them my black and blue and extremely swollen foot. It did not help that I had climbed with it! I told them that I was going home to rest. At the same time, however, I told them that I believed I was healed.

Going across to my house, directly opposite the main office of the church parking lot, I made my way slowly up the stairs to our bedroom. I found my wife in the bedroom putting away our clothes. Slowly and painfully, I pulled the shoe and sock off of the broken foot. What a mess! It was fat, swollen, black and blue all over. I put a pillow down at the end of the bed, and carefully pulled myself up onto the bed. Lying on my back, I tenderly placed my broken, black, and blue, swollen foot onto the pillow. No matter how I positioned it, the pain did not cease. I just laid there squirming, moaning, and sighing.

As I was lying there trying to overcome the shock that kept hitting my body, I heard the audible voice of **God**. He said to me: "What are you doing in bed?" **God** really got my attention when I heard Him with my natural ears. My wife would testify that she heard nothing. Immediately, in my heart, I said: "Lord, I am just resting." Then He spoke to my heart with the still small voice, very clearly, "Do you always rest at this time of day?" I replied: "No, Lord." It was about 3 o'clock in the afternoon.

He spoke to my heart again and said: "I thought you said you were healed?"

At that moment the gift of **Faith** exploded inside of me. I said: "Lord, I am healed!" Immediately, I pushed myself up off the bed, grabbed my sock and shoe, and struggled to put them back on. What a tremendous struggle it was! My foot was so swollen that it did not want to go into the shoe. My wife was watching me as I fought to complete this task. You might wonder what my wife was doing this whole time as I was fighting this battle of **Faith**.

She was doing what she always does, just watching me and shaking her head. I finally got the shoe on my swollen, black and blue foot. I put my foot down on the floor and began to put my body weight upon it. When I did, I almost passed out. At that moment, a holy anger exploded on the inside of me. I declared out loud: "I am healed in the name of **Jesus Christ** of Nazareth!" With that declaration, I took my right (broken) foot and slammed it down to the floor as hard as I possibly could.

I felt the bones of my foot break even more. Like the 4th of July: an explosion of blue, purple, red, white, and black exploded in my brain and I passed out. I came to, lying on my bed. Afterward, my wife informed me that every time I passed out, it was for about ten-twenty seconds. The moment I came to, I jumped right back up out of bed.

The gift of **Faith** was working in me mightily. I got back up and followed the same process again: "In the name of **Jesus Christ** of Nazareth I am healed," and slammed my foot down once more as hard as I could! For a second time, I could feel the damage in my foot increasing. My mind was once again wrapped in an explosion of colors and pain as I blacked out.

When I regained consciousness, I immediately got up once again, repeating the same process. After the third time of this happening, I came to, with my wife leaning over the top of me. I remember my wife saying, as she looked at me: "You are making me sick. I cannot watch you do this." She promptly walked out of our bedroom and went downstairs.

The fourth time I got up declaring: "In the name of **Jesus Christ** of Nazareth I am healed," and slammed my foot even harder! Once more, multiple colors of intense pain hit my brain. I passed out again! I got up the fifth time, angrier than ever. This was not a demonic or proud anger. This was a divine gift of violent I-will-not-take-no-for-an-answer type of **Faith**. I slammed my foot down the fifth time: "In the name of **Jesus Christ** of Nazareth I am healed!"

The minute my foot slammed into the floor, for the fifth time, the power of **God** hit my foot. I literally stood there under the quickening power of **God** and watched my foot shrink and become normal. All the pain was completely and totally gone. I pulled back my sock and watched the black and blue in my foot disappear to normal flesh color. I was healed! Praise **God**! I was made whole! I went back to the office, giving glory to the Lord and showing the staff my healed foot.

HERE ARE EXAMPLES OF BEING FAITH BASED OUTCOME INDEPENDENT

Doc Yeager: Back in 2013, I was lying in bed when I heard the **audible voice** of **GOD**. **HE** said to me: **"The violent take it by force!"** For a while now, this has been marinating in my soul.

Sometimes when **GOD** speaks to me, it takes time for it to become a reality. It could be four years later, or maybe even decades later, as the spirit of **GOD** is at work on my insides. You could say it is rather like a pregnant woman: life is growing inside of her womb. **FAITH** begins as a seed and must grow within us, in our hearts. We have a lot to do with that **FAITH** growing, expanding, enlarging, and becoming mature.

Please understand, everybody has **FAITH**. Everyone was born with a measure, a proportion of **FAITH.** When **JESUS** shared the parable of the ten virgins who were asleep, He said they all woke up when the trumpet sounded; but there were five foolish virgins and five wise virgins. It was only the five wise virgins that had enough oil to take them to the arrival of their Husband to be. I believe that one of the realities of the oil **JESUS** was speaking of is the **oil of FAITH**. I believe it is **FAITH** in **GOD** and **FAITH** in **JESUS CHRIST**.

People who do not have sufficient **FAITH,** in this time period, are going to have it rough. They are going to try to find somebody that does have **FAITH**, but it will be too late. Then there are those who do have **FAITH**, but it has been in hibernation. **FAITH** can be lying dormant inside of you for many years. Then suddenly, something supernatural happens, and it begins to come forth, like a bear coming out of hibernation!

Hebrews 11:32-34 And what shall I more say? for the time would fail me to tell of Gedeon, and of Barak, and of Samson, and of Jephthae; of David also, and Samuel, and of the prophets: 33 Who through FAITH subdued kingdoms, wrought righteousness, obtained promises, stopped the mouths of lions, 34 Quenched the violence of fire, escaped the edge of the sword, out of weakness were made strong, waxed valiant in fight, turned to flight the armies of the aliens.

Revelation 12:11 And they overcame him by the blood of the Lamb, and by the word of their testimony; and they loved not their lives unto the death.

FAITH BASED OUTCOME INDEPENDENT

PASTOR MIKE: WHY DO YOU GET ATTACKED SO MUCH BY THE DEVIL? You see, I have been HEALED of at least **Twenty** major ailments! Without the use of medicine or doctors!!

#1 Healed of major allergies

#2 Healed of loss of the sense of smell

#3 Healed of birth defects in the bones of my ears

#4 Healed of a speech impediment

#5 Healed of a broken back

#6 Healed of burned-out vocal cords

#7 I was raised from the dead by my wife

#8 Healed of painful tumors in my abdomen

#9 Healed of a serious hernia

#10 Healed of a broken and crushed kneecap

#11 Healed of a dangerous attack of conjunctivitis

#12 Healed of arthritis

#13 Healed instantly of a broken foot

#14 My son was Healed from rabies

#15 Healed from prostate cancer

#16 Healed from life-threatening colon cancer

#17 Healed instantly of a broken, twisted index finger

#18 Healed overnight of second-degree burns

#19 Healed of gushing bright red blood

#20 And many Healings, on a daily basis since February 18, 1975.

PLEASE UNDERSTAND I AM BRAGGING ON JESUS!

I have experienced the enemy trying to Kill Me - and my loved ones - over **Sixty** times! In all those dangerous situations (many times it looked like I was a goner!), **GOD** miraculously stepped in and delivered me. You might ask: **But How Pastor Mike?** I would tell you that it was: a **Violent FAITH that says: I Will Not Take No as an Answer Type of FAITH in CHRIST** that preserved me, and My Loved Ones.

*In the natural, I should have been dead when the gang leader tried to stab me to death.

*When the same man shot me with a 12-gauge shotgun.

*I should have been dead when the Yupik Indians tried to steam me to death.

*I should have been dead when I fell into the Bering Sea in rough weather.

*I should have been dead when my motorcycle flipped out underneath me, on black ice, on the main Highway.

*I should have been dead when the demon-possessed woman kept stabbing me in the face with a knife etc…..

I COULD TELL YOU STORY AFTER STORY!

(Well over 2000 to date)

I asked the Lord: "**FATHER**, why in the world have I gone through so much?" He spoke to my heart and said: **"I Will Use You As an Example Of What I Can Do in a Person's Life - If They Will Have FAITH in Me!"** But, I said Lord: "Why Me?" And He answered: **"I Use the Foolish To Confound the Wise!"**

1 Corinthians 1:27 But GOD hath chosen the foolish things of the world to confound the wise; and GOD hath chosen the weak things of the world to confound the things which are mighty;

Do Not Think for a moment that I am bragging on Mike Yeager. I wrote a book called: **"I Need GOD Because I'm Stupid."**

FAITH BASED OUTCOME INDEPENDENT

That book was written for the total purpose of causing people to realize that Mike Yeager is nobody. It is **JESUS CHRIST** that we put our complete confidence and hope in. If **GOD** can use Mike Yeager: I can guarantee that He can use anybody! It is our **FAITH** in **CHRIST** that gives us the victory.

1 John 5:4-5 For whatsoever is born of GOD overcometh the world: and this is the victory that overcometh the world, even our FAITH. 5 Who is he that overcometh the world, but he that believeth that JESUS is the Son of GOD?

I Pray with All My Heart That As You Continue to Read This Book **FAITH** will come exploding into your inner being. And that **FAITH** in **CHRIST** will bring you into a place Of Amazing Victory!

MY ATTITUDE ABOUT PAIN

I know that many people who read this probably will not believe me, but that is okay because its true! Who cares about the suffering? Who cares about the agony or about the end results? I am going to trust and believe **God**. Over 14 times I found through Matthew, mark, Luke, and John, where the life of **Jesus** was threatened. And who knows how many more times than that, where they tried to kill him. They tried to snuff him out. They connived, manipulated, and lied about him. He was not afraid to suffer because he was in the will of the **Father**. Now I'm talking about suffering because you're in the will of **God**. I am not talking about a little bit of rejection. We have a whole society who afraid of being rejected.

As a child I went through a lot of rejection. How many of you went through that? I did. And I went through rejection because I had hearing problems. I could hardly hear. And I had a speech impediment to where you could not understand me till I was 19 years old when **God** took it away. I went from Catholic school from third grade to fourth grade in the public school, and they continually picked on me. You don't think kids can be cruel? Children can be cruel. I mean, they tormented me until where I finally quit school at 15 years old. It caused me to get all wrapped up in drugs and alcohol and all that mess and trouble that goes along with it. I joined the Navy when I was 17 years old, thinking I could escape the mess, but it was worse in the Navy.

Committing Suicide February 18th

I was a complete mess I. **However, Supernaturally one night, God stepped into my life, instantly and radically changing me forever!** My last three months of military life was so amazingly transformed that I was put in charge of working parties and details from time to time. **God** instantly delivered me from all of my devices including all of my foolish behaviors. I was a new creature in **Christ! Christ** had **Supernaturally** set me free from the tormenting demonic powers that had possessed my life for so long!

Here is what happened! On my 19th birthday, I was overwhelmed with a demonic **Spirit** of self-pity and depression. I decided to end it all by slitting my wrist! I went into the bathroom with a large, survival hunting knife. I put the knife to my wrist with full intentions of slitting my artery. I was determined to kill myself. I held the knife firmly against my wrist and took one more last breath before I slid it across my wrist. I was going to make sure that I was going to go all the way down into the bones of my wrist. We had a young man who tried to cut his wrist in boot camp. All he succeeded in doing was messing his hand all up.

Blanket of Fear

Suddenly, invisible presence came rushing down upon me like a blanket. It was a tangible, overwhelming presence of mind-boggling fear. It was the fear of **God**, and it overwhelmed me! Instantly, I realized with the crystal-clear understanding that I was going to hell. I deserved hell; I belonged in hell, and hell had a right to me. Furthermore, I knew if I slit my wrist, I would be in hell forever.

And great fear came upon all the church, and upon as many as heard these things (Acts 5:11).

Overwhelming Love

I walked out of that little military bathroom to my bunk. I fell on my knees, reached my hands up toward heaven and cried out to **Jesus** with all my heart. All of this was **Supernatural** and strange. I did not ever recall any time when anyone ever shared with me how to become a Christian or how to be converted. I knew how to pray.

I cried out to **Jesus** and told Him I believed He was the Son of **God**, had been raised from the dead, and I desperately needed Him. I not only asked Him into my heart but I gave Him my heart, soul, mind, and life. At that very instant, a love beyond description came rushing into my heart. I knew what love was for the first time in my life.

At the same time, I comprehended what I was placed on this earth for—I was here to follow, love, serve, and obey **God**. A deep love and hunger to know **God** grabbed my heart. I was filled with love from top to bottom, inside and out—inexpressibly beyond belief. **Jesus** had come to live inside of me!

Rivers of waters run down mine eyes, because they keep not thy law (Psalm 119:136).

Completely Delivered

I was instantly delivered: from over three packs of cigarettes a day, from worldly and satanic music, from chewing tobacco; from cussing and swearing, from drugs and alcohol, and from a filthy and dirty mind.

Some might ask why my conversion was so dramatic. I believe that it's because I had nothing to lose. I knew down deep that there was not one single thing worth saving in me. The only natural talent I ever possessed was the ability to mess things up. At the moment of salvation, I completely surrendered my heart and life to **Jesus Christ**.

I am crucified with Christ: nevertheless I live; yet not I, but Christ liveth in me: and the life which I now live in the flesh I live by the Faith of the Son of God, who loved me, and gave himself for me (Galatians 2:20).

OBSESSED WITH A DEEP HUNGER FOR GOD'S WORD!

I remember after giving my heart to **Jesus Christ** that I got up from the floor born again, saved, and delivered, I was a brand-new person. Immediately hunger and thirst for the Word of **God** took a hold of me. I began to devour Matthew, Mark, Luke, and John. I just could not get enough of the word of **God** because of my love for **Jesus Christ** and his **Father**.

Jesus became my hero in every area of my thoughts and daily life. He became my reason for getting up and going to work, eating, sleeping, and living. I discovered that everything I did was based on the desire of wanting to please Him. I carried my little green military Bible with me wherever I went.

FAITH BASED OUTCOME INDEPENDENT

Whenever I had an opportunity, I would open it up and study it. It wasn't very long before I believed for a larger Bible. This larger Bible gave me much more room to make notes, highlight and circle certain Scriptures. The more I fed on the Scriptures, the greater my hunger became for them. I probably was not saved even for two months when I was asked to speak for the 1st time at a small Pentecostal church.

I believe it was called Adak Full Gospel Church. As far as I know, it was the only Pentecostal church on this military base situated on an Aleutian Island in Alaska. Since 1975 I have never lost my hunger or my thirst for **God**'s word. I can truly say even what the psalmist said!

Psalm 104:34 My meditation of him shall be sweet: I will be glad in the Lord.

This hunger for **God**'s word has caused me to memorize over a 3rd of the New Testament. I am not bragging or boasting; I'm just simply saying that **God**'s word is the joy and rejoicing of my heart. There are People Who Love to Swim, People Who Love to Work out, People Who Love to Do Push-Ups and Chin-Ups and Lift Weights, but we need people who love **God**'s word!

Instantly I Knew I Was Called to Preach

The day I gave my heart to **Jesus Christ** and had this radical transformation where I had experienced the terrible fear of the **Lord**, but then at the same time his overwhelming love, I knew that I knew that I knew within my heart of hearts that I was called to preach the Gospel.

Now, precisely what that meant at that moment, I had no idea because I didn't even know what a preacher was.

I had been raised in Catholicism my whole life, and I had never been to a Protestant or Pentecostal church.I did not know what it meant to preach. Now, to be honest, I might have seen Billy Graham or maybe I had seen Oral Roberts several times on our black and white TV set.

 All I know is at that moment I was called of **God** to preach the Gospel, not even realizing that **Christ** had given gifts to the church!

CHAPTER SEVEN

LOW SELF-ESTEEM IS NO EXCUSE FOR A BELIEVER

You see all my life up to I was 19 years old; I was in an environment where most people ever thought anything good about me. I mean, I was considered in those days, mentally retarded. They had me in the special ed class. Now if they spoke evil of **Jesus**, they're going to speak evil of you and me if we live for **God**. In the community that I pastor for almost 40 years they have claimed I am a Jim Jones, a David Koresh without any proof. Many people through the years and have told me that they were told to stay far away from us.

Now, why would the community say such a thing? Well, I'm originally from Wisconsin, so I'm an outsider. The second reality is that we are **Pentecostals, Full Gospel, Word people**. Most of these people in this surrounding area are Lutherans or Catholics. Most so-called Christians have no concept of what real Christianity looks like. If they would read the four Gospels and the book of Acts, things would be different, but many of them are Bible illiterates.

What is strange is that even the full Gospel Pentecostal churches in the community will tell people that we are a cult. If they would simply look up what this word means they would discover very quickly that we are anything but a cult. We are simply **Bible believing, God fearing, Jesus loving people**. We take **God** at His

169

Word!

Wikipedia Article

In modern English, a cult is a social group that is defined by its unusual religious, spiritual, or philosophical beliefs, or its common interest in a particular personality, object, or goal. This sense of the term is controversial, having divergent definitions both in popular culture and academia, and has also been an ongoing source of contention among scholars across several fields of study.[1][2]:348–56 The word "cult" is usually considered pejorative.

While the literal and original sense of the word remains in use in the English language, a derived sense of "excessive devotion" arose in the 19th century.[i] Beginning in the 1930s, cults became the object of sociological study in the context of the study of religious behavior.[4] Since the 1940s the Christian countercult movement has opposed some sects and new religious movements, labeling them "cults" because of their unorthodox beliefs. Since the 1970s, the secular anti-cult movement has opposed certain groups, and in reaction to acts of violence which have been committed by some of their members, it has frequently charged them with practicing mind control. Scholars and the media have disputed some of the claims and actions of anti-cult movements, leading to further public controversy.

Sociological classifications of religious movements may identify a cult as a social group with socially deviant or novel beliefs and practices,[5] although this is often unclear.[6][7][8] Other researchers present a less-organized picture of cults, saying that they arise spontaneously around novel beliefs and practices.[9] Groups labelled as "cults" range in size from local groups with a few followers to international organizations with millions of adherents.[10]

In the church, I pastor, the only one that we have ever exalted is **Jesus Christ**. The pastor is really nothing but a servant to the people to wash their feet spiritually speaking and to help them to grow spiritually. How do I respond to their Constant accusations? I simply let it slide off my back like water off a ducks back. I do not concern myself with it whatsoever.

We just had an incident where the local authorities came and claimed that we had drugs, felons and a catch of weapons. They went Through our buildings and discovered there was no such thing. Will this stop them from spreading the rumors and the slander? Absolutely not, because they were listening to the wrong voices.

Now it's amazing, how many Christians wear their feelings on their sleeves. If you look at them wrong or do not shake their hands, or say something exactly right, they become highly offended! To them it seems like the end of the world.

Well, guess what? Their eyes are not on **Jesus**. Look at **Jesus**. Look at the pain, the suffering, the agony, and what he went through for us. If I got what I truly deserved, do you know where I would be? I would be hell wouldn't I! But many believers are afraid of suffering. I think what's happening to our nation, is that we are finding out where people really are at spiritually. You see, we ought to have a **Faith** that's based on nothing but **Christ**, regardless of the outcome.

So, when the government begins to mandate that we have to disobey **God** to obey them, we should have stood up. The believer should have stood up and said: I will obey **God** like the three Hebrew children: We're not bowing our knees. This is not out of arrogance, or out of pride, but out of love, out of devotion, out of commitment, faithfulness to **God**. **God**, I am committed to you.

Paul said: ***Romans 14:8 For whether we live, we live unto the Lord; and whether we die, we die unto the Lord: whether we live therefore, or die, we are the Lord's.***

My heart breaks for from the minute that the government came along and told us, you are not going to obey the word of **God** when it came to gathering, most pastors complied. They simply surrender with no fight. Were they full of fear? They were afraid, but **God**, hasn't given us a spirit of fear:

2 Timothy 1:7 For God hath not given us the spirit of fear; but of power, and of love, and of a sound mind.

I'm not writing this to criticize pastors, but I tell you what we need is some standard setters. We need some men and women with some holy ghost, boldness. Some people who will say, **God**, I'm going to obey you and be an example. I am willing to pay the price. I am willing to suffer for you. There is scripture after scripture that reveals the early church suffered because they were obeying **God**, trusting **God**, looking to **God**, depending upon **God**, following **God**. And because of this they were persecuted, prosecuted, imprisoned, beaten. Yet the Bible said they rejoiced.

Acts 5:41 And they departed from the presence of the council, rejoicing that they were counted worthy to suffer shame for his name.

---

1 Peter 4:13 But rejoice, inasmuch as ye are partakers of Christ's sufferings; that, when his glory shall be revealed, ye may be glad also with exceeding joy.14 If ye be reproached for the name of Christ, happy are ye; for the spirit of glory and of God resteth upon you: on their part he is evil spoken of, but on your part he is glorified.

Philippians 1:29 For unto you it is given in the behalf of Christ, not only to believe on him, but also to suffer for his sake;

Paul talks about his sufferings for **Christ**: *2 Corinthians 11:24 Of the Jews five times received I forty stripes save one.25 Thrice was I beaten with rods, once was I stoned, thrice I suffered shipwreck, a night and a day I have been in the deep;26 In journeyings often, in perils of waters, in perils of robbers, in perils by mine own countrymen, in perils by the heathen, in perils in the city, in perils in the wilderness, in perils in the sea, in perils among false brethren;*

---

2 Corinthians 12:10 Therefore I take pleasure in infirmities, in reproaches, in necessities, in persecutions, in distresses for

Christ's sake: for when I am weak, then am I strong.

Scripture after scripture, especially in Philippians, that talks about the blessedness of partaking of the sufferings of **Jesus**. Have you ever been a partaker of the sufferings of **Jesus**? Have you ever been attacked and physically abused Because of your love for **Jesus**? Have you ever been in a situation where you stood your ground, you chose us to believe **God** and let the pieces fall where they may?

*Tuck Going to Beat Me to a Pulp

I knew a big Texan in the Navy who rode bulls in rodeos at one time. We called him Tuck; to this day, I don't know why. We also called him TEX. After I gave my heart to **Jesus Christ**, as a 19-year-old kid, I shared the gospel with him, his friends, and as many as I could. The Spirit of the Lord had begun to move upon one of Tuck's friends. Tuck was extremely irritated at me for causing this man to come under **Conviction**. Up until the time I had given my heart to **Jesus**, tuck had been a good friend of mine. But now that I was in love with **Christ**, he did not want anything to do with me. Whenever he looked at me, it was with great disdain.

One-night, Tuck came into my room completely intoxicated with alcohol. He woke me up banging on my door like a madman. I went out to see what he wanted. When I entered the foyer, he grabbed me by the neck with his large left hand. He picked me up off the floor by my neck and slammed me against the wall.

He clenched his right hand into a fist right in front of my face pulling it back as if getting ready to hit me with all of his might. It seemed as if his fist were as big as my face. He told me that he would pulverize me if I did not promise to leave one of his drinking buddies alone. The man he was speaking about had taken an interest in the gospel.

In the natural, my heart should have been filled with great fear because, without a shadow of a doubt, he could easily beat me to death. I could see and feel the devil in him. His face was all red, and his steely blue eyes were bulging, but instead of fear, what rose up in my heart was great compassion for his soul.

Right there on the spot, as I was hanging from my neck with his hand pinning me against the wall, I began to weep for him. I told him that he could do whatever he wanted to do to me, but I would never stop preaching and exalting **Jesus Christ**. I told him that I loved him, and he needed to get right with **God**.

He began to shake violently like a leaf in a strong wind. His fist was moving back and forth in front of my face. His mouth was moving erratically, with foam coming between his teeth and hanging on his lips. During this time the other men in my barracks had heard the commotion and were all standing around watching this event unfold. After what seemed a long time, Tuck finally lowered his fist and put me down. He turned around without a word and walked away from me. From that moment up until I left the Navy, he never spoke to me again.

Many years later, I was talking with Willie, the cowboy. Willie had become a master chief in the Navy, and his expertise was underwater demolition. I asked what had happened to Tuck. Right after that event with me, he said, Tuck lost his mind. He took his Colt 44 magnum pistol, walked up to our military base commander, and put the gun against his head.

Thank **God** he did not shoot the man, but of course, he was arrested and court-martialed. Tuck ended up being an alcoholic, which caused him to lose his wife and family, and then he was diagnosed with cancer.

Up to this point, it would look like there was no hope for Tuck at all. Oh, how wrong we can be. **God** is more than able to intervene when people stand in the gap. When Tuck was going to beat me to a pulp until I heard about him years later, I never stopped lifting him before the Lord in **Prayer**.

Years later, Willie, the cowboy, contacted me and told me the rest of the story. My heart was filled with tremendous joy when he told me Tuck got right with **God**. The day will come when I meet Tuck on the other side.

Tucks Tragic Beginning but a Glorious End

Now the story does have a wonderful ending. Willie, the cowboy, told me that he was not right with **God** when he knew me. But the spirit of **God** had arrested him, and he had gotten right with **Jesus**.

It turns out that Willie, the cowboy, had stayed in contact with Tuck all of those years and eventually had a chance to speak to him about the Lord. Before Tuck died, Willie had the opportunity to lead Tuck to **Christ**, and he was gloriously born again. Shortly after that, Tuck died and went home to be with **Jesus**. Someday I will see him again. Only this time, we will have sweet fellowship.

Not by works of righteousness which we have done, but according to his mercy he saved us, by the washing of regeneration, and renewing of the Holy Ghost (Titus 3:5).

Radical Muslim Going to Kill Me

A Radical Muslim was going to kill my son, so I took his place!!!

I had my family with some members of the church ministering on the streets of Baltimore. We were at one of my favorite fishing holes, Lexington market. We had finished feeding the people. My wife and daughter had sung some songs. And now my son Michael was preaching a compassionate message on salvation and giving one's heart to **Jesus**. It was getting pretty late in the day so we were preparing to leave.

About a block away from us there were some radical Muslims preaching a message of hate and racial bigotry. We always left them alone, never attacking their philosophy but simply preaching **Jesus Christ** is the only answer for the sin-sickened soul. As my son Michael was finishing up his message, an African-American Muslim came charging at him. He got right into my son's face screaming and yelling, cussing and swearing, getting ready to do him bodily harm.

I immediately saw what was happening and intervened. I stepped between my son and this screaming madman. I turned my face away from the Muslim, telling my son to pack up the equipment and get everybody into the van. Then I turned back to face this man who was full of the devil.

My heart was filled with love for him and those who have been deceived along with him. Now that my son was out of the picture, this man's total focus was on me. He had his right hand in his pocket gripping onto something. I could see that it was in the shape of a gun pressing against the cloth of his jacket. The barrel of this gun was aimed right at my belly from all appearances.

There was absolutely no fear in my heart whatsoever as I spoke softly to him. I just kept on speaking about **Jesus** as he kept yelling at me. He seemed to get more infuriated that I was not intimidated. He purposely began to spit in my face as he was yelling and screaming. There were many people out on the street that day. It seemed like everything had stopped as they were watching and waiting to see what would happen. I could sense the spirit of murder and death was permeating the air.

I truly believe that people were waiting for him to gun me down. There was absolutely no fear in my heart but a great sadness that I would leave behind my wife and my children. I'm sure that tears roll down my face along with his spittle as I prepared myself in my heart to die. My wife and children and those of the church had cleared away from the area. I could see them out of the corner of my eye loading into the van. My heart was filled with peace knowing they were safe.

This man would scream and yell and spit, then walk away just to come running back to me again. This continued, it seemed, for at least 15 minutes if not longer. I just was speaking to this Muslim softly about **Jesus Christ** when suddenly, he just simply walked away. I stood there watching him leave when an African American lady walked up to me. She looked me straight in the eyes and said this to me. I have never in my whole life seen anything like that. You just stood there as he screamed and spit on you. We could all see there was no fear or anger in your heart. You just kept responding with kindness and gentleness.

That was my opportunity to share **Jesus Christ** with her, telling her that it was not me but **Jesus** inside of me. The Lord had spared me once again to live another day to preach the glorious gospel of **Jesus Christ**.

John 15:13 Greater love hath no man than this, that a man lay down his life for his friends.

JESUS SUFFERED FOR US

He knew before he ever created us what he was going to go through for us. But he was willing to go through it. Now his sufferings was not just the fact that he was made sin for us, but he was denied by his, disciples.

The prophet Isaiah had amazing **VISIONS**. He had **VISION** after **VISION** with such clarity of heavenly and spiritual realities: it is virtually impossible to improve on his descriptions. One amazing **VISION** he had was a declaration of the sufferings of **CHRIST**, discovered in Isaiah 53.

Isaiah 53:3-5 He is despised and rejected of men; a man of sorrows, and acquainted with grief: and we hid as it were [our] faces from him; he was despised, and we esteemed him not. 4 Surely he hath borne our griefs, and carried our sorrows: yet we did esteem him stricken, smitten of GOD, and afflicted. 5 But he [was] wounded for our transgressions, [he was] bruised for our iniquities: the chastisement of our peace [was] upon him; and with his stripes we are healed.

We need to realize that all we have from **God** is a gift that has been given to us by Him. It is imparted to us by **Faith** in **Jesus**. **Jesus** through His earthly Life, Teachings, Deeds, Words, Example, Sufferings, Crucifixion, Death, and Resurrection has opened the windows of Heaven to pour himself out into His people! Imparted Healing, Imparted Authority, Imparted Wisdom, Imparted Peace, Imparted Joy, Imparted Love, Imparted **Faith**, Etc. All is given to us as a gift from the love of the **Father** of Lights!

Death if you remain in sin!

You see, my friend, if you remain in your sinful condition, **God** has no choice but to allow you to go to a place where you can do no harm. And in that place, he cannot allow you to continue in your sin. So, it is a place where pain and misery will never cease. Your mind will not be able to dwell on wrong thoughts because of the pain that you will be experiencing. This is not the will of **God** for your life. He gave us His only begotten son so you would not have to go to an ETERNAL HELL!

FAITH BASED OUTCOME INDEPENDENT

And fear not them which kill the body, but are not able to kill soul: but rather fear him which is able to destroy both soul and body in hell. Malt 10:28

But I will forewarn you whom ye shall fear: Fear him, which after he hath killed hath power to cast into hell; yea, I say unto you, Fear him. Luke 12:5

Raging waves of the sea, foaming out their own shame; wandering stars, to whom is reserved the blackness of darkness forever.   Jude 1 :13

Surely thou wilt slay the wicked, 0 God: depart from me there ye bloody men. Psalms 139:19

And whosoever was not found written in the book of life was cast into the lake of fire. Rev 20:15

And in hell he lift up his eyes, being in torments, and seeth Abraham afar off, and Lazarus in his bosom. Luke 16:23

And cast ye the unprofitable servant into outer darkness: there shall be weeping and gnashing of teeth. Matt 25:30

"For God so loved the world, that he gave his only begotten Son, that whosoever believeth in him should not perish, but have everlasting life" (John 3:16).

    Jesus did not die just to forgive us of our sins but to destroy the sinful and selfish nature of the devil that is in our flesh and soul. You see, my friend, **God**, is coming back to take a bride for His Son out from the midst of the wicked human race. It will be a glorious bride absolutely head over heels in love with her groom, which is **Jesus Christ**. This bride will be made up of people who want to love **God** and His Son more than anything else. I hope you are part of this church. And if you are not, there is still hope that you can become a part of the body and bride of **Christ**.

"Who will have all men to be saved, and to come unto the knowledge of truth" (1 Tim. 2:4).

"The Lord is not slack concerning his promise, as some men count slackness; but is longsuffering to us-ward, not willing that any should perish, but that all should come to repentance"(2 Pet. 3:9).

God gave us **Jesus** in order to provide us with victory over our filthy, sinful, wicked, self-seeking, self-pleasing, self-centered, self-loving, and self-obsessed lives. **Jesus Christ**, Emanuel, who is **God** in the flesh, took upon Himself the sins of the world—your sins and mine. The Creator, Author, and Maker of all things died upon the cross. That is amazing and awesome love. He did this so that we could be free from sin and selfishness from the nature of the devil. **Jesus** is the only remedy we have from our sinful hearts. He is the only antidote from the wrath and anger, and tribulation and anguish of the righteous judgment of a holy **God**.

You see, a righteous judge must always give a punishment worthy of the crime that was committed. The penalty which is required for the crime reveals the seriousness of that which transpired. The price that **Christ** had to pay demonstrates the horrendous severity of the situation. And one sin, not covered under the blood, deserves eternal damnation. Hell, with all of its torments, reveals how grievous sin really is. It is so wicked that we see that in order for man to be redeemed, **God** had to suffer and die upon the cross for the selfishness of humanity.

How much more do we deserve, seeing that our sins are piled higher than the mountains of this world? But, you might ask why such a place as hell? First, we need to realize that man is an immortal soul, which means that we are eternal. When **God** created us, He made us in His likeness and in His image. We are made of a divine substance. It declares in Genesis that when **God** breathed into the body of man, he became a living soul.

"So God created man in his own image, in the image of God created he him; male and female created he them" (Gen. 1:27).

"And the LORD God formed man of the dust of the ground, and breathed into his nostrils the breath of life; and man became a living soul" (Gen. 2:7).

SMITH WIGGLESWORTH

Your Mind in Agreement

Many things happened in the lives of the apostles to show the power of **Christ** over all flesh. In regard to paying tribute, **Jesus** said to Peter, "We are free, we can enter into the city without paying tribute; nevertheless, we will pay." I like that **Thought**, that **Jesus** was so righteous on all situations. It helps me tremendously. Then **Jesus** told Peter to do a very hard thing. He said, "Take that hook and cast it into the sea.

Draw out a fish and take from its gills a piece of silver for thee and Me." This was one of the hardest things Peter had to do. He had been fishing all his life, but never had he taken silver out of a fish's mouth. There were thousands and millions of fish in the sea, but one fish had to have a piece of silver in it. He went down to the sea as any natural man would, speculating and **Thinking**, "How can it be?" But how could it not be, if **Jesus** said it would be? Then the perplexity would arise, "But how many fish there are, and which fish has the money?" Brother, if **God** speaks, it will be as He says.

What you need is to know the **MIND** of **God** and the **Word** of **God**, and you will be so free you will never find a frown on your face, nor a tear in your eye of unbelief again. The more you know of the mightiness of the revelation of **God**, the more everything in the way of fearfulness pass away.

To know **God**, is to be in the place of triumph. To know **God** is to be in the place of rest. To know **God** is to be in the place of absolute victory. No doubt many things were in Peter's **MIND** that day, but thank **God** there was one fish, and he obeyed. Sometimes to obey in blindness brings the victory. Sometimes when perplexities arise in your **MIND**, obedience means **God** working out the problem. Peter cast the hook into the sea, and it would have been amazing if you could have seen the disturbance the other fish made to move out of the way, all excepting the right one. Just one among the millions of fish **God** wanted. **God** may put his hand upon you in the midst of millions of people, but if He speaks to you, that thing that He says will come to pass.

On this occasion, **Jesus** said to Peter and the rest, that when they went out into the city they would see a man bearing a pitcher of water, and they should follow him. It was not customary in the East for men to carry anything on their heads. The women always did the carrying, but this had to be a man, and he had to have a pitcher.

One day there was a man preaching and he said it was quite all right for **Jesus** to go and arrange, for a colt to be tied there, and another preacher said it was quite easy to feed all those thousands of people, because the loaves in those days were so tremendously big, but he didn't tell them it was a little boy that had the five loaves. Unbelief can be very blind, but **Faith** can see thru a stone-wall. **Faith** when it is moved by the power of **God** can laugh at every adversity.

They said to the man with the pitcher, "Where is the guest chamber?" "How strange it is that you should ask," he replied, "I have been preparing that, wondering who wanted it." It is marvelous when **God** is leading how perfectly everything works into the plan. He was arranging everything. You **Think** He cannot do that today for you?

People who have been in perplexities for days and days, He knows how to deliver out of trouble; He knows how to be with you in the dark hour. He can make all things work together for good to them that love **God**. He has a way of arranging His plan, and when **God** comes in, you always know it was a day you lived in **God**. Oh to live in **God**! There is a vast difference between living in **God** and living in speculation and hope.

FAITH BASED OUTCOME INDEPENDENT

There is something better than hope; something better than speculation. "They that know their **God** shall be strong and do exploits," and **God** would have us to know Him.

"And when the hour was come, He sat down and the twelve apostles with Him." "When the hour was come". That was the most wonderful hour these men had ever experienced. There never was an hour, never will be an hour like that hour on earth again. What hour was it? It was an hour of the passing of creation under the blood. It was an hour of destruction of demon power. It was an hour appointed of life coming out of death.

 It was an hour when all that ever lived came under a glorious covering and cleansing of the blood of **Christ**. It was an hour when all the world was coming into emancipation by the blood of **God**. It was an hour in the world's history when it emerged from dark chaos, a wonderful hour! Praise **God** for that hour! Was it a dark hour? It was a dark hour for Him, but a wonderful light dawned for us. It was horribly dark for the Son of Man, but praise **God** He came thru it.

An Amazing and Wonderful Thought

There are some things in the Scriptures which move me greatly. I am glad that Paul was a man. I am glad that **Jesus** was a Man. I am glad that Daniel was a man, and I am also glad that John was a man. You ask Why? Because I see that whatever **God** has done for other men, He can do for me. And I find **God** has done such wonderful things for other men that I am always acknowledging that these things are possible for me. **Thinking** about this is a wonderful **Thought** to me.

 Jesus said in that dark and trying hour: "I have a desire to eat this Passover with you before I suffer." Desire? What could be His desire? His desire because of the salvation of the world. His desire because of the dethronement of the powers of Satan. His desire because He knew he was going to conquer all the works of the enemy and make every man free that ever lived. It was a great desire, but what lay between it?

Just between that and his resurrection was the cross and Gethsemane! Some people say that **Jesus** died on the cross. It is perfectly true, but is that the only place? **Jesus** died in Gethsemane. That was the tragic moment! That was the place where He paid the ultimate debt. It was in Gethsemane, and Gethsemane was between Him and the resurrection. He had a desire to eat this Passover and knew Gethsemane was between Him and the resurrection.

I want you to **Think** about Gethsemane. There alone, and with the tremendous weight, the awful effect of all sin and disease upon his body, He cries out, "If it be possible, let it pass." Oh could it be! He could only save when He was man, but here in a great chaos of darkness He comes forth: "To this end I came."

It was His purpose to die for the world. Oh dear saint, will it ever be spoken thru your lips or your **MIND** that you will ever have a desire to serve **Christ** like that? Will you and I, under every **Circumstances** take up your cross so fully, to be in the place of any ridicule, any surrender? **Jesus** desired to eat the Passover with His disciples, knowing what it meant? It can only come out of the depths of love we have for Him that we can say this morning, "Lord **Jesus**, I will follow." Oh how very wonderful is this decision in our **HEART**! **God** knows the **HEART**. You do not always have to be on the house-top to shout to indicate the condition of your **HEART**. He knows your inward **HEART**. You say, "I would be insanity not to be willing to suffer for **Jesus** when he so earnestly desired to suffer in order to save me." "With desire," He says.

I know what it is to have the kingdom of heaven within you. He said that even the least in the kingdom of heaven is greater than John the Baptist, meaning those who are under the blood, those who have seen the Lord by **Faith**, those who know by redemption they are made sons of **God**. I say to you, He will never taste again until we are there with Him. The kingdom will never be complete and it could not be fulfilled until we are all there at that great Supper of the Lamb where there will be millions and trillions of redeemed, which no man can number. We shall be there when that Supper is taking place. I like to **Think** upon these realities.

I hope you will take a bold step into these truths with **God** and believe it. It is an act of **Faith God** wants to bring you into; a perfecting of that love that cannot fail to accomplish **God's** will. It is a fact that He has opened the kingdom of heaven to all believers, and that He gives eternal life to them that believe. The Lord, the Omnipotent **God**, it is He that knows the end from the beginning, and has arranged by the blood of the Lamb to clans the guilty and make intercession for all believers. Oh it is a wonderful inheritance of **Faith** to find shelter and forgiveness through the blood of **Jesus**!

I want you to see that He says, "Do this in remembrance of Me." He took the cup, He took the bread, and He gave thanks. The very attitude of giving thanks for His shed blood, giving thanks for His broken body, overwhelms the **HEART**. To **Think** that my Lord could give thanks for His shed blood which he is about to pour out for us! To **Think** that my Lord could give thanks for His broken body which is about to be broken for us!

Only Almighty **God** can reveal this heroic act of **Jesus** to our human **HEART**! The natural man cannot receive it, but the spiritual man, the man who has been created anew by **Faith** in **Christ**, he is able to receive it. The man who believes **God** comes in into our **HEART**s with the eternal seed of truth and righteousness and **Faith**, and from the moment he sees the truth by **Faith** he is made a new creation.

The flesh from that moment begins to wither, and the spiritual man begins take over. One begins to passes off, the other begins to passes on, until a man takes on the image and the likeness of **God**. I say the Lord brings a child of **Faith** into a place of rest, and causes him to sit with **Christ** in heavenly places, giving him a language in the Spirit and making him know he no longer belongs to the law of sin and death.

You see this bread which represents His broken body? The Lord knew He could not bring us any nearer to His broken body. Our bodies are made of bread. The body of **Jesus** was made of that bread, and He knew He could bring us no nearer. He took the natural elements and said, "This bread represents my broken body." Now will it ever become that body of **Christ**? No, never. You cannot make it so. It is foolishness to believe it, but I take it as an emblem, and illustration and when I eat it, the natural leads me into the supernatural, and instantly I begin to feed on the supernatural by **Faith**, One leads me into the other.

Jesus said, "Take eat, this is my body." I have a Revelation of knowledge of **Christ** thru this emblem, symbol. May we take from the table of the riches of His promises. The riches of heaven are before us. Fear not, only believe, for **God** has opened the treasures of His Holy **Word**.

Stir up your Faith

I will tell you one incident that will stir up your **Faith**. I am not here to brag about me. I am here to impart divine truth into you concerning the **Word** of **God**, that after I leave, you can experience the same things I have. I went to Switzerland, and after I had been there for some weeks a brother said, "Will you not go to meeting tonight?" "No," I said, "I have been at it all this time, you can take charge tonight." "What shall we do?" he asked. "Do?" I said, "Paul the apostle left people to do the work and passed on to another place: I have been here long enough now. You do the work." So he went to the meeting.

When he came back he said, "We have had a wonderful time." "What happened?" He said, "I invited them all out, took off my coat and rolled up my sleeves and prayed, and they were all healed. I did just like you did."

Jesus says, "I give you power over all the power of the enemy." [Lk 10.19] They entered into the houses and healed the sick that were therein. The ministry of divine power at work in us is wonderful, but who would take upon himself to say, "I can do this or that"? If it is **God**, it is all right; but if you **Think** it is you, it is all wrong. When you are weak, then you are strong. [2Co 12.10] When you are strong in your own strength, you are weak. You must realize this and live only in the place where the power of **God** rests upon you, and where the Spirit moves within you. Then **God** will mightily manifest his power and you will know as **Jesus** said, "The Spirit of the Lord is upon me." [Lk 4.18]

God brings a remarkable, glorious reality to our **MIND**s tonight: The healing of a little helpless girl. The physicians had failed. The mother said to the **Father**, "There is only one hope that if we can see **Jesus**! As sure as we can meet **Jesus**, our daughter will live." Do you **Think** it is possible for anybody anywhere to go looking for **Jesus** without seeing him? Is it possible to **Think** about **Jesus** without **Jesus** drawing near? No. This man knew the power there was in the name of **Jesus**: "In my name shall ye cast out devils." [Mk 16.17]

He purposes to Transform Us

Beloved, we may do much praying and groaning, but we do not receive from **God** because we do not believe. And yet sometimes it takes **God** a long time to bring us through the groaning and the crying before we can

FAITH BASED OUTCOME INDEPENDENT

believe.

I know this, that no man by his praying can change **God** for you cannot change Him. Prayer does not change **God**, but it changes us. Finney said, "Can a man who is full of sin and all kinds of ruin in his life, change **God** when he starts to pray?" No, it is impossible. But when a man labors in prayer, he groans and travails because his tremendous sin is weighing him down, and he becomes broken in the presence of **God**; and when properly melted he comes into perfect harmony with the divine plan of **God**, and then **God** can work in that clay.

Up to this moment He could not change us. Prayer changes **HEART**s, but it never changes **God**. He is the same yesterday, and today, and forever and is full of love, full of compassion, full of mercy, full of grace, and ready to bestow his blessings upon us as we come in **Faith** to Him.

Believe that when you come into the presence of **God** you can have all you came for. You can take it away, and you can use it, for all the power of **God** is at your disposal in response to your **Faith** in **Christ**. The price for all was paid by the blood of **Jesus Christ** at Calvary. Oh, He is the living **God**, the One who has power to change us! "It is He that hath made us, and not we ourselves." And He purposes to **Transform** us so that the greatness of His power may work through us. Oh, beloved! **God** delights in us, and when a man's ways please the Lord, then He makes all things to move according to His own blessed purpose.

We read in Hebrews 11.5, "By **Faith** Enoch was translated that he should not see death.... Before his translation he had this testimony, that he pleased **God**." I believe it is in the **MIND** of **God** to prepare us for translation. But remember this, translation comes only in the round of holy obedience and a walk according to the good pleasure of **God**. We are called to walk together with **God** by the Spirit. It is delightful to know that we can talk with **God** and hold communion with Him.

Through this wonderful Baptism in the Spirit which the Lord gives us, He enables us to talk to Himself in a language that the Spirit has given, a language which no man **understand**s but which He **understand**s, a language of love. Oh, how wonderful it is to speak to Him in the Spirit, to let the Spirit lift, and lift and lift us until He takes us into the very presence of **God**! I pray that **God** by His Spirit may move all of us so that we walk with **God**, even as Enoch walked with Him.

But beloved, it is a walk by **Faith** and not by sight, a walk of believing the **Word** of **God**. I believe there are two kinds of **Faith**. All people are born with a natural **Faith**, but **God** calls us to a supernatural **Faith** which is a gift from Himself. In the 26th chapter of Acts Paul tells us of his call, how **God** spoke to him and told him to go to the Gentiles, "to open their eyes, and to turn them from darkness to light, and from the power of Satan unto **God**, that they may receive forgiveness of sins, and inheritance among them which are sanctified by **Faith** that is in Me."

The **Faith** which was in **Christ** was by the Holy Spirit to be given to those who believed. Henceforth, as Paul yielded his life to **God**, he could say, "I am crucified with **Christ**: nevertheless I live; yet not I, but **Christ** liveth in me: and the life which I now live in the flesh I live by the **Faith** of the Son of **God**, who loved me, and gave Himself for me". The **Faith** of the Son of **God** communicated by the Holy Spirit to the one who puts his trust in **God** and in His Son.

I want to show you the difference between our **Faith** and the **Faith** of **Jesus**. Our **Faith** is limited and comes to an end. Most people have experienced coming to the place where they have said, "Lord, I can go no further. I have gone so far, and I cannot go on." But **God** can help us and take us beyond this. I remember one night, being in the north of England and going around to see some sick people, I was taken into a house where there was a young woman lying on her bed, a very helpless case. Her **reason** was gone and many things were manifested that were absolutely Satanic, and I knew it.

She was a beautiful young woman. Her husband was quite a young man. He came in with a baby in his arms, leaned over and kissed his wife. The moment he did so she threw herself over on the other side of the bed, just as a lunatic would do, with no consciousness of the presence of her husband, or baby. It was **HEART**-breaking.

The husband took the baby and pressed the baby's lips to the mother. Again there was a wild frenzy. I said, to the sister who was attending her, "Have you anybody to help?" She answered, "We have done everything we could." I said, "Have you no spiritual help?" Her husband stormed and said, "Spiritual help? Do you **Think** we believe in **God** after we have had seven weeks of no sleep and this maniac condition? If you **Think** we believe in **God**, you are mistaken. You have come to the wrong house."

FAITH BASED OUTCOME INDEPENDENT

There was a young woman about eighteen who grinned at me as she passed out of the door, as much as to say, "You cannot do anything." But this brought me to a place of compassion for this poor young woman. And then with what **Faith** I had I began to penetrate the heavens by prayer. I was soon in heaven by the Spirit!

I tell you I never have seen a man get anything from **God** who prayed on the fleshly level. If you get anything from **God** you will have to pray right into heaven, for all you want is there. If you are living an earthly life, all taken up with sensual things, and expect things from heaven, they will never come. **God** wants us to be a heavenly people, seated with Him in the heavenlies, and laying hold of all the things in heaven that are at our disposal.

I saw there, in the presence of that demented girl, limitations to my **Faith**; but as I prayed there came another **Faith** into my **HEART** that could not be denied, a **Faith** that grasped the promises, a **Faith** that believed **God's Word**. I came from the presence of the glory back to earth. I was not the same man. I confronted the same conditions I had seen before, but in the name of **Jesus**. With a **Faith** that could shake hell and move anything else, I said to the demon power that was making this young woman a maniac, "Come out of her, in the name of **Jesus**!" She rolled over and fell asleep, and awoke fourteen hours later perfectly sane and perfectly whole.

Enoch walked with **God**.

During those many years of his life he was penetrating the heavens, laying hold of and believing **God**, living with such co-operation and such a touch of **God** upon his life that heaven came to him on earth. He became so heavenly in his **HEART** and **MIND** that it was not possible for him to stay on earth any longer. Oh, hallelujah!

I believe **God** wants to bring all of us into this place with His will, so that we shall penetrate into the heavenlies and become so empowered that we shall see signs and wonders and divers gifts of the Holy Spirit in our midst on a daily basis. These are wonderful days and these are days of the outpouring of the Holy Spirit. You ask me, "When would you have liked to have lived on the earth?" My answer is, "NOW. It is wonderful to know that I can be filled with the Holy Spirit. That I can be a temple in which **God** dwells, and that through this temple there shall be a manifestation of Gods power that will bring glory to His name."

Enoch walked with **God**. I want to live in constant communion with **God**. I am so grateful that from my youth up, **God** has given me a hunger for the Bible. I find the Bible food for my **SOUL**. It is strength to the believer. It develops the character of **God** in us. And as we receive with meekness the **Word** of **God**, we are being changed by the Spirit from glory to glory. And by this Book comes **Faith**, for **Faith** cometh by hearing, and hearing by the **Word** of **God**. And we know that "without **Faith** it is impossible to please Him."

I believe that all our failures come because of an imperfect **understanding** of **God's Word** and will. I see that it is impossible to please **God** on any other order then by **Faith**, and everything that is not of **Faith** is sin. You say, "How can I obtain this **Faith**?" You see the secret in Hebrews 12.2, "Looking unto **Jesus** the author and finisher of our **Faith**." He is the author of **Faith**. Oh, the might of our **Christ** who created the universe and upholds it all by the might of His power! **God** has chosen Him and ordained Him and clothed Him, and He who made this vast universe will make us a new creation. He spoke the **Word** and the stars came into being. Can He not speak the **Word** that will produce a mighty **Faith** in us? Ah, this One who is the author and finisher of our **Faith** comes and dwells within us, quickens us by His Spirit, and molds us by His will. He comes to live His life of **Faith** within us and to be to us all that we need. And He who has begun a good work within us will complete it and perfect it; for He not only is the author but the finisher and perfecter of our **Faith**.

"The **Word** of **God** is living and powerful, and sharper than any two-edged s**Word**, piercing even to the dividing asunder of **SOUL** and spirit, and of the joints and marrow, and is a discerner of the **Thoughts** and intents of the **HEART**." How the **Word** of **God** severs the **SOUL** and the spirit. The **SOUL** which is corrupted by carnality, and filled with selfishness and evil! Thank **God**, the Lord can sever from us all that is earthly and sensual, and make us a spiritual people. He can bring all our selfishness to the place of death, and bring the life of **Jesus** into our being to take the place of that earthly and sensual thing that is destroyed by the living **Word** and Spirit. The living **Word** pierces right to the very marrow.

When I was in Australia, so many people came to me with double curvature of the spine; but the **Word** of the Lord went right down to the very marrow of their spines, and instantly they were healed and made straight, as I laid hands on them in the name of **Jesus**. The divine Son of **God**, the living **Word**, through His power, and Spirit moved upon those curvatures of the spine and straightened them out. Oh, thank **God** for the mighty power of the **Word**!

The **Word** of **God** comes in to separate us from everything that is not of **God**. It destroys. It also gives life. He must bring to death all that is carnal in us. It was after the death of **Christ** that **God** raised Him up on high, and as we are dead with Him we experience the revelation that we are raised up and made to sit in heavenly places in the new life that the Spirit gives.

God has come to lead us out of ourselves into Himself, and to take us from the ordinary into the extraordinary, from the human into the divine, and make us after the image of His Son. Oh, what a Savior! What an ideal Savior! It is written, "Now are we the sons of **God**, and it doth not yet appear what we shall be: but we know that, when He shall appear, we shall be like Him; for we shall see Him as He is." But even now, the Lord wants to **Transform** us from glory to glory, by the Spirit of the living **God**. Have **Faith** in **God**, have **Faith** in the Son, have **Faith** in the Holy Spirit; and the Triune **God** will work in you, working in you to will and to do all the good pleasure of His will.

Smith - "Perfect love will never want the preeminence in everything, it will never want to take the place of another, it will always be willing to take the back seat."

The most important thing

The one thing that counts, is to see that we are filled with the Holy Spirit, filled to overflowing. Anything less than this is displeasing to **God**. We are commanded by **God** to be filled with the Spirit, and in the measure you fall short of this you will not be able to fulfill all of the plan of **God**. The Lord would have us moving on from **Faith** to **Faith**, from glory to glory, from fullness to overflowing. It is not good for us to be ever **Thinking** in the past tense, but we should be moving on to the place where we dare believe **God**. He has declared that after the **Holy Ghost** is come upon us we shall have power. I believe there is an avalanche of power from **God** to be apprehended if we will but catch the vision, and believe his **Word**.

Paul wrote at one time, "I will now come to visions and revelations." **God** has put us in a place where He expects us to have His latest revelation, the revelation of that marvelous fact, **CHRIST** IN US, and what this really means. We can apprehend **Christ** fully only as we are filled and overflowing with the Spirit of **God**. Our only safeguard from dropping back into our natural **MIND** from which we can never get anything, is to be filled and yet filled again with the Spirit of **God** and to be taken on to visions and revelations on a new level.

The **reason** why I emphasize the importance of the fullness of the **Holy Ghost** is that I want to get you beyond all human plans and **Thoughts** into the fullness of vision, into the full revelation of the Lord **Jesus Christ**. Do you want rest? It is in **Jesus**. Do you want to be saved from everything the devil is bringing up in these last times? Receive and continue in the fullness of the **Holy Ghost**, and He will be ever revealing to you that all you need for all times is in **Christ Jesus** your Lord.

I desire to emphasize the importance of the Spirit's ministration and of the manifestation of the Spirit which is given to every man to profit withal. As you yield to the Spirit of the Lord He has power over your intellect, over your **HEART**, and over your voice. The Holy Spirit has power to unveil **Christ** and to project the vision of **Christ** upon the canvas of your **MIND**, and then He uses your tongue to glorify and magnify Him in a way that you could never do apart from the Spirit's power.

Never say that when you are filled with the **Holy Ghost** you are "obliged" to do this or that. When people say that they are "obliged" to do this or that I know it is not the Spirit of **God**, but their own spirit moving them on to do that which is unseemly and unprofitable. Lots of people spoil meetings because they scream. If you want to do that kind of thing you had better get into some cellar. That is not to edification. I believe that, when the Spirit of **God** is upon you and moving you to speak as He gives utterance, it will always be to edification.

But don't spoil the gathering because when you ought to stop you go on. Who spoils the meeting? The man who starts in the Spirit and finishes in the flesh. Nothing is more lovely than prayer, but a prayer meeting is killed if you will go on and on in your own **SOUL** when the Spirit of

FAITH BASED OUTCOME INDEPENDENT

God is finished with you. You say as you come from some meetings, "That was a lovely message if the preacher only had stopped half an hour before he did." Learn to cease immediately the unction of the Spirit lifts. The **Holy Ghost** is jealous. Your body is the temple, the office of the **Holy Ghost**, but He does not fill the temple for human glorification, but only for the glory of **God**. You have no license to continue beyond a "Thus saith the Lord."

There is another side to this. **God** would have the gathering as free as possible, and you must not put your hand upon the working of the Spirit or it will surely turn sourer. You must be prepared to allow a certain amount of extravagance in young and newly baptized **SOUL**s. You must remember that when you were brought into this life of the Spirit you had as many extravagances as anybody, but you have now become somewhat more mature. It is a pity that some do get to sober, for they are not where they were in the early days. We have to look to **God** for wisdom that we do not interfere or dampen the Spirit or quench the power of **God** when it is manifested in our meetings. If you want to have an assembly full of life you must have an assembly full of manifestation. Nobody will come if there is no manifestation. We need to look to **God** for special grace that we do not move back to looking at things from a natural viewpoint.

The preacher, after he loses his unction, should inwardly repent and get right with **God** and get the unction back. We are no good without the unction of the Spirit of **God**. If you are filled with the grace of **God** you will not be judging everybody in the assembly, and you will not be easily frightened at what is happening.

You will have a **HEART** to believe all things, and to believe that though there may be some extravagances, the Spirit of **God** will take control of things and will see that the Lord **Jesus Christ** Himself is exalted, glorified, and revealed to hungry **HEART**s that desire to know Him. The Lord would have us wise unto that which is good and simple concerning evil, free from distrust, entering into a divine likeness to **Jesus** that dares believe that **God** Almighty will surely watch over all. Hallelujah!

The **Holy Ghost** is the One who magnifies the Lord **Jesus Christ**, the One who gives illumination of Him. If you are filled with the **Holy Ghost**, it is impossible to keep your tongue still. Talk about a dumb baptized **SOUL**! It is not to be found in the Scriptures or outside of the Scriptures. We are filled with the Spirit in order that we may magnify the Lord, and there should be no meeting in which the saints do not glorify, magnify, praise, and worship the Lord in Spirit and in truth.

I would like to give one **Word** of caution, for failure often comes through our not recognizing the fact that we are always in the body. We will need our bodies as long as we live. But our body is to be used and controlled by the Spirit of **God**. We are to present our bodies, holy and acceptable unto **God**, which is our **reason**able service. Every member of our body must be so sanctified that it works in harmony with the Spirit of **God**. Our very eyes must be sanctified.

 God hates the winking of the eye. From the day that I read in the Proverbs what **God** had to say about the winking of the eye (Prov. 6:13 and 10:10) I have never winked. I desire that my eyes may be so sanctified that they can always be used for the Lord. The Spirit of **God** will bring within us a compassion for **SOUL**s that will be seen in our very eyes.

God has never changed the order of things, first there comes the natural, and then the spiritual. For instance, when it is on your **HEART** to pray, you begin in the natural and your second **Word** will probably be under the power of the Spirit. You begin and **God** will end. It is the same in giving forth utterances under the Spirit's power. You feel the moving of the Spirit within and you begin to speak and the Spirit of **God** will give forth utterance. Thousands have missed wonderful blessings because they have not had **Faith** to move out and begin in the natural, in **Faith** that the Lord would take them into the realm of the supernatural. When you receive the **Holy Ghost** you receive **God's** Gift, in whom are all the gifts of the Spirit.

 Paul counsels Timothy to stir up the gift that was within. You have power to stir up **God's** Spirit within you. The way you stir up the gift within you is by beginning in **Faith**, and then He gives forth what is needed for the occasion. You will never begin if you **Think** you have to be full of **God**. When we yield to timidity and fear we simply yield to Satan. Satan. Whispers, "It is all self." He is a liar. I have learned this, if the Spirit of **God** is stirring me up, I have no hesitation in beginning to speak in tongues, and the Spirit of **God** gives me utterance and gives me the interpretation. I find that every time I yield to the Lord on this order I get a divine touch, I get a leading **Thought** from the Spirit of **God** and the meeting is moved into the realm of **Faith**.

You attend a meeting in **Faith**, believing that the Lord is going to meet you there. But perhaps the evangelist is not in harmony with **God**. The people in the meeting are not getting what **God** wants. The Lord knows it. He knows His people are hungry. What happens? He will take perhaps the smallest vessels and put His power upon them. As they yield to the Spirit they break forth in a tongue.

Another yields to the Spirit and there comes forth the interpretation. The Lord's church has to be fed, and the Lord will take this means of speaking to His people. Pentecostal people cannot be satisfied with the natural message. They are in touch with heavenly things and cannot be satisfied with anything less. They feel when there is something lacking in a meeting, and they look to **God** and He supplies that which is lacking.

When a man is filled with the Spirit he really has very little **understanding** of what he has. We are so limited in our **understanding** of what we have received. The only way we can know the power that has been given to us is through the ministration and manifestation of the Spirit of **God**. Do you **Think** that Peter and John knew what they had when they went up to the temple to pray? They were limited in **Thought**, and limited in their expression. The nearer we get to **God** the more conscious we are of the poverty of our human **SOUL** and we cry with Isaiah, "I am undone, I am unclean." But the Lord will bring the precious blood and the flaming coals for cleansing and refining and send us out to labor for Him empowered by His Spirit.

God has sent forth this outpouring that we may all be brought into a revelation of our son ship - that we are sons of **God**, men of power, that we are to be like the Lord **Jesus Christ**, that we are to have the powers of son ship, the power to lay hold of that which is weak and to quicken it. The Baptism of the Spirit is to make us sons of **God** with power. We shall be conscious of our human limits, but we shall not limit the Holy One who has come to dwell within. We must believe that since the **Holy Ghost** has come upon us we are indeed sons of **God** with power. Never say that you can't. All things are possible to them that believe. Launch out into the deep and believe that **God** has His all for you, and that you can do all things through Him who strengthens you.

Peter and John knew that they had been in the upper room, they had felt the glory. That they had been given divine utterances. They had seen conviction on the people. They knew that they had come into a wonderful thing. They know that what they had would be ever increasing and that it would be ever needful to cry, "Enlarge the vessel that the

Holy Ghost may have more room within." They knew that all the old things were moved away and they had entered into increasing and ever increasing knowledge of **God**, and that it was their Master's wish that they should be filled with the Spirit of **God** and with power every day and every hour. The secret of power is the unveiling of **Christ**, the all-powerful One within, the revelation of **God** who comes to abide within us.

 As they looked upon the crippled man at the Beautiful Gate they were filled with compassion. They were prompted by the Spirit to stop and speak with him. They said to the lame man, "Look on us." It was **God's** plan that the man should open his eyes with expectation. Peter said, "Of silver and gold we have none. But we have something and we will give it to you. We don't know what it is, but we give it to you. It is all in the name of **Jesus**." And then began the ministry of **God**.

You begin in **Faith** and then you see what will happen. It is hidden from us at the beginning, but as we have **Faith** in **God** He will come forth. The coming forth of the power is not of us but of **God**. There is no limit to what He will do. It is all in a nutshell as you believe **God**. And so Peter said, "Such as I have I give to thee: in the name of **Jesus Christ** of Nazareth rise up and walk." And the man who had been in that way for forty years stood up, and began to leap, and entered into the temple walking and leaping and praising **God**.

"For to one is given by the Spirit the Word of wisdom." I want you to keep in **MIND** the importance of never expecting the gifts of the Spirit apart from the power of the Spirit. In coveting the best gifts, covet to be so full of **God** and His glory that the gifts in manifestation will always glorify Him. We do not know all and we cannot know all that can be brought forth in the manifestation of the **Word** of wisdom.

One **Word** of wisdom from **God**, one flash of light on the **Word** of **God**, is sufficient to save us from a thousand pitfalls. People have built without a **Word** from **God**, they have bought things without a **Word** from **God**, and they have been ensnared. They have lacked that **Word** of wisdom which will bring them into **God's** plan for their lives. I have been in many places where I have needed a **Word** from **God** and this has been my place of refuge.

I will give you one instance. There is one thing I am very grateful to the Lord for, and that is that He has given me grace not to have a desire for money. The love of money is a great hindrance to many; and many a man is crippled in his ministry because he lets his **HEART** run after financial matters. I was walking out one day when I met a godly man who lived opposite me and he said, "My wife and I have been talking together about selling our house and we feel constrained to sell it to you." As we talked together he persuaded me to buy his place, and before we said good-by I told him that I would take it.

We always make big mistakes when we are in a hurry. I told my wife what I had promised, and she said, "How will you manage it?" I told her that I had managed things so far, but I did not know how I was going to get through this. I somehow knew that I was out of divine order. But when a fellow gets out of divine order it seems that the last person he goes to is **God**. I ended up relying on an architect to help me, but that scheme fell through. I turned to my relations and I ended up with mud on my face as one after another turned me down. I tried my friends and managed no better. My wife said to me, "Thou hast never been to **God** Yet." What could I do?

I have a certain place in our house where I go to pray. I have been there very often. As I went I said, "Lord, if You will get me out of this mess, I will never trouble You on this line again." As I waited on the Lord He just gave me one **Word**. It seemed a ridiculous thing, but it was the wisest counsel. There is divine wisdom in every **Word** He speaks. I came down to my wife, saying, "What do you **Think**? The Lord has told me to go to Brother Webster." I said, "It seems very ridiculous, for he is one of the poorest men I know." He was the poorest man I knew, but he was also the richest man I knew, for he knew **God**. My wife said, "Do What **God** says, and it will be right."

I went off at once to see him, and he said as he greeted me, "Smith, what brings you so early?" I answered, "The **Word** of **God**." I said to him, "About three weeks ago I promised to buy a house of a man, and I am short 100 pounds ($500). I have tried to get this money, but somehow I seem to have missed **God**." "How is it," he asked, "that you have come to me only now?"

I answered, "Because I went to the Lord about it only last night." "Well," he said, "it is a strange thing; three weeks ago I had 100 pounds. For years I have been putting money into a co-operative system and three weeks ago I had to go and draw 100 pounds out. I hid it under the mattress. Come with me and you shall have it. Take it. I hope it will bring as great a blessing to you as it has been a trouble to me." I had a **Word** from **God**, and all my troubles were ended.

This has been multiplied in a hundred ways since that time. If I had been filled with the **Holy Ghost**, I would not have bought that house and would not have had all that pressure. I believe the Lord wants to loose us from things of earth. But I am ever grateful for that **Word** from **God**. There have been times in my life when I have been in great crises and under great weight of intercession.

I have gone to the meeting without the knowledge of what I would say, but somehow or other **God** would give by the Spirit some **Word** of wisdom, just what some **SOUL**s in that meeting needed. As we look to **God** His **MIND** will be made known, and His revelation and His **Word** of wisdom will be forth coming.

"If thou shalt confess with thy mouth JESUS AS LORD, and shalt believe in thine HEART that God hath raised him from the dead, thou shalt be saved" (Romans 10:9).

"For TO THIS END Christ died and lived again, THAT HE MIGHT BE LORD of both the dead and the living" (Romans 14:9).

Smith - "I know that **God's Word** is sufficient. One **Word** from Him can change a nation. His **Word** is from everlasting to everlasting. It is through the entrance of this everlasting **Word**, this incorruptible seed, that we are born again, and come into this wonderful salvation. Man cannot live by bread alone, but must live by every **Word** that proceeded out of the mouth of **God**. This is the food of **Faith**. "**Faith** cometh by hearing, and hearing by the **Word** of God."!

CHAPTER EIGHT
Overcoming Depression by the Word

Before I was born again, I was a manic depressant, and suicidal. After I gave my heart to **JESUS**, February 19, 1975, I was delivered. Now here it was the winter of 1978, and depression was hitting me massively. I was living in that old chicken house with the evangelist and his wife.

I had moved all the way down the hallway to the farthest bedroom. I was sleeping on a plywood bed frame in my sleeping bag, in a room with no heat. The truck that I had just bought was sunk in a septic system, with a transmission that had gone out. I was having to walk almost 3 miles away to Belleville to go to work.

Wave after wave of depression was hitting me. I did not have enough money to fix my truck. There really was no food in the house. I allowed this to go on probably for better than a month. One morning I got up to study and pray. That morning something snapped within my heart and mind. Enough was enough. I put my Bible on the floor and stood on my Bible in my stocking feet.

I boldly declared: in the name of **JESUS** you lying spirit of depression, go from me, now! I am not going to put up with it one more moment, because **JESUS** has set me free. The minute I spoke the word of **GOD** against this depression, it released me. From that day forward I was free. Whom the Son Sets Free, Is Free Indeed.

*We quit McDonald's with no money

When we began to work for McDonald's, as newlyweds attending Bible School, we informed the manager that we needed to work together. That when he hired us he would have to hire us as a team. We explained to him that in order to go to the college we were attending we needed both to have an income. That we only had one vehicle, and that if we were working separate hours, it would not work.

I also informed him that if the day ever came where he called for just one of us, that on that day, and at that time, we would quit on the spot. I emphasize this because he needed to understand that this is the only reason we would accept employment there. He completely and wholeheartedly agreed with this mandate.

A number of months went by and everything was working wonderful. With both of our income from McDonald's, it was just keeping our nose above the water. One day the manager of McDonald's called our phone, which we had installed at the apartment. I picked up the phone, and he told me that they would not need me today. That only my wife should come in for work.

I told him that she would not be coming in. He asked why? I reminded him of the agreement we had. I said: my wife and I as of today quit. We will be in to pick up our last check later on. I could tell that he was stunned, but what was done, is what was done. I hung up the phone.

I told my wife that we were no longer working at McDonald's. She asked me: what are we going to do for money? She said: I'll drop out of Rhema, and you can attend. I will go get a job and support us. I told her: no Kathleen **GOD** sent us here for both of us to go to school. We are both going no matter what it takes. She said: well what are we going to do then? We will believe **GOD**, and he will provide. Almost immediately after this took place, somebody I knew came to me and informed me that the Broken Arrow school district was hiring janitors. Praise **GOD**, I was hired immediately.

Now the income from this job was not enough to cover all of our bills. I would still be over $500 short every month, which was a lot of money in those days. But supernaturally by the time that we left Oklahoma from the Bible college, all of our bills were paid up to date.

Empty Cupboards Overflowing

November 1978 was our first Thanksgiving together as a couple. Things did not look too cheerful around our apartment. We had eaten the last bit of food left in the house. We had been surviving on pancakes and spaghetti for the longest time. Plus, we had no gas in the truck again. We had met a couple who lived in the same apartment complex who were going to the same Bible school as we were, so we would catch a ride with them to school and back. When he went to school that day, we decided to sow our last five-dollar bill into the offering. We would never tell anybody our needs because **GOD** was our source.

After we got home from school, we sat back and rested a little bit. I was to leave for work at about two o'clock. Kathleen and I sat together on the couch and held hands to agree in prayer for food and money. We were sitting on a miracle because when we had arrived in Broken Arrow, the only piece of furniture that we had with us was Kathleen's pink canopy bed. The Lord opened up this small apartment in which the last tenants left behind all of their furniture except the bed!

As we were praying, there came a knock at our door. I opened the door, and there was our next-door neighbor, who was a heavy pot-smoking hippie. He and his wife's apartment was directly across from ours. Sometimes I would look over at their apartment and it looked like a "cloud of glory" was coming out of their window because of all the dope they smoked. I had shared the gospel with them many times.

When he had come to my door, I asked him what he needed. He told us that he and his wife were going away for Thanksgiving and they did not want to leave food in the house. He wanted to know if we could use some food. Praise the Lord! **GOD** had answered our prayers by using our next-door neighbor hippies. I told him "Yes we could use it!"

I thought he would bring one or two bags over to our apartment. Instead, he brought us bag after bag, and box after box of food. He brought so much food that it literally filled all of our kitchen cabinets! It did not make any natural sense because much of the food was in cans and jars, items that would not go bad for months, or even years. However, we did not argue with them; we simply thanked them with grateful hearts.

After they had left, we decided that we should bless someone else even as we had been blessed. We knew a single mother in the apartment complex that was really struggling. So we took a good portion of it to her apartment. I remember her crying with gratefulness. Right as I was getting ready to leave for work, there was another knock on the door.

I opened the door and there was a brother in **CHRIST** I knew standing there. He reached out his hand gave me a handshake, shoving a roll of money into the palm of my hand as he did so. This had to be **GOD** because Kathee and I did not tell anyone of our needs. I now had the money I needed to put gas in my truck to go to work!

Give, and it shall be given unto you; good measure, pressed down, and shaken together, and running over, shall men give into your bosom. For with the same measure that ye mete withal it shall be measured to you again (Luke 6:38).

Who's the Turkey?

Kathleen and I had been attending Bible College in Broken Arrow, Oklahoma. It was to be our first Thanksgiving together. We had just given away our last five dollars as an act of **FAITH**. When we arrived back at our apartment, to our wonderful amazement, **GOD** sent people to bless us with groceries and money. I had to go to work that night but before I walked out the door of our apartment, Kathleen said to me, "Let's pray and believe **GOD** for a turkey." I'm sorry to say that arrogance and pride rose up in my heart.

I very ignorantly raked her over the coals. I told her that I was doing all that I could do to believe **GOD** and if she wanted a turkey (at that moment she had one for a husband) she would have to believe **GOD** for one all by herself. She looked me straight in the eyes saying, "Okay, I will." As I stood there, she prayed crying out to **GOD**. "Lord, will you please give me a ten-pound Butterball turkey for Thanksgiving? And now Lord, I thank you for that ten-pound Butterball turkey. Amen." I laughed at her, turned my back to her, got into my truck and went to work.

I thought in my heart that **GOD** was not going to answer her prayers because *I* was the man of **FAITH**. At this time, I was working for the Broken Arrow school district as a janitor. About eight o'clock at night, I took my break for my meal. Kathleen had made me a bagged lunch, so I had to go out to the truck to get it.

As I went to the parking lot and walked towards my truck, I noticed that there was something sitting on the hood. It was a cold, frosty night with the wind blowing slightly. As I got closer, I could see that it was a grocery bag. I grabbed it off the hood in order to look inside. I opened the bag, and, to my utter amazement, it was a turkey —not just any turkey but a ten-pound Butterball turkey! **GOD** had heard my wife's prayers and had someone put a turkey on my truck at work.

There were two turkeys out in the cold that November night. Was Kathleen ever elated when both of her turkeys came home that night. We ate one of the turkeys and the other still lives with her. We discovered later that a good friend of ours had a newspaper delivery route and he had recently obtained so many new customers that his company had given him an extra turkey.

As he was driving down the road, not knowing what to do with this extra turkey, he saw my pickup truck sitting at this elementary school. It was quickened in his heart to give us the turkey. The only problem was that my truck was locked. It was such a cold night that he knew that the turkey would be okay on the hood.

Ephesians 3:[19] and to know the love of **CHRIST***, which passes knowledge, that ye might be filled with all the fullness of* **GOD***.[20] Now unto him that is able to do exceeding abundantly above all that we ask or think, according to the power that worketh in us, [21] unto him be glory in the church by* **CHRIST JESUS** *throughout all ages, world without end. Amen.*

GAVE IT ALL AWAY

All these years, we've been married, we always been givers. A lot of times it looked like we were being stupid. Many times, the Lord would have us to give in **Circumstances** that seemed to be completely insane. For, another words, we needed every penny we had plus a lot, lot, lot more, and we didn't have it. And the Lord would speak to me and tell us to empty our bank account and give it away. Isn't that crazy? No, it's the obedience of **Faith**. It's living by **Faith**. It's not easy. It's an audacious **Faith**. It's a **Faith** that says, you know what? All I know is what **God** it is telling us to do,

FAITH BASED OUTCOME INDEPENDENT

and we are going to be obedient.

A Good Description of How FAITH In CHRIST Operates.

I love this quote from Smith Wigglesworth Who was Mightily used of **GOD**:

"Natural" men see things only as they appear, but "spiritual" men see things completely differently. There is a divine, and inward violence called **FAITH** that refuses to agree with the devil. It refuses to call **GOD** a liar by disagreeing with Him. **No Matter What Men of FAITH** understand that **Change Will Not Come Without Confrontation.**

We must confront ourselves, our **Circumstances**, and the demonic world: without compromising our character, attitude, or personality.

I HAVE LEARNED TO NOT BE MOVED BY CIRCUMSTANCES

 Paul the apostle reveals within the epistles that he wroter that he had learned how to live by **Faith – Based Outcome Independence!**

Philippians 4:11 Not that I speak in respect of want: for I have learned, in whatsoever state I am, therewith to be content. 12 I know both how to be abased, and I know how to abound: every where and in all things I am instructed both to be full and to be hungry, both to abound and to suffer need.

We're talking about **Faith** that is rooted and grounded, deep into **God**. A **Faith** that is not moved by the **Circumstances**. We will not allow ourselves to be driven out of the will of **God** by whatever problems confront us. A perfect example is the three Hebrew children, who refused to bow before the statue of Nebuchadnezzar.

Fed Me Duck Head, Guts, Feet

When I was with the Alaskan Yupik Indians as a 19-year-old kid out in the bush of Alaska, they would purposely feed me the worst of the hunt. I knew this was for two reasons.

#1 I was a rotten white man that they thought had stolen Alaska away from them. (At least that's what they thought)

#2 I was a radical, on fire, in love with **JESUS**' 19-year-old kid that they could not entice to do their drugs, alcohol, and Un**god**ly activities. I just kept preaching the love of **JESUS**, and the salvation of **CHRIST** to them. I ate the duck feet, duck guts, and sucked the brains and the eyeballs out of the duck heads they put on my plate.

You might say, Pastor Mike, why would you do that? Because the Bible says whatever they put on your plate when you enter into the house where you are to eat. I take that literally. The common American **Christian** is very picky in what he eats. He will not eat anything that his flesh does not like.

Luke 10:8 And into whatsoever city ye enter, and they receive you, eat such things as are set before you:

I Quit as a Janitor

(1978) During the time my wife and I were attending Rhema Bible training center I got a job working for the Broken Arrow school district. This job lasted approximately six months. One day I went to work, as usual, not knowing this would be my last day of employment with the school district. **GOD** was about to give me a job at Rhema on their maintenance team.

One evening as I was waxing and buffing a classroom floor (at the same time praying quietly under my breath)when out of the blue my boss came storming into the classroom. He asked me what in the #@!#@ did I think I was doing. I just looked at him and kept working. He became more aggravated, yelling and screaming like he had lost his mind. (He was quite demon oppressed.) I knew he was living a perverted and very twisted lifestyle because he talked and bragged about it all the time. I had not condemned him for his sin but simply strove to live a holy life in front of him and all of the other workers.

My boss finally got in my face and tried to push me around. As I was standing there, I heard the Lord say; it's time to quit; you have done all that you can here. Now, in the natural, I really needed this job for my wife and me to keep going to Bible school and to pay bills and food. However, the Spirit of the Lord said to me, your job here is done. I had shared **CHRIST** with all of the workers. I had worked very diligently and hard to be a good witness. There was nothing more in the natural that I could really do to help these people.

I have learned through the years that if **GOD** tells you to do something, then you better do it, because HE knows what HE is doing. Whenever I have ignored the voice of **GOD**, the results have always been tragic. So right on the spot I turned off the floor buffer, looked at this man and said," I quit!"

He said, **"What?"**
I said, **"I quit!"**
He said to me, **"You can't quit!"**
I said, **"Oh, yes I can, and I just did!"**

I walked right past him out into the hallway of the school. He was yelling and screaming at me as I walked down the hallway. I simply ignored him and kept walking. **GOD** in my Ford F250 pickup truck, and headed home to our apartment where my wife was waiting for me. The question was: Now what was I going to do now?

I went home and told Kathleen what I had done. She took the news with a gentle acknowledgment that **GOD** would provide. That's one wonderful thing about my lovely wife. She has been in very difficult situations with me, and yet she just keeps on loving, praying, and standing on the word. **GOD** will give you the desires of your heart, especially when those desires are led and directed by HIS Spirit.

Working at Rhema

I asked the Lord if I could have a job working at the Bible school (Rhema) we were attending. It would be the perfect place to work because I wanted to be around **GOD**ly people and get more connected to the ministry.

Several days later as Kathee and I sat in class, there was an announcement over the loudspeaker that the school was hiring people to work with their yard and maintenance crew. My heart leaped for joy. Immediately after that class was completed, I went to the main office and filled out an application.

The next day, I went back to the office, and they informed me that I had been hired. They wanted me to start that very day. Kathleen caught a ride home with some friends back to our apartment because I needed to stay at work. Working for the Broken Arrow school district had prepared me for this job. If I had not quit when the Spirit of the Lord had quickened me, I would have missed this opportunity.

FAITH BASED OUTCOME INDEPENDENT

Why I Canceled My FREE Health Care Policy 1981 up to Present

I Told the Church Board to Cancel My Health Insurance Policy: which the church was paying for! My wife and I were pasturing an Assembly of **GOD** church in three Springs Pennsylvania. This was back in 1979. This church automatically gave free health insurance to their pastors. I asked to have a special meeting with the board. I informed the board that I wanted to save them money. They asked me how I could save them money. I told them that they could cancel our health insurance policy because we did not need it. My wife and I had agreed previously that we did not need this health insurance policy.

To many people (**Christ**ians) this would seem preposterous and blatantly arrogant. But you see at 19 years old when I gave my heart to **CHRIST**, I had a divine Revelation of healing. I saw within a vision **CHRIST** upon the whipping post. I saw the cat of nine tails striking his back. I saw the flesh and the blood splashing in all directions. I saw the overwhelming pain and agony upon the face of **JESUS** as he took those 39 lashes.

As I was seeing this open vision when I heard the Lord say to me: By My Stripes, You Are Healed! **From 1975, up to the present, I have looked to GOD for my healing**. Before this time, I was always at the doctor's or laid up in a hospital bed. Pastor Mike have you ever taken your family to the doctors? Yes, I have, and they know that if they ask me to take them to the doctors I will, with no condemnation upon them! **GOD** will always work with us where we are at. But our whole motive should be to go deeper, higher, and wider with **CHRIST** in our walk of **FAITH**.

My children and my wife have been healed many times as we prayed together and looked to **CHRIST** for their healing. Yes, there's been a number of times when there were minor operations upon their bodies, but overall, we have lived a doctor free life. The great physician has been there for us.

Many times, when it seemed hopeless as I would cry out to **JESUS** sometimes all night long, even for months on end for myself, **CHRIST** the Great Physician would show up and would heal my children, my wife, and me. You see I do not think it is **GOD**'s will to heal me, and my family, I Know It Is His Will! Many times, through the years people contact me wanting me to fight the fight of **FAITH** for them. Oh, and how I wish I could, but it is their responsibility to take a hold of **GOD**, and not let go.

Now the board members agreed to my request at three Springs Assembly of **GOD**. From the time my wife and I have been married in 1978, up to present we do not have healthcare insurance. I know the government is trying to require us to do so, but truly we would rather look to **JESUS**. We will obey the laws of the land if it is required, but **CHRIST** is our healer. It is my greatest desire to bring people into this place of freedom.

Where CHRIST is our all in all! This is not a matter of pride. If I felt in my heart I needed help from the medical world (because I was not where I needed to be spiritual), I would get it. My three sons and daughter who are now all in their 30s live in this same realm. None of them have health care insurance because they are strong in **FAITH** when it comes to their own personal healing.

The minute that any one of us begins to get symptoms of sickness immediately we lay hands upon each other, commanding the illness to go, and for our bodies to be healed. Does the healing manifest right away, all the time? The answer to that is: **NO!** Why? Because it is what The Word of **GOD** Says That We Have Need of **Patience!**

That is the time from which you pray and believe, unto

the manifestation of the healing. During this time, we just keep rejoicing and thanking **GOD** that it is done based upon the fact that: By the Stripes of **JESUS** we are he healed! Now what has happened to me in the past when I have perceived that I was not where I needed to be spiritually to receive my healing, I would simply dig in deeper. I would once again begin to cry out to **GOD**, hide HIS word in my heart, and go radically after **JESUS**. **He Has Never Failed to HEAL Us!**

Kept Burning My Hands

The church did not have very much money. The amount of fuel oil we went through to keep it warm was ridiculous. I decided to put a wood stove in the parsonage. I put it in the half-basement of the house.
The floor of the basement was nothing but rocks and dirt. The wood-burning stove was a long, deep, cast-iron outfit. Using an existing chimney in the basement, I connected the wood stove to this chimney. It was a very old system, however, with a very little draft.

That made it extremely hard to get it started with a good fire going. In the process of trying to maintain the fire, I would consistently somehow place my hands against the stove. I do not know how many blisters I got from that wood stove. It seemed as if I could not help but burn my hands! You would have thought that I would have begun to believe **GOD** for wisdom not to burn my hands but that's not what I did. Instead, I began to confess verses about the fire not being able to burn me.

Isaiah 43:2 When thou passes through the waters, I will be with thee; and through the rivers, they shall not overflow thee: when thou walks' through the fire, thou shalt not be burned; neither shall the flame kindle upon thee.

This went on for many weeks and sure enough, without fail, I would touch the stove by accident. But I was getting burned less and less. My hand or fingers would simply turn red. One day, I again touch the stove when it was literally glowing red. That's how hot the stove was. Instantly, my hand hurt. I put my other hand over the burnt part of my hand and commanded the pain to cease. I confessed that I would have no blister. From that point for I would be thanking and praising **GOD** that my hand was healed. Sure enough, the pain left, and my hand was only slightly pink.

Victory over Painful Tumors

(1980) I woke up one morning with tremendous pain in my lower abdomen. I lifted up my shirt and looked down where the pain was. There was a lump on my abdomen about the size of an acorn. I laid my hands on it immediately, commanding it to go.

I said, "You lying devil, by the stripes of **JESUS** I am healed and made whole." After I spoke to the lump, the pain became excruciating and overwhelmingly worse. All that day I walked the floor crying out to **GOD** and praising him that His Word is real and true.

I went for a walk on the mountain right behind the parsonage. It was a long day before I got to sleep that night. When I awoke the next morning the pain was even more severe. It felt like somebody was stabbing me in my gut with a knife. I lifted up my shirt and looked and there was another lump. Now I had two lumps in my lower abdomen.

I laid my hands on them, commanding them to go. Tears were rolling down my face, as I spoke the Word. I lifted my hands toward heaven and kept praising **GOD** that I was healed. Even though I did not see any change, I kept praising **GOD**. All the symptoms were telling me that **GOD**'s Word is a lie and that I was not healed by the stripes of **JESUS**. But I knew that I was healed. It was another long day. It seemed as if I could never get to sleep that night. The pain was continual and non-stop!

When I got up the next morning the pain had intensified even more. Once again I looked at my abdomen and to my shock, there was another lump the size of an acorn. Now I had three of these nasty lumps and each was about the size of an acorn. I did not think that the pain could get any worse, but it was. Once again I laid my hands on these tumors, commanding them to go in the name of **JESUS CHRIST** of Nazareth.

I declared that by the stripes of **JESUS** I am healed! It felt like a knife sticking in my gut all that day and night. I lifted my hands, and with tears rolling down my face, kept praising **GOD** that I was healed.

By **FAITH** I began to dance before the Lord a victory dance, praising **GOD** that I was healed by the stripes of **JESUS**. I went to bed that night hurting worse than ever. All night I tossed and turned and moaned, all the while thanking **GOD** that I was not going to die but that I was healed. I got up the next morning, and all of the tumors and pain were gone. They have never come back.

*And he said, Let me go, for the day breaketh. And he said, I will not let thee go, except thou bless me. And he said unto him, What is thy name? And he said, Jacob. And he said, Thy name shall be called no more Jacob, but Israel: for as a prince hast thou power with **GOD** and with men, and hast prevailed (Genesis 32:26-28).*

RED HOT SKILLET COULD NOT BURN MY HANDS

I was cooking breakfast one morning, having just put oil in a cast-iron skillet. I was making eggs, bacon, and hash browns. As I was busy making breakfast, there was a knock on the door. When I opened the door, one of my parishioners named Paul was there. Paul and I were very good friends and would spend hours together praying and witnessing. He probably was fifteen years my senior. I invited him into the house and we began to talk about the things of **GOD**. I had completely forgotten about the cast-iron skillet on the stove.

The next thing that I knew, my wife was screaming. I went into the kitchen and saw that the oil in the skillet had exploded into fire, with flames reaching as high as the old kitchen cupboards. I knew if I did not move fast the whole house would go up in flames.

The house was a firetrap waiting to happen. I was not thinking. I yelled for Paul to open the outside door as I was running for the stove and the skillet. I scooped the red-hot skillet up into my hands, spun around, and carried it out the door. Paul was standing out of the way and my wife was watching everything as it happened. I ran outside and flipped the pan upside down on the ground.

After a while the flames went out. I was standing and looking down at the cast-iron skillet when I suddenly realized what I had done. I was in such a hurry that I did not even grab a towel or any kind of heat pads before I scooped up the frying pan. I had literally picked it up with my bare hands. I looked down at my hands in complete amazement.

They should have been severely burned all the way to the bones. All that happened was that they became a little red. Not only that, but why didn't the flames of the burning oil not burn me? In just a brief period, all the pain and the redness in my hands were gone. If my wife and Paul had not seen me do it, I would truly doubt it myself. But **GOD** and his word are amazing!

Who through FAITH subdued kingdoms, wrought

righteousness, obtained promises, stopped the mouths of lions, Quenched the violence of Þ re, escaped the edge of the sword, out of weakness were made strong, waxed valiant in fight, turned to fight the armies of the aliens (Hebrews 11:33-34).

Bought Tickets to Germany

We were getting ready to move from the parsonage of the church we had been pastoring. As I was in prayer one morning, the Spirit of **GOD** spoke to my heart, Go to Germany! It was very strong that I needed to go to Germany. When I shared this with my wife, without hesitation she agreed. We had to raise money in order to buy the tickets and go.

We put our car on the market and sold it within a couple of days. That was a miracle within itself. That was the Sports Granada that I had outfitted with ridiculous equipment. It was an older gentleman that bought the car. We tried to sell whatever else we could. What we could not sell, we put in storage. We then bought round-trip tickets to Frankfurt, Germany. My wife Kathleen, Michael (who was now three months old) and I caught a plane and landed in Frankfurt, Germany.

Frankfurt Germany, Now What?

When we entered the airport terminal I did not know what else to do. This pattern is how **GOD** has led me to the majority of my spiritual life. I do not try to figure out what to do—I simply take one baby step at a time. As I was standing in the terminal, simply being quiet and waiting to hear what the Spirit would say, the Spirit quickened my heart to go to the American military welcome center at the airport.

I remember walking towards the military welcome center with my wife and child. Standing right outside of the glass window office area was a gentleman who was dressed in military clothing. Because I had been in the navy and not in the army, I did not know their ranking system. This particular military man, who was an older Hispanic man, was some type of officer. I walked up to him and simply started talking. It turns out he was a sergeant, and he was stationed at the local American military base. He asked me what we were doing in Germany.

I told him that I was a minister, and how the Spirit of **GOD** quickened my heart to come to Germany to minister and that we had come by **FAITH** with no connections in the **Christian** community. He then informed me that he himself was a pastor and had connections throughout Germany. As I was speaking to him, **GOD** moved on his heart to help us! He also invited us to come and preach to his congregation. We had a wonderful move of **GOD**'s Spirit in the church. Then the pastor helped us get the proper papers and IDs to go to any military base in Germany. The doors began to swing open for us!

And the angel of the Lord spake unto Philip, saying, Arise, and go toward the south unto the way that goeth down from Jerusalem unto Gaza, which is desert (Acts 8:26).

GOD Provides an Apartment

We had been ministering in a church in the industrial part of Germany. **GOD** had moved in a wonderful way. The pastor and congregation did not realize it, but we had nowhere to go after this service. We did not have any more services lined up at the moment.

I did not tell this pastor anything about our situation. I like the opportunity to watch **GOD** work. If I would have told the people our needs or what was going on, then most likely they would have responded out of compassion to help us. But I love to live at the forefront of watching **GOD** perform perfectly-orchestrated divine events. For this reason, Kathee and I did not tell anyone what was going on.

We simply held hands together and **prayed**, asking **GOD** for somewhere to stay that night. After the meeting, a German woman in her 50's approached us very timidly. She informed us that her husband was working in Saudi Arabia for the oil industry and that she had an apartment in the area. She was leaving for Saudi Arabia the next day and was desperate for someone to stay at her apartment.

She asked us if we could possibly stay at her home until she got back within the next month. Remember, this lady had just met us and we were complete strangers to her. Not only that, but we were foreigners from America.

Kathee and I both looked at each other, knowing once again the Lord had come through for us. We told her that we would be willing to do that for her. She also encouraged us to eat all of the food that there was in her house, and we were glad to accommodate her request!

I have been young, and now am old; yet have I not seen the righteous forsaken, nor his seed begging bread (Psalms 37:25).

Thanking GOD For Food & Money

We continued to minister in the local area where we were staying in Germany. Eventually, we had also consumed all of the food in the sister's apartment as she has given us the liberty to do. All of our finances were completely depleted. We did not even have any money for gasoline.

I got up early in the morning - as per my usual routine - it was time for me to talk to **GOD**: about our needs. We were in Germany at this time, doing missionary work. We were also completely out of food, money and gas for our car. Our one-year-old son was having to depend on mom for all of his nourishment. The apartment we were staying in, at this time, had a long hallway leading to all rooms: straight ahead was a very small front room (with sliding doors); on the right-hand was a small kitchen and on the left-hand was the bedroom.

I was in the front room praying and crying out to **GOD**. I never complain, gripe, or tell **GOD** what is wrong when I pray. Prayer, supplication, and thanksgiving are the order of the day. So, I was talking to the **FATHER,** in the name of **JESUS**, and I knew, that He already knew what we needed. Still, He tells us in His Word to let Him know what we need.

After I was done talking to the **FATHER**, I stepped into the realm of praise and thanksgiving. I lifted my hands and began to dance before the Lord. My dance is not elaborate, orchestrated, symbolic or performance. It is just me, lifting my feet (kind of kicking them around) and jumping a little bit - in a rather comical, childlike fashion. Some people really believe that they have to get into some kind of elaborate system of swinging their arms and bodies: I just keep it really simple, sincere, and from my heart.

While I was seeking **GOD**, my wife was in the kitchen, cleaning up. During my singing in tongues and dancing before the Lord, there was a knock on the apartment door, which I did not hear. My wife, however, did hear the knocking. She put down the dishes and headed for the door.

Now, as far as we were aware, no one knew where we were staying.

My wife opened the door to a tall, distinguished-looking, German gentleman. He informed her that he had been looking for us. He said he'd been actually hunting us down because **GOD** had used us in a service where he'd experienced his first supernatural encounter.

My wife came to inform me about the gentleman at the door. So, I walked down the skinny hallway, to where this gentleman was standing, to speak to him. I did have a recollection of meeting him at a previous service; I'd prayed for him to be filled with the **Holy Ghost** and I remember him speaking in tongues. At the time, I had no idea of his background. He gave me quite an impressive resume of who he was; it turns out he was a professor at a local German college.

He shared with us how he had struggled to believe in the supernatural, because of his superior intellect, but when he came to the service I was ministering at, his world was turned upside down! He had experienced **GOD**! When he left that meeting, he said, the Spirit of the Lord was upon him. He also said the Lord spoke to him for the first time he could ever remember. The Lord told him specifically that he was to find me and give me a certain amount of money.

Ever since the Lord had spoken to him (a number of days previously) he had been trying to find us. He had just learned of our address from someone at a church we had been ministering at. Now … here he was! Standing at our door, during the exact same time when I had been praying— praising and thanking **GOD** for the finances and food we needed. Before he left, he handed us an envelope. When he'd gone we opened up the envelope and it was exceedingly abundantly above all that we could ever ask or hope for. We did not have any more financial worries or needs until we left Germany.

JESUS saith unto them, Fill the waterpots with water. And they Þ lled them up to the brim. And he saith unto them, Draw out now, and bear unto the governor of the feast. And they bare it. When the ruler of the feast had tasted the water that was made wine, and knew not whence it was: (but the servants which drew the water knew;) the governor of the feast called the bridegroom (John 2:7-9).

Chiseled a Hole through a Bomb Shelter

We were ministering at a church in the western part of Germany, the industrial area. Because I had no meetings during the day, it came into my heart to help this church. They had a two-story building that had been built during World War II. The upstairs area was being used as their sanctuary and offices. They wanted to use the downstairs for youth and a tea room. In America we would call it a coffee house. There is only one major problem. There were no windows in this basement which actually was level with the ground outside.

As we were talking about evangelizing the youth in the area, they had said that someday they wanted to put a window approximately 4' x 6' into this room. The only problem was that when this building was built the downstairs was built to be a bomb shelter. The walls were approximately 3 feet wide, being built from mortar and bricks. It was designed to withstand bombs that were being dropped by the Americans and the British.

This ministry at the time did not have the people, for the finances to have someone open up the room. It came into my heart that I would do this for them. I told them that I would like to do this project. They told me they did not have the money to pay me nor did they have the money for the mortar that would need to be used to finish the project. I told them there was not going to be any cost involved on their side. That the Lord had laid it upon my heart to do this for them. Now, this was not my profession, but it was basically grunting labor.

I got myself a large sledgehammer, plus a small sledgehammer in a steel wedge. So my project began. My wife and son were in the same large room with me through all of this process, but far enough away to where the flying bricks and the mortar would not hit them. Day after day I began to chisel. It was a very slow process because the mortar the Germans used was extremely hard. It literally took me days on end until finally, I broke through to the other side with a very small hole.

From that very small hole, I began to work my way to the left, the right, up, and down. I was aiming for a 4' x 6' window. That was the window they already had been provided by a donation. Hour after hour, day after day, for approximately two weeks I worked on this project. My hands were bruised, bleeding and hurting. More times and I can remember I would hit my hand with the sledgehammer.

Why were you doing this Pastor Mike? Because **GOD** laid it upon my heart, and it was for Him and Him alone that I was laboring! The day came when the opening was completed. Then I had to go and by the mortar, make it up in a large mortar pan, and began to basically plaster the sides, the top, and the bottom. When I finished the project I'll have to admit it was exactly what they were looking for. They had men in the church they were able to install the proper hardware and the window.

Once this project was done, then they fixed up the rest of the room to be a gathering for the youth and the congregation to fellowship and to do Bible studies.

The Great Escape

After nine months in Germany with many signs and wonders, the Spirit was tugging at our hearts to get back to America. The only problem is that we had ended up being involved with a ministry that wanted us to stay with them. They provided housing and food for us.

It's not that they were controlling but every time I would talk about leaving; they would convince me to stay. Don't misunderstand me. They were beautiful people. It's just that it was time for us to leave! Please realize, we were still a young married couple. My wife went through tremendous emotional stress because I was being so insipid. We had only been married for four years. During that time, it seemed as if I had always known what the will of **GOD** was but now I was confused.

I finally realized that I was out of the will of **GOD** and we just needed to leave. I did not want to discuss this with these people again because I did not trust myself —they might convince me to stay longer. Their theology was that we needed to have a plan for every step we took. **GOD** doesn't lead me in that way. It is simply one little step after another, placing the future into His hands.

We were staying in this church's coffee and tea shop where the youth gathered and held special meetings. I woke Kathleen up early one morning. Michael was sleeping, so we bundled him up in some blankets. Then we very quietly tiptoed out of the facility. After we put Michael in his car seat, Kathleen sat behind the steering wheel. She put the car in neutral as I got behind the car and began to push it. Once the car was coasting and we were out of their compound and the parking lot, I jumped in and Kathleen started the vehicle. She put it in gear and away we went. Hallelujah! We were free from my indecision and wavering.

We followed the map back towards Frankfurt, Germany. We got on the Audubon and I opened that little car up to eighty kilometers an hour. There is no speed limit on the Audubon, so we were slowpokes compared to everyone else. From Wesel, we had approximately a 280-kilometer journey to get to the airport in Frankfurt.

As we were driving on the Audubon, the car began to act very strangely. We had just begun the journey when the car began to slow down. I kept pumping the gas and the car would speed up. We had plenty of gas in the car so that was not the problem. Then the engine began to sputter and make loud knocking noises.

There was something drastically wrong with our automobile. There was no way that we were going to miss getting to the Frankfurt airport because we needed to get back to America.

Kathleen and I began to command the car to keep running in the name of **JESUS**. By this time, everybody was passing us. The vehicle was slowing down to as little as ten kilometers an hour. Many times, it seemed to almost come to a standstill.

We laid our hands on the dashboard, commanding it to keep on running in the name of **JESUS**. Then the car would speed up again and I would sink the pedal to the floor. We would hit up to 120 kilometers an hour and then the cycle would start all over again —going back down to ten kilometers an hour, if not less. We kept speaking to that car all of the way to the airport. I refused to pull off the road and turn it off. In the name of **JESUS**, we were going to make it to the airport! Smoke was pouring out of the back end of the vehicle.

This journey seemed to take days to complete, but of course, it did not. We finally saw the exit signs for the American military base where we knew someone we could leave the car with. As we pulled into the parking space in front of the military house of the people we knew, the car died completely.

It was dead, never to live again. We heard later on that they simply hauled it away and scrapped it. The engine had completely frozen up and it was mechanically impossible for the engine to be repaired. Someone gave us a ride to the airport. We were just in time to catch the plane back to the USA.

Go on TV audible voice

Right after my wife gave birth to Daniel, we had some good friends come and stay with us. They were our spiritual parents to an extent. Mary was helping my wife clean the house and care for Michael.

I basically stayed out of their way. While they were cleaning the kitchen, I was upstairs in my **prayer** room spending time with the Lord in **prayer** and meditating on the Word. When I was finished, I got up and started to come down the stairs.

As I was coming downstairs, I heard the audible voice of **GOD**. This is what He said to me, and I quote, **"Go on TV!"** That's what I heard. The audible voice of **GOD** was so real, that I instantly fell to my knees. I said, "Lord, the church does not have the money to put me on TV!" ($250 for one half-hour program every Sunday)

Then He began to communicate with me in His still quiet voice. He spoke to my heart and said, **the church will not pay for your TV time. You will believe and trust Me for it!** I said, Yes, Lord! He then quickened to my heart that the first TV station I would be on would be Channel 25 out of Hagerstown, Maryland.

The Spirit literally informed me about the specific time I would be on would be Sunday Mornings at 6:30 a.m. Once again, I told the Lord I would obey Him.

Now my wife is always very supportive of me. (Or maybe I should say she never tries to stop me!) She is a real trooper. In fact, she is so much of a trooper that she was up and about within twenty minutes of giving birth to Daniel.

After the Lord had finished speaking to me, I went downstairs to share this with her. When I told her this, she became very upset with me. I believe part of the reason is that financially we were already in need of some miracles. We did not even have money for fuel oil to heat our house.

We probably only had enough fuel oil for one more day. She was so upset with me that she went and told Mary. (Mary, by the way, is an aggressive pioneer woman.

To date, Mary and her husband Paul have done many wonderful works in the countries of Africa. She is a mother of **FAITH**. I'm sure it did not help that my wife was distraught and had just given birth to Daniel.)

My Wife Extremely Upset

When I entered the kitchen, Mary cornered me. She tried to speak some sense into me. She basically skinned me alive! Of course, I didn't blame Mary or my wife, but I had heard from **GOD**!

Humble yourselves therefore under the mighty hand of GOD, that he may exalt you in due time: Casting all your care upon him; for he careth for you (1 Peter 5:6-7).

GOD Supplied Fuel Oil

Later that day as I was praying, a brother who had been saved and filled with the **Holy Ghost** in our church, Andy, knocked at our front door. He was self-employed and he had been cleaning up people's properties.

He asked me how Kathee and I were doing, and how was our newborn son? He then informed me that he had two fifty-five gallon barrels of fuel oil on the back of this truck and wanted to know if I knew anyone that needed heating oil. I said, "Yes, Andy, we do!" He backed his truck up, and he put the fuel into our fuel tank.

Channel 25 Hagerstown Just for you

After hearing the Lord telling me to go on TV, the very next day I called Channel 25, WHAG in Hagerstown, Maryland, asking to be transferred over to their sales department. When someone else answered the phone, I told this person that I was interested in purchasing a half-hour slot on their channel. I did not tell them what day of the week or time I wanted.

I simply said that I was going to produce a half-hour program. (How I was going to produce these programs I did not know). The sales personnel was a lady who informed me that they did not have any time available, and did not know when another slot would be available. I asked her if she would go to their programming department and discuss with them if there was anything they could do. She said she would, even though she thought it would not make any difference because they had no time available.

Approximately three days later, the sales personnel called me back, telling me that they had called a special meeting to discuss my request. She informed me that normally they do not have their TV station on the air until seven o'clock on Sunday mornings, but they had unanimously agreed to bring their station on the air at 6:30 a.m. just for me! From the very first day of our broadcast, we had a tremendous response. All the finances that we needed to stay on the air came in. ($250 for one half-hour program every Sunday)

Eventually, we were on seven TV stations one day a week. Then I was on with Dr. Lester Sumrall's network five days a week. Dr. Sumrall later came to our church and ministered for us. Until the day Dr. Sumrall died, my ordination papers were with him and his ministry.

But he that shall endure unto the end, the same shall be saved. And this gospel of the kingdom shall be preached in all the world for a witness unto all nations; and then shall the end come (Matthew 24:13-14).

FAITH BASED OUTCOME INDEPENDENT

Embrace The Sufferings Of CHRIST

I heard a very interesting story from another minister of the gospel. Supposedly (if I have the story correct) he was in China, ministering. At the end of his service, he was having a conversation with another Chinese believer. They were talking about the sufferings, persecutions, and afflictions that were taking place in China, against the body of **CHRIST**. This particular man said he knew of a situation where the government had arrested a pastor. The pastor was taken to prison for quite a long time.

When the pastor was in prison, they began to torture him, afflict him, and do terrible things to him in order that he would renounce his **FAITH**. But, thank **GOD**, he never did. I do not know how long this went on before he was finally released, but it was implied that it was for quite a while. When he was finally let go, he eventually made it back to the church he had pastored. He stood before his congregation and shared with them his testimony: how **GOD** had preserved him and kept him - that he had not denied the **FAITH**. He also shared, in detail, all of the terrible things that had happened to him while he was in prison. All of the sufferings, tortures, and pains he had endured for **JESUS CHRIST**. That day, the entire congregation, all believers, broke out in weeping and crying.

When the Chinese believer had finished telling his story, a visiting American minister said: "They must have really loved their pastor." The Chinese believer looked at him oddly and he asked: "What do you mean?" The American minister replied: "The way they were weeping and wailing, and crying for him." **The Chinese believer replied: "Oh! No! You have it all wrong! You completely misunderstand!** They were not crying because the pastor was tortured. They were weeping and crying because they felt there was something wrong with them, in the fact that they had not been arrested themselves, and tortured for **CHRIST**! They were literally jealous of their pastor for being so blessed in being tortured for **CHRIST**."

Acts 5:41 And they departed from the presence of the council, rejoicing that they were counted worthy to suffer shame for his name.

1 Peter 4:13-16 But rejoice, inasmuch as ye are partakers of **CHRIST***'s sufferings; that, when his glory shall be revealed, ye may be glad also with exceeding joy. 14 If ye be reproached for the name of* **CHRIST***, happy are ye; for the spirit of glory and of* **GOD** *resteth upon you: on their part he is evil spoken of, but on your part he is glorified. 15 But let none of you suffer as a murderer, or as a thief, or as an evildoer, or as a busybody in other men's matters. 16 Yet if any man suffer as a* **Christian***, let him not be ashamed; but let him glorify* **GOD** *on this behalf.*

We, as Western believers, seem to have no concept of what it really means to be **GOD**'s people. I have heard from very reliable sources that the believers in China really feel sad for us. They literally pray and weep for us, because of the fact that we are so fleshly and worldly; self-centered, self-serving and self-seeking. We are nothing but slaves to our emotions and to carnality.

You cannot believe how many people, so-called believers, in America, believe we are more spiritual and more mature than most other people in other countries! This could not be further from the truth. **GOD** has allowed me to be in the midst of other believers in poverty-stricken countries, where they have nothing, yet many of them are more spiritually mature then we are. They literally put us to shame! **May GOD have mercy on our souls.**

Terrible Warts Gone Over Night

A poverty-stricken couple began to come to our church. We watched as **JESUS** set this couple free from drugs, alcohol, violence, and immorality. We helped install a new bathroom in their little house. The wife became one of the main workers in the church. She was always there trying to help people.

One day they brought one of their young daughters to us. They told us she had a problem they did not know how to resolve. They had taken her to the doctor, but there didn't seem to be anything they could do. The girl was hiding behind them so her mother brought her to the front. Then she had the girl held out her little hand. It was terrible.

Her little hand was completely covered with warts front and back. We are not talking about twenty or thirty warts. It literally looked like hundreds of warts. We laid our hands on her little hand. We then commanded these foul warts to come off of her hand in the name of **JESUS CHRIST** of Nazareth, and for her hand to be completely healed.

As we looked at her hand, it did not seem as if anything happened. We told them that when you pray in **FAITH**, you must believe that those things you asked for in **FAITH** are done. We explained that what we need to do is begin to thank **GOD** that she is healed—that the warts are gone in the name of **JESUS**. Both the husband and the wife agreed that it was done. They took their little girl, got in their car, and left.

Later that day I received numerous calls from the couple telling me there was no difference. Each time I encouraged them just to keep praising **GOD** that it was done. At about 10 pm they once more called me, and once again I told them **GOD** has done it, and you will see it . I said this laughter in my voice because my heart had been quickened by the **Holy Ghost**! I knew that I knew that I knew it was done!

The next morning, I received a phone call from the mother. She was extremely excited and bursting with happiness. She told us that when her little girl went to bed that night nothing had changed. The warts were just as bad as ever.

When she went to get her the next morning, every single wart was gone but one. They brought the little girl back to us to look at her hand. Sure enough, in one-night **GOD** had removed every single wart but one, which was in the palm of her hand! The skin on her hand was smooth and normal just like the other one, as smooth as baby skin. We declared that the last remaining wart would have to leave also!

How GOD Healed Me of a Hernia

***I Kept Radically SHOVING my intestines back into where they belonged with my fingers for two weeks.**

Day after day we were putting up the steel for our new church facility. We only had the use of the crane for one day. The crane had handled all of the heaviest beams. All of the rest of the steel had to be carried up to the top of the building and placed by hand. I'm not a very large man, as I only weighed about 140 pounds at the time. I was pulling and tugging, walking on steel beams, and balancing precariously with large steel purlins over my shoulder over 20 feet above the ground.

One day, as I was trying to put a heavy beam into place, I felt something rip in my lower abdomen. Later that day I noticed I had a small bulge in my abdomen area. I had torn loose some stomach muscles. I had a hernia! I did not tell anyone. I found a quiet place and cried out to **GOD**. I laid my hands over the hernia, commanding it to go in the name of **JESUS CHRIST** of Nazareth, and I went back to work because the building had to be put up.

Every day I kept on lifting heavy steel. The hernia did not go away so I kept looking to **GOD**, trusting, and believing. The only one who became aware of the hernia was my wife. Honestly, I do not even remember telling her.

Why would I not tell anyone? It wasn't because I was afraid that they would have a poor opinion of me because I wasn't getting healed. I've never worried in the least about people thinking I did not have **FAITH**. **FAITH** is the substance that is or is not. The Bible says if any man has **FAITH**, let him have it to himself.

Romans 14:22 Hast thou FAITH? Have it to thyself before GOD.

In my heart, there was nothing I needed to prove to anyone, but to **GOD** himself. You see, my confidence is in **JESUS CHRIST**, the heavenly **FATHER**, and the **Holy Ghost**, and the Word of **GOD**! If I have to go to the doctor, or use medication, it's nobody's business.

For over two years this hernia remained with me. Actually, I thought it was three, but my wife says it was two. Every time this hernia would bother me, I would lay hands over the top of it, and command it to go, thanking **GOD** that I was healed.

Eventually, this hernia began to get very serious. It began to bulge so far from my body that I knew eventually it would strangle. A strangled hernia is very dangerous.

A strangulated hernia is a hernia that is cutting off the blood supply to the intestines and tissues in the abdomen. Symptoms of a strangulated hernia include pain near a hernia that gets worse very quickly and may be associated with other symptoms.

I knew in my heart that it was time to get very serious about this situation. You see the kingdom of heaven sufferings violence and the violent take it by force. I knew that I knew that I knew that by the stripes of **JESUS** I am healed. I literally began to take the fingers of my right hand shoving this hernia back up into my stomach lining, and speaking to my stomach lining and commanding it to be healed. For approximately two weeks I kept on aggressively shoving this hernia back into my body, declaring that it was healed.

In the world they say: it's the early bird that gets the worm. In **Christ**ianity: It's the Spiritually Violent Man That Gets the Answer.

Now, this type of **FAITH** needs to be developed. It's absolute unwavering, and total confidence, I cannot be defeated attitude and **GOD**.

Hebrews 6:18that by two immutable things, in which it was impossible for GOD to lie, we might have a strong consolation, who have fled for refuge to lay hold upon the hope set before us:

 I went to bed one night approximately two weeks after I had become aggressive with my **FAITH** in **CHRIST** and woke up the next morning to an amazing miracle. The hernia was completely gone. That has been over 30 years ago, and it has never come back. **FAITH** is the substance of things hoped for, the evidence of things not seen.

CHAPTER NINE
To the Rescue on a Snowmobile
KNEE SEVERLY DAMAGED!

The knee is made up of four components: bones, cartilage, ligaments, tendon. Every part of my knee severely damaged! (1992)

Mike to the rescue, or so I thought. I dressed up in all my winter trappings. I then went out and brushed the snow off my John Dear snowmobile and laid my hands on it, commanding it not to give me any problems. I should have prayed over myself first.

I started the old machine up, revving the throttle as I headed out of the church parking lot. I turned to my right going down the deserted, main highway. There I was, having the time of my life and doing it for the fire department! Here I was doing about 50 miles an hour or faster when I hit a section that was nothing but black ice.

The snowmobile's back end spun to the right out of control. I went flying through the air as it threw me for a lopper. I slammed my right kneecap extremely hard on the asphalt road. I felt my kneecap rip, break and tear as I kept sliding down the road for quite a distance. The snowmobile had continued on its way, spinning out of control.

The snowmobile itself eventually stopped because my hand was no longer cranking the throttle. Fortunately, it was not damaged because there was nothing but snow in every direction. There I was, lying in the dark on the ice-covered road in the snow and freezing wind, clutching my busted up knee, alone and in tremendous pain! It felt like blood was running down my leg. Immediately, I cried out to **JESUS** and repented for being so stupid and for not using **God**ly wisdom.

My theology is that almost everything that goes wrong in my life is usually my own stupid fault. Even if the devil is involved in it, it is most likely because I first opened the door for him. After I was done repenting and confessing to the Lord, I went aggressively after my healing.

I commanded my kneecap to be put back into its normal condition in the name of **JESUS CHRIST** of Nazareth. I commanded every broken part of my kneecap to be made whole. You see, I could grab my patella and move it all around. It was no longer attached to my knee. It seemed to have become completely disconnected, no longer restrained by its associated ligaments.

Probably at this juncture, 99.9% of people would have called it quits when it comes to completing the mission they set out on. But that is not my mode of operation. If I declared that I was healed then I needed to act upon it. I discovered a truth a long time ago, **GOD** cannot lie!

Numbers 23:19**GOD** is not a man, that he should lie; neither the son of man, that he should repent: hath he said, and shall he not do it? or hath he spoken, and shall he not make it good?

But let me say this; I had been hiding **GOD**'s WORD in my Heart! So, I slowly crawled back over to my snow machine and pulled myself back into the seat. I painfully swung my left leg over the seat into its proper position. At that very moment, wave after wave of pain overwhelmed me.

Years of experience walking in **FAITH**, however, caused me to declare that I am healed in the name of **JESUS**. In the name of **JESUS**, I am healed. Over and over I kept saying this to myself all along this painful journey! I opened the throttle and proceeded on the way to pick up the equipment operator. I kept proclaiming the truth.

On the way, there were a lot of areas where my snowmobile just would not go. The snow was way too deep in some areas to go or the road was flooded with water in others. The storm had dumped a combination of rain, ice, and snow. One would need a boat to go through some of the areas where I went. Admittedly, at times I took chances that I should not have taken. I would accelerate to high speed and just zip across the flooded areas.

The back end of the snowmobile would begin to sink as if I wasn't going to make it. But, I would constantly revert back to the old trusted declaration: In the name of **JESUS**, in the name of **JESUS**, in the name of **JESUS**, I will make it. There are a lot of wonderful messages preached on **FAITH** but that's not what wins the victory. It is when the Word has been quickened in your heart that you know, that you know, that you know, that you know that **GOD** and His Word are true.

I cannot describe to you enough the immense pain and agony that I was going through, yet I did not merely think that I was healed, I knew that I was healed! **FAITH** is not thinking, hoping, or wishing. It is knowing that you know, that you know, that you know. About 45 minutes later I finally reached my first destination which was a miracle!

The township worker saw me pull up outside of his house. As he came to the machine, he could not see my face because of my helmet and my ski mask. I did not tell him that I had an accident and shattered my kneecap.

I do not adhere to bragging about the devil or his shenanigans, lies or deceptions. This was no little man that I had to carry on the back of my machine either. He must have been over six feet tall, and heavy set. He mounted up and we were on our way. It took major **FAITH** to keep ongoing.

We had to take numerous detours before I finally got him to the big earthmover that he was tasked to operate. He jumped off my snowmobile and thanked me for the ride. I told him it was no problem as I opened up the throttle and headed home.

This time, I decided to take a different route because the last route was so bad. It took all the **FAITH** that I could muster to get back to the parsonage. I was cold, wet, tired and completely overwhelmed with pain from the shattered knee. When I got home, I just kept thanking

GOD that I was healed. During the next couple of days, I refused to pamper my leg. I did not put any ice or heat upon it.

I did not take any kind of medication or painkillers. I did not call anyone asking them to please pray for me and to believe **GOD** for my healing. I know this may seem extremely stupid, but I knew in my heart that I was healed. It has got to be in your heart! My head, my body, and my throbbing, busted kneecap were all telling me that I was not healed, but let **GOD**'s Word be true and every symptom a lie.

When the next Sunday rolled around, the roads were clear enough for people to make it to church. During that time, you might have called me Hop-Along Cassidy because of the way that I was walking. I do not deny the problem, but I sure as heaven denied the right for it to exist! One of our parishioners, who was a nurse, saw me limping badly. She asked me what happened and I told her. She informed me that this was a major problem. She tried to explain to me in medical terms exactly what she thought I had done to my knee.

Medically, in order to reattach and repair my patella, I would have to endure at least one major surgical procedure. She recounted to me that she had once had a similar injury although it was nowhere near as bad as mine. She went on to elaborate that even after extensive operations, her knee was still giving her major problems. I thanked her for this information and went back to trusting and believing that by the stripes of **JESUS CHRIST**, I was healed.

I sure as heaven was not going to let go or to give up on **GOD**'s promises. I wrestled with this situation day after day, commanding my knee to be to function as **GOD** had designed it to do. Thanking **GOD** over and over I was Healed!

When the pain would overwhelm me, I would tell it to shut up, be quiet and work! When it seemed like my leg would not carry me, I would command it to be strong in the name of **JESUS**.

This went on for well over a month. One morning I crawled out of bed and my knee cap was perfectly healed. You would think that when the healing manifested that I would begin to sing, shout and dance, but I did not and I do not! You see I had already done all of my rejoicings in advance because I believe that the minute I prayed, I received! That was over 25 years ago and I am still healed!

19 GOD is not a man, that He should lie; neither the son of man that he should repent: hath He said, and shall He not do it? or hath He spoken, and shall He not make it good? Num 23:19

Typical Missionary Journey

I arrived in the Philippines with some kind of stomach flu or virus, and I became deathly sick. On top of the sickness, I was extremely tired because of jet lag. The trip over was a nightmare! I had used a foreign airline to get a low price, but you get what you pay for. It was a crowded flight, with babies crying and filling their diapers.

The air in the airplane was extremely hot and stuffy; it stunk so badly that I almost had to breathe through my shirt. The seats on the plane were very small and uncomfortable. The person sitting next to me was practically sitting on my lap! The journey was almost twenty-four hours long. When I arrived in Manila, I had to catch another small plane which would take me to the province of Samar, to the town of Calbayog City.

I waited about four hours before I boarded the small plane to get to Calbayog. When I landed at the airport in Calbayog, I had to take what they call a Jeepney, which looks like a Willies Jeep, only it's about ten times bigger. I had to ride this Jeep, crowded with other travelers, all the way out to where I was to meet up with the believers I was working with.

There are no windows in the Jeepney - except for the very front windshield. Because of this, I breathed in diesel fuel for hours while traveling on rough, bouncy roads. Filipinos were pushing up against me all the way. I felt like an animal crowded in a cage.

After more than thirty hours without sleep, my head was throbbing so bad I could hardly handle it. I felt like I was going to pass out at any minute. I was sicker than sick. Finally, after what felt like a never-ending nightmare, I arrived at Catarman, where I was scheduled to preach. In the natural, I was in no condition to preach or minister. Yet, I made it to my first meeting. The building had a tin roof, walls made of block, and the seats were wooden benches with no backs.

I almost fell over, right then and there, but I buckled down and gritted my teeth. When it was time for me to speak, the Spirit of **GOD** quickened my mortal flesh. I preached like a house on fire! For the next twenty days, nonstop, I preached every chance they gave me. My mind, heart, and body were energized and quickened by the **Holy Ghost**. This is the life of **No Matter What FAITH**!

By FAITH Purchased $250,000.00 C-Band

As I was memorizing scriptures one day, my fax machine began to print a page. I picked up the fax, not yet knowing who it came from. It was a picture of a very large, thirty-foot satellite uplink system. I discovered that it came from a good friend of mine who lived in Ohio. A lot of our TV equipment had come from him; which he provided at tremendous discounts. I have no idea why in the world he would fax this information to me. Not in any stretch of the word was I looking for a C-band uplink satellite system. However, the minute I looked at the fax, the Spirit of **GOD** quickened within my heart, and said, buy this system.

I said to the Lord, Why, Lord?

FAITH BASED OUTCOME INDEPENDENT

He replied because you are going to be transmitting my word across America, twenty-four hours a day by satellite."

I asked, Lord, why would you have me do this?

He responded because you have been **Faith**full in hiding My Word in your heart.

Now the original value of this thirty-foot Vertex uplink dish, with its pedestal and transmitter building, had been valued at over $250,000. That cost is not including all of the equipment that would have to go with it, and its transportation. It was located in State College, Texas, at the Westinghouse factory, where they had been using it for teleconferencing.

I have always hated raising money. I'm not good at it and do not like it. I told the Lord, Lord I do not want to raise this money!

He spoke to my heart saying, you will not have to. I will move upon the hearts of the people, and all the money will come in, as you share with them what I am speaking to you now.

I went before the congregation the next Sunday and shared with them the experience that I had, exactly the way the Lord told me to. Almost nonchalantly, I told them that if they would like to donate towards this project they could. The finances began to come in, just as He told me they would!

And they came, every one whose heart stirred him up, and every one whom his spirit made willing, and they brought the LORD'S offering to the work of the tabernacle of the congregation, and for all his service, and for the holy garments. And they came, both men and women, as many as were willing hearted, and brought bracelets, and earrings, and rings, and tablets, all jewels of gold: and every man that offered an offering of gold unto the LORD (Exodus 35:21-22).

Poured Massive Concrete for Up-Link

When **GOD** told me to buy a **C-band uplink system** (originally $250,000) that my friend had faxed to me. I contacted the broker to made arrangements to purchase the uplink system.

As the money came in through the following weeks, we wired the money into a Westinghouse account. During this time, we also applied for our C-band uplink license through the FCC.

Westinghouse sent us the blueprints we needed to begin to prepare and pour the foundation. I think there were over fifteen yards of concrete alone that we needed to pour. That was not including the precise placement of hundreds of feet of rebar's, which needed to be placed into the concrete pad - before we could pick up the dish.

Across Wet Land

Westinghouse informed me that where the satellite uplink system was located was a very wet area, and if there was any type of water on the ground when we tried to take a crane or an 18 wheel truck back into that area, it would sink - up to its windshield. They insisted it must be a very dry time before I could pick it up. I shared this with the whole congregation so that we could believe in the dry spell that we desperately needed. As we came into the fall, rain began to fall heavily all the way from out West to the East Coast. It rained, and rained, and rained!!

On a Saturday, right before Thanksgiving, the **Spirit of the Lord spoke to me** - out of nowhere - and told me it was time to go get the uplink system. **I knew it was the voice of GOD,** so I contacted the men in my church who had volunteered to help pick up the equipment. (What I'm about to share with you could be a book in and by itself, so I will try to keep it brief.)

FAITH BASED OUTCOME INDEPENDENT

The men I had contacted to help me go pick up the system, challenged me a little about going. Nevertheless, they had been with me through numerous life storms, and they knew that I could hear from **GOD**.

I told them to come to the Sunday morning church service and be prepared to leave right after the service. We had a Dodge Caravan, that six of us could cram into, with an attached covered trailer that would carry our air compressor and tools.

That Sunday morning, I informed the congregation of our intentions to go pick up the satellite uplink system. Some of the people became extremely upset - since it had been raining for weeks on end. After all, I had verbally told them that we could not pick up the system unless we had a thoroughly **dry season**. On top of that, we were still $8,000 short of the money we needed to complete the transaction! However, I told the congregation that I knew in my heart that the Lord had spoken to me, so we would be going.

We are talking close to a 1,400-mile trip. If I had not heard from heaven correctly … we were in big trouble! As we pulled out of the parking lot that Sunday afternoon, it was cold, wet, and raining everywhere. All through the day, we drove in the rain. We did not stop through the night but drove straight through to the next day. As we pulled into State College, Texas, it was still raining.

I told the men, even though it's the end of the day, let's go look at the **C-band uplink system**. We followed the directions to the Westinghouse factory. As we pulled onto the property, something strange seemed wrong with their yard. All their grass was **brown and dead**. We pulled up to a parking spot right outside of the main office; then we went inside to introduce ourselves to the personnel.

There was a woman behind a glass sliding window at a countertop. We commented to her about the grass is brown and dead on their property. She told us it was the strangest thing that they had ever seen or experienced.

It had rained everywhere else in their area, but not one drop of rain had fallen upon the Westinghouse ground. There was absolutely no explanation for it.

At least that's what they believed; we knew different! We were smack-dab, right in the middle of the will of **GOD** and **GOD** had kept their land dry.

---

*I beseech you therefore, brethren, by the mercies of **GOD**, that ye present your bodies a living sacrifice, holy, acceptable unto **GOD**, which is your reasonable service. And be not conformed to this world: but be ye transformed by the renewing of your mind, that ye may prove what is that good, and acceptable, and perfect, will of **GOD** (Romans 12:1-2).*

By FAITH I Said Money is in the Account

The Westinghouse factory informed us that the C-band uplink system was around the back. However, it was going to take special equipment to dismantle this sophisticated piece of equipment. One company had told them it would take about a week to dismantle, with the cost of $40,000. Well … we were all just a bunch of country hicks with an air compressor and regular tools!

They also informed us we would need a large crane, with a specially designed truck, to carry the equipment. In addition, it would be impossible during this week, because it was Thanksgiving. They also informed us that they would need to have all the money wired into their account – in advance - before we would even be allowed to touch, let alone disassemble, the system.

FAITH BASED OUTCOME INDEPENDENT

I told them this was acceptable to us, because we needed a good night's sleep anyway, and we would be back early in the morning to dismantle the system: to have it shipped to our facility in Gettysburg, Pennsylvania.

Some of the men asked me what we were going to do, because we did not have the money, the equipment, nor did we have the truck. I told them everything was okay.

The gift of FAITH was at work in my heart

I called up the church office, just to double-check about the $8,000 that we still needed, and they informed me nothing had come in, yet.

Even though I had been informed that the $8,000 we needed still had not come in, we were up bright and early. We headed out to have a good breakfast before arriving at Westinghouse. I called up our church office, after 8:00 a.m. EST, to ask if the money was there yet. They said: **"No Pastor, there is no sign of it … and we don't know what to tell you."** I told them that it was okay. That we did not need the money until we got to the factory to pick up the equipment.

We arrived at the factory, walked up to the front office counter, and informed them that we were ready to begin dismantling the uplink satellite system. They said that there was still a problem - with us being short $8,000.

I told them to access their account and they would discover the money had been wired. The lady went to her computer and came back a few minutes later and said, **"Yes, it had just been wired."** **Hallelujah!** The money had been wired to Westinghouse's account! To this day, I am not certain where all the money came from, but **GOD** had supplied.

GOD Supernaturally Enabled Us

We drove the minivan and trailer to the uplink system. It was one *big* satellite dish. (You can come and see it at our church.) I had all the men gathered in a circle, holding hands to pray. I prayed that **GOD** would give to us a spirit of wisdom and understanding in the knowledge of what we needed to do, and how to do it, quickly and speedily - with no damage to the system! After we were done praying and thanking **GOD**, I discussed with the men what needed to happen next.

The Spirit of **GOD** came upon all of us. I began to watch the men crawl over the satellite dish; like a well-organized and experienced team. It was so amazing, that the personnel, technicians, and scientists came out of the Westinghouse factory to watch us. They were snapping pictures as we were working! They were absolutely flabbergasted and kept talking about how it was supposed to take a week for the dish to be disassembled and packed - not two days!

As our men were working, I began to make phone calls. The Lord provided a crane company to come for the day. Of course, once they arrived, they tried to charge us way more than what they agreed upon over the phone. But **GOD** gave me gentle, holy boldness to deal with it. So, they eventually came back down to their original verbal agreement.

Special Truck on Thanksgiving Weekend

FAITH BASED OUTCOME INDEPENDENT

I then contacted a trucking terminal out of Houston, Texas and told them the kind of truck we were looking for. They informed me that they did not have that type of truck available, and they did not know where to send us to find one. Not only that, but there was nobody there, being only a couple of days before Thanksgiving. I asked them to please just go ahead and look around.

The man on the phone said: "Hold on! There is a man and woman standing outside of my office right now. I need to ask them what they want."

To his amazement, they were a married couple looking to carry a load back East. He put the man on the phone with me. Amazingly, it was exactly the kind of truck we desperately needed! The couple arrived with the truck and backed up to the large satellite dish. The truck did not sink down in the least, because the ground was so dry, and hard. The panels of the uplink dish were all stacked off to the side, so we only needed the crane for one day. All the cranes had to do was load up the main pedestal and the transmission shed.

The next morning, we came back to finish the packing. We had a wonderful time-sharing **CHRIST** with the married couple that owned the truck. I am convinced that both are probably saved now because we asked if we could pray for them before they left with our equipment. I saw the gift of **FAITH** come upon them as we laid our hands on them. We loaded the truck and found that the transmitter building itself was too tall to fit under the bridges.

Not only was the equipment too high to fit under bridges, and overpasses, but our satellite equipment succeeded in the legal weight limit of what the truck was allowed to carry.

We told the couple that we did not know what we could do, but that we'd certainly be praying for them. The driver informed us not to worry about them getting our equipment to us.

How he brought our uplink system to Pennsylvania is another amazing story. As he was driving his truck on the main highways, he would slow down as he approached a bridge, and let the air out of his air shocks.

He'd crawl slowly under the bridge and would speak to other truck drivers by CB, those who were ahead of him, to find out if the weigh stations were open. If they were open, he would pull over until they had too many 18 wheelers to inspect, and then he'd pass by safely. He did this all the way from Texas to Gettysburg, Pennsylvania!

When the uplink dish finally arrived, we had a crew of men and women ready. The huge concrete slab, which was over three feet deep, and the rebar that was needed in the concrete was cured and ready. Within three days we had this system installed, ready to operate, and ready to broadcast. However, the time to broadcast was not immediate.

And he that searcheth the hearts knoweth what is the mind of the Spirit, because he maketh intercession for the saints according to the will of **GOD***. And we know that all things work together for good to them that love* **GOD***, to them who are the called according to his purpose (Romans 8:27-28).*

LESTER SUMRALL OPERATED IN NO MATTER WHAT FAITH!

Rev. Dr. Lester Frank Sumrall (February 15, 1913 - April 28, 1996). I had the privilege of knowing Lester. Not only did Lester preach in the church I pastor, but he ordained me as a Minister of the Gospel. I will tell you right now that he was the real McCoy!

I heard a story about Dr. Lester Sumrall some years ago when he found himself in the middle of the Central American Rainforest. As he went about his ministry in that region, he came across a witch doctor. In today's rock and roll Hollywood scene, this witch doctor would look like a normal man ... but, in those days, this was a pretty strange fellow!

FAITH BASED OUTCOME INDEPENDENT

In one hand, the witch doctor would hold a bullfrog (always a symbol of satanic power). On the other hand, he held a mixture of human blood and alcohol, and this was placed in the bullfrog's mouth. Then the witch doctor would dance, make satanic incantations and worship demonic entities.

Fortunately, Dr. Sumrall wasn't raised in the modern-day school of humanistic, people-pleasing preachers. All he did was follow **JESUS**' biblical example and placed his hands on the side of the witch doctor's head, he said two words: **"Come out!"**

The witch doctor fell over with a thud. When he returned to his feet, the witch doctor was born again and started speaking in a heavenly language and glorifying **GOD**. Later that night, Dr. Sumrall returned to his room to go to bed. Since it was warm, and without air conditioning, he decided to open the windows while he slept.

As he lay down, a strange odor began to fill the room. Suddenly, all of the sultry heat of the night disappeared from the room. A damp chill filled the place and it was so cold that Dr. Sumrall began to shiver. A wind began to blow the curtains wildly on their rods. Then, the bed began to shake so violently that it moved all the way out into the middle of the floor!

Well, Dr. Sumrall had enough of this! He raised himself up from his bed and said: "You demon spirit, I recognize you. I cast you out earlier today. **In the name of JESUS CHRIST of Nazareth, you go now!"**

Immediately, the evil presence left the room. The heat returned, the curtains laid down against the wall, the bed stopped shaking and the horrible odor left the room.

Now, most modern-day preachers would have written a book right there! In fact, they would have written seven books: and told how the devil obeyed them. But ... that wasn't Dr. Sumrall's way.

Instead, he rose back up in his bed, looked out of the window and shouted: **"Hey devil! Get back in here!"**

Immediately the curtains began to stick out on end as a wind rushed through the room. The coldness returned … the smell returned … the bed began to shake violently and almost shook him out of bed. Dr. Sumrall sat up in his bed and said: "Devil … When I came into this room, my bed was against that wall. **Now, in the name of JESUS, PUT IT BACK!"**

The bed went shaking back across the room and settled down against the wall. **"Now"** Dr. Sumrall ordered, **"get out of here!"**

Most people will not believe a story like this, but I have personally experienced manifestations of evil spirits in the physical realm. One of the major keys to dealing with devils is that you never glorify them. You never speak highly of them or exalt them. So many of those who think they are called into the deliverance ministry make a major mistake in this area. It is simply because they do not have **FAITH** in **GOD**, who created these entities, and He is so much greater than they are – it's no big deal for Him to cast them out

Smith Wigglesworth "GOD Shall Operate"

On one occasion, (1930) Smith Wigglesworth ended up with a terrible affliction of gallstones. He was informed by a specialist that the only way to deliver him from the gallstones was by an operation. Smith's son-in-law, James Salter, said that during the whole three years of this trial, Smith never stopped preaching, never complained, or told anyone. Even though Smith Wigglesworth was in great pain, and bled a great deal, he continued to minister to the sick, even with **blood running down**

his legs, filling his socks and shoes, as he laid hands on the sick. He did end up spending many days in bed, in great pain, but he would get up to make it to the meetings where he was to minister. This test went on day, after day, after another day, and night, after night.

It is reported that the meetings he conducted during this time were powerful, with many attesting to the wonderful miracles of **GOD**'s healing power. When deliverance finally manifested in Smith's body, it was almost instantaneous; with all twenty-plus gallstones removed. Smith Wigglesworth was made completely and perfectly whole. Smith put those stones in a small tin can and on occasions he would show the stones to different people as he told them of **GOD**s **Faith**fulness'.

Some of the stones were quite large: others were jagged and needle shaped. All of the stones not only caused tremendous pain but penetrated his innards in such a way that it caused constant hemorrhaging. Smith was a man who understood what it meant to have **FAITH**, and he worked by patience. He had an unshakable **FAITH** that caused him to agree with **GOD**, and to disagree with the **Circumstances** - no matter the pain, or problem.

Dr. Michael H Yeager: Whenever we exalt the devil through sickness or the afflictions or problems of our lives, we are operating in a spirit of unbelief. I am not saying that we cannot share privately, with people of **FAITH**, what we are going through, so that they can agree and believe with us. In over forty years of walking with **CHRIST**, I have shared very little with people of what I was being confronted with. I knew that most people were not truly going to be believing with me, but would simply tell others what I was going through.

Dangerous Attack of Conjunctivitis
(1994)

Doc Yeager: I am sharing this story to help you understand how to take hold of your healing. The minute any type of physical affliction attacks your body is the very moment you need to take a hold of **GOD**'s Word and come against the enemy of your soul. Your body is the temple of the **Holy Ghost**, and the enemy has no right to afflict it!

John 10:10 The thief cometh not, but for to steal, and to kill, and to destroy.

*James 4:7 Submit yourselves therefore to **GOD**. Resist the devil, and he will flee from you*.

A brother from the church I pastor had accompanied me to the Philippines. We were ministering in the province of Samar, which is one of the five provinces of the Philippines. It takes an airplane ride from Manila, and then a transfer to ground vehicles. The trip is rather long, tiring and challenging. Not including the fact that we were in the territory of the New People's Army, which is an anti-government communist movement. Believe me when I say they would kill you in a heartbeat.

So, when we finally arrived at our destination, the Filipinos that we would be working with were waiting for us. The local pastors, and believers, had already prepared the way for us to hold crusades in different towns and villages. In the natural, they really did not need us, because they were all walking in the realities of **GOD**. To some extent, we Americans were like White Elephants in that we drew a crowd. However, we did not have any more of the Holy Spirit or the Word of **GOD** than they did.

As we made our way to the first set of meetings, all of our team, including myself, were attacked with conjunctivitis, commonly called: "Pinkeye." Conjunctivitis is caused by a virus that can be dangerous in two ways: Firstly, the person with the infection can lose some of their vision - in severe cases, they can totally lose their eyesight - this could be for a short time, or it could be permanent. Secondly, the infection can spread very rapidly and is highly infectious. People with "Pinkeye" often get conjunctivitis germs on their hands by rubbing their eyes, then leave germs on objects they touch.

The first sign of this affliction is that your eyes begin to feel dry and irritated. Then it gets to the point where it literally feels like someone has grabbed a handful of sand and shoved it into your eyes; grinding your eyeballs slowly with the sand. The whites of your eyes eventually turn pink and can become blood-red when it's bad.

The minute my eyes started to feel irritated, I found a quiet place of prayer. I simply spoke to my heavenly **FATHER** and thanked Him for what **JESUS** had done for me when He received the stripes upon His back. After meditating upon this for a short while, it was time to take the authority that **CHRIST** has given to all believers.

I spoke to this affliction in the name of **JESUS**, commanding it to go: Now! Now! Now! In the name of **JESUS CHRIST** of Nazareth! No ifs, and or buts. I followed with thanksgiving and praise - I thanked **GOD** that I was healed. Not that I was going to be healed, but, that I <u>was</u> healed already! From that moment forward it did not matter how I felt or looked. I knew that I knew that I knew that I was healed. I just kept on thanking and praising **GOD**, quietly, and in my heart.

I went on my way – rejoicing! Even though I did not feel any different or look any different. Not one more word came out of my mouth about this affliction; or how terrible my eyes felt. Within less than two days all the symptoms were gone!

I'm sorry to say that this was not the case for the rest of the team. A lot of these precious people were going through terrible irritation. The brother I had brought with me began to get much worse. Eventually, the whites of his eyes turned blood-red. I knew in my heart that if we did not do something he could go blind.

This continued for over a week; then he finally told me that he had to get back to America. I learned a long time ago not to be critical of people, but to work with them - where they are at. He told me that I could continue with the meetings - but he was leaving! I informed everyone that I would travel back to America with this brother and make sure he got back home. He was my responsibility; I was his pastor and the spiritual authority of these meetings.

Of course, my precious Filipino brothers were slightly upset and disappointed, because there were meetings that still needed to be fulfilled. I informed them that I was sorry, but my first responsibility was to this brother, and the **Holy Ghost** would move through them, and speak through them.

To cut our trip short, it was going to take **FAITH** to get on the plane earlier than we were scheduled to leave. And we also had to believe that we were not going to be stopped by customs because of the highly contagious affliction in his eyes. All the way home he wore dark sunglasses. Through a series of miracles, we were able to board a plane early and get back to America.

The infection he had picked up in the Philippines did not leave him, without medical help. Thank **GOD** he did not lose his eyesight. **JESUS** always works with us - where we are at. My position is one of being there for people, no matter what. We help, pray and encourage where we can. If we do not see a miracle, we simply keep our eyes on **JESUS**.

If we fall short, we just determine in our hearts to get back up and keep on going. If I run into situations where it does not seem like I can receive healing, I just go deeper into **GOD**, His Word, and His will for my life. **GOD** will never let you down!

Rough Salvage Yard Owner Saved

There was a local auto salvage yard that I would periodically go to in order to purchase parts for my vehicles. The Lord laid it into my heart to begin to go down there on a regular basis to witness to the owner and his son. This was a man who had a rough exterior, but on the inside, I could sense a unique and tender-hearted person. He was the kind of man that I could relate with.

You see, I was raised in a very rough and tumble world. My grandpa, who was a large tell man, (I do not know what happened to me, I am only 5 feet 8 inches) and was the original Texas kid! Grandpa was born in the late 1800s. Up until he died in 1973, he had a famous reputation. You did not mess with him. I still remember him with his cowboy hat, chewing tobacco in his mouth, and a large stogie in his hand.

Back to the salvage yard. I would try to go there at least once a week to just chat with the owner, Dale. Plus, I kept lifting him before the Lord. It really did not seem like I was getting anywhere with him spiritually, but I just kept at it. One day I received a phone call from him, which was highly unusual because he never called me. He seemed to be rather upset and distressed. He asked if I could come by and see him. I told him absolutely, and that I would be right down. When I got to his place of business, he began to share what was going on.

He said that he had not been feeling very well lately, so he set up a doctor's appointment to go see what was wrong. When they were done with all of the tests and examinations, the prognosis was not very good. They informed him that he had cancer, and not just any cancer, but a very deadly form of cancer. I believe it was in his bone marrow and throughout his whole body. They told him there was no hope and that there was nothing they could do for him. They would not even give him chemotherapy, or radiation. When he was done telling me this tragic news, he asked me what he should do.

I could tell he was extremely serious. He was ready to do whatever it took. I told him he needed to give his heart to **JESUS CHRIST**. I said to him, "Put your hand into the hands of **JESUS**, and no matter what the outcome of this situation is, you need to walk with **GOD**." Right then and there, Dale gave his heart willingly and openly to **JESUS CHRIST**. (I could tell that he was a true conversion, and he immediately became **Faith**full in coming to hear the Word at church.)

I laid my hands on him and began to take authority over this spirit of cancer and death. I cursed it from its roots and commanded it to go in the name of **JESUS CHRIST** of Nazareth. We proclaimed life and healing. I continued to pray as the Spirit of **GOD** spoke to my heart. Dale was in complete agreement.

When we were done, I told him, "**GOD** requires us to have prayer-supplication and thanksgiving. Now you need to begin lifting your hands and praising **GOD** that you are completely healed and made whole and thank **GOD** that the cancer is gone and that you have been set free by the stripes of **JESUS CHRIST** and His precious blood." At that very moment, he felt something happen in his body. He told me he began to feel extremely good. He even went back to work. Then he set up an appointment to go see the doctors. Their prognosis was amazing! They said almost all of the cancer was completely gone. It was in complete remission. They had given Dale just a couple weeks to live, but now they were saying that the cancer was in total remission. This was to their total amazement!

I wish I could say this story ended well. It did in the sense that Dale is on the other side of eternity waiting for us now. I have seen this happen more times than I want to relate. **GOD** does wonderful miracles, and the medical world intrudes, stepping in to try to complete what **GOD** has begun. The doctors told Dale and his family that even though the cancer was in total remission, just in case, they would give chemo and radiation!

They would not help him before because they said he was completely lost according to their estimates. But now that **GOD** had intervened, the medical world wanted to help Dale. The chemo and radiation took dale's life. I watched as his hair fell out, and he became a shadow of the man he was! I saw Dale in the last couple of hours before he died.

He said goodbye to me. He said he was tired of fighting, and he just wanted to go home to be with **JESUS**. I hugged him goodbye with tears rolling down my face. The next time I see Dale, it will be a glad reunion day in heaven.

*But I would not have you to be ignorant, brethren, concerning them which are asleep, that ye sorrow not, even as others which have no hope. For if we believe that **JESUS** died and rose again, even so them also which sleep in **JESUS** will **GOD** bring with him (1 Thessalonians 4:13-14).*

Arthritis Could Not Stay

There are generational curses that are passed on from one generation to another. These are satanic strongholds that must be broken. In my family lineage, there were quite a number of these strongholds. My personal family members and I have and had numerous physical infirmities.

When I gave my heart to **JESUS CHRIST** and began to intensely study the word of **GOD**, I discovered that I was free from the curse of the law. I began to aggressively take what **CHRIST** had purchased for me with the stripes on His back. By **FAITH**, I began to cast down these physical strongholds

Not only did I receive healing for my own personal body, but I also declared that in the name of **JESUS** these physical afflictions would not be passed on any longer. My sons and daughters and their children would not have these afflictions.

One of these afflictions that were passed on from generation to generation is arthritis. My sister Deborah began to experience arthritis in her late 20s. At one time she had been a very gifted typist and piano player, but before she was in her 40s, her fingers had become gnarled and almost unusable. Arthritis had entered her body so dramatically that I remember her crying with pain and great suffering.

By my late 20s and early 30s arthritis began to try to manifest itself in the joints of my fingers. The minute that pain came to my hands I began to speak to them even as **JESUS** declared in the gospel of Mark 11:23 and 24. I submitted myself to **GOD**, resisted the devil by speaking to the affliction and commanding it to go. And then I began to praise **GOD** and thank **GOD** that by **FAITH** I was healed In the Name of **JESUS**. No matter how my hands or fingers felt I thank **GOD** that I was healed.

Sure enough, after a day or two, the stiffening and pain would completely dissipate from my joints. Through the years it has tried to come back, but I have not allowed it. I know this may sound braggadocios, but it's not. This is a reality that **CHRIST** has given to every believer. At the writing of this book I am 66 years old and free from arthritis!

Driving under the Influence of Holy Ghost

FAITH BASED OUTCOME INDEPENDENT

We had left the island in the morning, and we were now holding meetings in a town called Pambujan, which was about 19 miles away. **GOD** was moving in a wonderful way. The Philippine brother who was over all the work in this area is named Danny. He also had two other brothers, Jonathan, and Hurley, who are also ministers of the gospel. (You can friend them on Facebook if you like).

I personally knew their **FATHER**, Reese Monte's (who has since gone home to be with the Lord), who was an amazing man of **GOD** who was instrumental in starting over five hundred churches throughout the Philippines islands.

The name of the organization was "**FAITH** Tabernacle. These men are all apostolic in nature. If I understand correctly, Danny has been instrumental in starting over seventy churches. Now here I was ministering with Danny. Danny came to me late one night and said he was homesick. He had never been away from his wife this long. We were approximately 32 miles from his home in Catarman.

This may not sound like a long-distance to you, but believe me with the road conditions, the weather, and the communist it was quite a distance, especially if you are going to travel in the night. In this area, I never saw any vehicles out on the road after the sunset.

Now I had earned a reputation for being good on a motorcycle. In all reality, though I wasn't very good on a motorcycle at all. It is simply that the Spirit of **GOD** would quicken me as I would take a motorcycle up into the mountains to preach the gospel to the natives. I'm kind of hyperactive, so in between Crusades and conferences. When everyone else was taking a siesta, I would find someone who was willing to go with me to interpret for me, and I would head up into the mountains.

We were deep in a heavily populated area where there were known to be anti-government radicals, Communists, the NPA, and it was extremely dangerous to be there and especially at night. Brother Danny came to me one night asking me if I would be willing to take him home on a motorcycle that someone had driven who was on our team.

It was a very rainy and foggy night. Now the motorcycle that was available was an old machine—I believe it was a Kawasaki 250. This motorcycle had some issues though. The headlights were very dim, and at times the shifting mechanism would fall off if you were not very careful.

When Danny asked me to take him home, the Spirit of **GOD** quickened my heart and said: take him. It was like when David had said he was thirsty for the waters of the well in Bethlehem. Three of his mighty men broke through the host of the Philistines and drew water out of the well in Bethlehem for David to drink. This quickening in my heart was so strong that without any hesitation I told Danny I would take him home to see his precious wife and children.

Danny informed me with almost a whisper that we must not stop along the way no matter what because the Communists would be out in full force. He also said we would have to be very careful because the Communists (if they heard us coming) would stretch a thin cable wire across the road in order to kill us. I saw a video one time where this is exactly what they had done, and it was captured on film. The motorcyclist was cut right in half. It was not a very pretty image.

He also informed me that if they got their hands on us, we would be dead men. Even with this dire warning from Daniel, I had total and perfect peace. There was a divine excitement within my heart to go on this journey. This is not something you can explain to a person who has never experienced the quickening, moving, empowering presence of the **Holy Ghost**.

FAITH BASED OUTCOME INDEPENDENT

As we began this journey, we had made one major mistake. We forgot that there was road construction all along the way and that the main bridge was out. If we would have remembered, then we would've taken a long way around. As it was, we took the regular route that would've been the shortest route to Danny's home.

Now, as I was driving the motorcycle, I could barely see where I was going. The rain and the fog were coding the shield of my helmet. The headlight was very dim almost nonexistent. I had to keep reaching up with my left hand to wipe my face shield to see where I was going. Danny was sitting behind me holding on tight as I was driving. I believe I was driving at approximately forty-five to fifty miles an hour.

After we had been on this rough construction road for several miles, I thought that I could see something very dark and threatening in the pathway ahead of us. In my mind it seemed to me to be an enemy and waiting, and yet I had total peace. I should have slowed down, but I just kept ongoing. The next thing I knew, Danny was yelling very loud in my ear with a great warning, "watch out."

I yelled back at Danny: Hold on, we are going to go through it! Whatever this object was, we slammed into it doing about 50 miles an hour. As it turned out, it was a very large pile of gravel and road material. We hit this very large pile of construction material which was almost vertically straight up. The bike without hesitation raced to the top of this pile of construction material and launched us up into the void of the night. During this event, Danny took his head and put it underneath my left forearm, under my armpit.

It turns out he had been in a terrible motorcycle accident before, and now he was trying to protect himself as much as he could from the disaster which was unfolding. In every scenario, this was going to be a major catastrophe.

Not only would-would be killed or extremely hurt when we hit the concrete road but then the communist would be upon us. There were no hospitals or help that would be available for us. We Surely Were Dead Men!

Here we were launched up into the darkness of the night. As I was up in the air on the back of this motorcycle, it truly felt like I was just sailing through the sky like when I used to fly airplanes. During this experience, I was supernaturally engulfed in an amazing bubble of peace and joy. I had absolutely no fear or anxiety whatsoever. I was operating in the REALM of the spiritual. It seemed like for the longest time we were not going to come down.

WE WERE TOSSED INTO THE VELVET BLACKNESS OF THE NIGHT AS WE HIT AN ALMOST VERTICAL HUGE PILE OF GRAVEL!

We were suspended in the heavens. Of course, we must've been sailing through the skies in an upward and downward flow. It was obvious when we hit the wet concrete roadway below us, that something would have to give. But when we make contact with the road, it was so smooth, so nonresistant, that it almost felt like putting on a pair of comfortable old bedroom slippers. This is the only way I can describe it. We did not skid, bounce, or slide in any sense of the word.

The only thing negative that happened when we met the road is that the gear shifter fell off the motorcycle. We were stuck in the Top Gear as we headed down the road. We had to stop and go back and look for it.

We went all the way back to the pile of gravel we had hit and started from the pile working our way out to find the shifter. I did not think to measure the distance of our jump. We looked and looked and looked with the dim headlight of the motorcycle.

FAITH BASED OUTCOME INDEPENDENT

By this time, Danny was very concerned about the Communists seeing the headlight of the motorcycle and hearing its engine running, so we decided to leave the motorbike in top gear and leave.

As we were headed down the road at about four hundred feet away from the pile of road gravel, I saw something gleaming on the road in front of us in the rain. We stopped, and there was the shifting mechanism! We put it back on the bike and went our way. How far we flew through the night sky that night, only **GOD** Knows! Now if you think this sounds incredulous, weight two ye hear about the next part of this journey. Danny Monte's can verify every bit of this journey.

But they that wait upon the LORD shall renew their strength; they shall mount up with wings as eagles; they shall run, and not be weary; and they shall walk, and not faint (Isaiah 40:31).

Evil Knievel would be Jealous

Over a 300' River We Go on Wet Slimy Planks in the Fog and Rain at Night, surrounded by communists!

Here we were on this unreliable motorcycle driving through the rain and the fog in the middle of the night. It seemed as if we had been on the road for an hour when we came upon the river. This river was over three hundred feet wide. It was a very deep and fast-moving river that flowed into the Philippine Sea. We forgot we had taken another way to get to Pambujan. The reason we had to take another way is that the bridge was out. I believe **GOD**'s hand was in this.

They had driven wooden pilings down into the bed of the river. It looked like they had placed rough sawn planks upon these pilings. These planks were approximately eighteen inches wide and were loosely attached on these pilings. This footbridge appeared to be four to five feet above the river. These planks were wet and slimy. I would not have wanted to walk on them in the daylight, let alone on a wet and extremely foggy night.

To get to the beginning of the planks we would have to to go down a muddy and slimy embankment. Then we had to go up a steep muddy dirt pile to get to the planks and unstable walking bridge.

There was just no way we could walk that motorcycle across this river. It was not wide enough to walk alongside other motorcycle and push it. There's no way somebody could stand in front of the motorcycle to control the handlebars, while somebody pushed behind. Even if we could it was too dark, wet, slimy, and foggy. If there is any communist around, they could easily pick us off with a gun within those 300 feet to the other side.

Danny asked, "What are we going to do?" The Spirit of **GOD** was upon me in the most indescribable way. I do not believe up to that moment I had ever experienced **GOD**'s presence so manifested in my flesh. There was not an ounce of fear or inadequacy in me at that moment. This was not pride, conceit, or self-confidence in my ability to drive this motorcycle. It was the spirit of the living **GOD** rushing through my veins, my mind, and my body.

I shouted to Danny you over the sound of the motorcycle engine, and the rain, "Hold on Danny!" I am sure that at that moment Danny Montes had no idea what as of about to do. I gave him the opportunity to try to stop me. He wrapped his arms tight around my waist as a revved the engine of the motorcycle.

With that declaration, I shifted into first gear, and release the clutch. I took off, shifting into second gear and then shifting into third gear going down the muddy bank. Then I went up the muddy embankment they had built to get to the planks. Remember this was only designed for foot traffic during the day. It was not designed to be used across at night, or for that matter to people on a motorcycle.

FAITH BASED OUTCOME INDEPENDENT

I came up onto the first plank. I gunned the throttle and drove the motorcycle onto the first wet, slimy, loose plank—not slipping one time. I still can remember the dim headlight of the motorcycle reflecting off the wet planks. The friend will of the motorcycle staying right in the middle of the narrow planks one after another. The rushing deep dark river about 5 feet below us. Just one slip, one miscalculation, one turning of the handlebars in the slightest direction, and we would've been swallowed up by the river never to be seen or heard from again.

Over 300 feet of the slimy plank in the rain, with fog, with a very dim headlight! THIS WAS **GOD** ALL THE WAY! If I would've gone to the left or to the right, either way, one foot, we would have plummeted into the raging river. It was the Spirit of **GOD** that took us across that three-hundred-foot river in the rain and fog, over a precarious bridge that was only made for foot traffic during the daytime. To make a long story short, the Lord saw us safely to Danny's house.

Years later I went on the internet to look at this river I had crossed. The internet image had been updated in 2010. The new bridge they were just beginning to build at that time has been completed. You can see the alternative road we had to take as another route until the new bridge had been built. I am overwhelmed at the amazing things I have watched **GOD** do.

I know after that experience Pastor Danny Montes named his next child Michael and his following daughter Kathleen which is my wife's name. A kind of always thought that maybe he did that because of the experience we had that night. Maybe someday he'll tell me if that's true or not.

For with GOD nothing shall be impossible. And Mary said, Behold the handmaid of the Lord; be it unto me according to thy word. And the angel departed from her (Luke 1:37-38).

CHAPTER TEN
My Busted Broken Finger Healed!

We all do stupid things; that is just a part of our humanity. The question is: Will **GOD** still heal us in spite of our stupidity? I have discovered many times that the answer to this question is yes! Here is another example of something stupid I did and **GOD** was still there for me.

One day I walked into my son Daniel's house. He was in his front room playing a videogame. It's something called PlayStation Move, where he was playing a game called Sports Champion. He held a wand in his hand, thrusting it and waving it back and forth aggressively. As he was doing this, there was another man on the big screen TV following his moves as a fighting opponent.

Right then and there I should have turned around and walked out, but curiosity got the better of me. He asked me if I wanted to play a game with him because you could have two players at one time fighting each other. I thought about it for a while and decided, yes I would play. So he handed me another wand, showing me how to activate it. The object of the game was to wave and thrust the sword on the video by waving the wand in my hand. The man on the screen would follow my movements and fight for me.

He started the game console, and we began. Of course, I had never played this game before nor do I make a habit of playing video games, so he was winning. I began to get more aggressive trying to win the game but no matter how much I tried, my son seems to be able to score points against me. I totally gave into my flesh and began to wave, stab and wave my make-believe sword everywhere.

I mean I aggressively got into this thing. In the process of trying with everything inside me to win this game, I did not notice that I had gotten close to hitting a heavy-duty metal case that he had in his front room. Before I knew what I did, I was sweeping the sword to the right down away from me with all my might and slammed my right hand into the corner of this metal cabinet.

I am telling you that I really slammed my hand extremely hard. My son Daniel said I hit the cabinet so hard that it put a dent in the cabinet. The minute I hit that cabinet with all my might, pain exploded through my body. I looked at my index finger and it was all mangled and twisted. Immediately, it swelled up turning black and blue and was twisted. Just looking at my busted-up index finger made me sick.

I began to jump around holding my finger with my other hand. And this is what I was crying out to **GOD** as I was jumping and screaming, "Lord, please forgive me for being so stupid. Lord, I will never play this game again. I'm so sorry, **FATHER GOD**, in the name of **JESUS** I repent. I kept jumping around holding onto my finger crying out to **GOD** saying: I repent, I repent, I repent. Forgive me, Lord!"

My son Daniel looked at the finger and said dad you broke it, you are going to have to go to the doctor. With my finger so full of pain and my other hand holding it, I told him I did not need a doctor that I had **JESUS CHRIST** and he is the great physician. After I made sure that I had sufficient repentance, I spoke to my finger. I commanded my bones to be knit back together and for my finger to be made completely whole. And then I began to thank **GOD** that I was healed. I just kept praising the Lord that my finger was made whole no matter how it felt or how it looked.

The spirit of **GOD** must have spoken through me at that moment because I told my three sons that by tomorrow morning my finger would be completely well, and you would not be able to tell that I had ever slammed it by being so stupid. When I was finished making this declaration of **FAITH**, I walked away from them holding onto my finger. Even though the pain was throbbing through my body, I just kept thanking **GOD** that I was healed.

My son Daniel still remembers very vividly how busted, twisted, broken, black and blue my finger was. I believe that he thinks it was rather funny how I was jumping around confessing and repenting and promising **GOD** to never do this again. I went to bed that night and fell asleep holding onto my finger, thanking **GOD** that I was healed. I was meditating on the Word and confessing that what **JESUS** did for me when he had taken the stripes on his back had the ability to completely make me whole from stupid accidents that were my fault.

The next morning when I woke up early to pray and seek **GOD**, I had completely forgotten about my finger. And then it hit me that there was no pain. I looked at my index finger and you could not even tell that I had busted, broken and bruised it. I was completely healed! I went and showed my three sons what **GOD** had done for me in spite of my own stupidity.

GOD is so awesome and amazing. All we have to do is cry out to Him and He will answer and deliver us from every situation if we simply trust, repent and obey him; giving praise and thanks no matter how it looks. How long do we keep thanking and praising **GOD**? We are to keep on knocking and to keep on asking until we receive the full manifestation of that which we believe for!

Matthew 21:14, And the blind and the lame came to him in the temple; and he healed them.

Casting out a Devil easily

As many of the congregation were laughing, shouting, crying I heard a burst of laughter that seemed to be out of sync. Now, I really cannot claim that I can play any instruments, though I did take drum lessons, and I did at one time try to learn to play the guitar. If you strum the strings of the guitar even if you're not a musician many times you will be able to tell when one of the strings is completely out of tune. As I'm standing in the front of the congregation, I heard one of the strings that seemed to be off.

I looked over to my left and there was one of the young men in our church. He was approximately 20 years old. This was a wonderful young man of **GOD**. I looked at him and he was laughing uncontrollably to the point where his face had completely turned beet red. As I looked at him the Holy Spirit said to me: this laughter is not of me.

You need to cast the devil out of him! This is very important that you hear this. There are many people laughing, and yet this man's laughter was not of **GOD**. This young man needed deliverance. The problem with many ministers today is they really do not know **GOD** to the place where they can discern what's of the Lord and what's not. If we are not mature in the things of the spirit, and if we do not know the voice of **GOD,** we can do much damage.

We can do damage in two ways. #1 by ignoring manifestations that are not of **GOD**. If we let them continue, it will bring death and destruction for the flesh profited nothing. #2 the second way we can do much damage is if we do not deal with this situation with love and wisdom. In my heart, I knew exactly what needed to be done.

I did not take the microphone and say to the congregation! Now, you all watch what I'm about to do. I am about to cast the devil out of brother so and so. Neither did I stop the service, and become paranoid over everybody else laughing. Just because one man's laughter was not of **GOD** did not mean that everybody's laughter was not of **GOD**.

As this young man was laying on the floor laughing hysterically, with his face completely beet red, I simply walked up to him. I put my hand on his body. I leaned down and very quietly with an authoritative voice I said: you Foul Unclean Spirit Come Out of him NOW in the name of **JESUS**! After I spoke this over him, I straightened up and backed off.

You see I knew, that I knew, that I knew this spirit had to come out of this young man. That I did not have to make a big show like Ed Sullivan. That I have authority with **CHRIST** because I was submitted to **CHRIST**! People who are not submitted to **GOD** will not be able to exercise this kind of authority. It is not that I'm super spiritual, but I just simply knew within my heart in every area of my life as far as I knew I was submitted to **GOD**.

I backed away from this young man about 10 feet. He was still laughing uncontrollably when suddenly by the gift of discernment I saw the spirit leave them. Immediately he stopped laughing. The beet red from his face completely disappeared. At that moment he began to weep uncontrollably.

He began to cry out to **GOD**, repenting from whatever sin he had been involved in. Tears filled my eyes as I watched this precious young man become delivered from an unclean spirit. Nobody in the congregation knew what was happening. I never said anything over the pulpit about this situation. Here it is over 20 years later when I am finally sharing this story. This young man went on to serve **GOD**. I never pulled him aside and told him we needed to go through generational deliverance. I never even said a word to him about what happened that day. I never asked him what sins he was involved in.

FAITH BASED OUTCOME INDEPENDENT

There is a natural tendency of people wanting to make a big to do out of deliverance. It is the **Holy Ghost** and the anointing of the spirit of the Lord that will set people free. Yes, we do need our minds renewed, but we do not need hours and hours of deliverance. When you exalt the devil, he will love to come. If we will exalt **JESUS CHRIST** the **Holy Ghost** will come flooding in like a mighty river, or like a mighty wind, or like a consuming fire! All glory and praise to **GOD**.

Remove the Life-Support Now

Our little 18-month daughter Naomi was seriously injured in the summer of 1998. For two months we had been staying at the Ronald McDonald House. Our little girl Naomi was in the Hershey Medical Center. Thank **GOD** for people who want to help people in need. Our daughter was in the intensive care unit. My wife and I were told that she was brain dead as they constantly tried to convince us to donate her organs.

We are not talking about just once or twice but on a consistent daily basis. They kept insisting that her organs could help others who were in critical need of a transplant. We had walked into a living nightmare. My wife and I kept crying out to **GOD**. After about a month, one night, as I was walking the floor at the Ronald McDonald House at about three o'clock in the morning, the Spirit of the Lord arrested me.

He told me that I was ashamed of the gospel of **CHRIST**. I asked, "Lord, what do you mean?" He informed me that I needed to go in and take authority; that the doctors and the medical staff were not my **GOD**. You need to go in and take charge, I was commanded.

The Spirit of **GOD** informed me that our daughter did not

need to be on life-support because she could breathe on her own. Furthermore, I learned later that many of the symptoms that she was experiencing was from the medication that they had overdosed her on. Early the following morning, I told my wife to get ready because it was going to be a rough day. I walked in that morning with my minister's collar with which I usually conduct official business.

Because I have a Ph.D. and a Doctor of Divinity, I always required that the medical personnel address me as Dr. Yeager. I went in and confronted the person who oversaw the hospital floor. I insisted for them to remove the breathing tube. They informed me that they could not because she could not live without it. I told the charge nurse that I wanted to speak to the next higher up.

Granted, I did get loud, but I was not ignorant, Un**god**ly, or nasty. Finally, after numerous interviews, the head doctor came. I told him enough is enough; take that equipment off my daughter! He finally agreed to do this. You need to understand that all this time they had been harassing us to donate her organs. The love of money is the root of all evil! When the man who was over the life-support equipment came, I stood by as he extubated her. He let slip a revealing statement.

He said this equipment should have been removed weeks ago. I said, what? He said yes, she does not need this equipment. When they removed the breathing equipment, she breathed easily on her own. As I retell the story, it is almost like it happened just yesterday.

*2 Timothy 1:8 Be not thou therefore ashamed of the testimony of our Lord, nor of me his prisoner: but be thou partaker of the afflictions of the gospel according to the power of **GOD**;*

Sixteen Hours on My Face for My Son Daniel Who Was dying from rabies

My son Daniel when he was 16 years old (in 2000) brought home a baby raccoon. He wanted to keep this raccoon as a pet. Immediately people began to inform me that this was illegal in the state of Pennsylvania. That to have a raccoon in Pennsylvania you had to purchase one from someone who was licensed by the state to sell them. The reason for this was the high rate of rabies carried among them. But stubbornness rose up in my heart against what they were telling me.

You see I had a raccoon when I was a child. Her mother had been killed on the Highway, and she had left behind a litter of her little ones. I had taken one of the little ones and bottle-fed it, naming her candy. I had a lot of fond memories of this raccoon, so when my son wanted this raccoon, against better judgment, against the law of the land, I said okay.

I did not realize that baby raccoons can have the rabies virus lying dormant in them for months before it will be manifested. I knew in my heart at the time that I was wrong to let him keep this raccoon, but like so many when we are out of the will of **GOD** we justify ourselves.

We do not realize the price that we will have to pay because of our rebellion and disobedience. Daniel named his little raccoon Bandit, and he was a bandit because he was constantly stealing and getting into everything. A number of months went by, and one day my son Daniel told me he had a frightening dream. I should've known right then and there that he needed to get rid of this raccoon. He said he had a dream where rascal grew up and became big like a bear, and that it attacked him and devoured him.

Some time went by and my son Daniel began to get sick, running a high fever. One morning he came down telling me that something was majorly wrong with Bandit. He said that he was wobbling all over the place and bumping into stuff. Immediately the alarm bells went off.

I asked him where his raccoon was. He informed me that rascal was in his bedroom. Immediately I went upstairs to his room, opening his bedroom door, and their rascal was acting extremely strange. He was bumping into everything, with spittle coming from his mouth. Immediately my heart was filled with great dread. I had grown up around wildlife and farm animals, and I had run into animals with rabies before.

No ifs, and or buts, this raccoon had rabies. I immediately went to Danny asking him if the raccoon had bitten him, or if he had gotten any of rascal saliva in his wounds? He showed me his hands where he had cuts on them, informing me that he had been letting rascal lick these wounds. He had even allowed rascal to lick his mouth. Daniel did not look well, and he was running a high-grade fever and informed me that he felt dizzy.

I knew in my heart we were in terrible trouble. I immediately called up the local forest ranger. They put me on the line with one of their personnel that had a lot of expertise in this area. When I informed him of what was going on, he asked me I did not know that it was illegal to take in a wild raccoon. I told him I did know, and that I had chosen to ignore the law.

He said that he would come immediately over to our house to examine this raccoon and if necessary to take it with him. I had placed rascal in a cage, making sure I did not touch him. When the forest ranger arrived I had the cage sitting in the driveway. He examined the raccoon without touching it. You could tell that he was quite concerned about the condition of this raccoon.

He looked at me with deep regret informing me that if he had ever seen an animal with rabies that according to his almost 30 years in wildlife service, this raccoon had rabies. He asked me if there was anyone who had been in contact with this raccoon with any symptoms of sickness. I informed him that for the last couple of days my son Daniel had not been feeling well. Matter of fact he was quite sick.

When I told him the symptoms that Daniel was experiencing, he was obviously shaken and upset. He told me that anybody who had been in contact with this raccoon would have to receive shots and that from the description of what my son Daniel was going through, and for how long, that it was too late for him! He literally told me he felt from his experience that there was no hope for my son, and he would die from rabies.

He loaded the raccoon up in the back of his truck, leaving me standing in my driveway weeping. He said that he would get back to me as soon as they had the test results and that I should get ready for state officials to descend upon myself, my family and our church.

I cannot express to you at that moment the hopelessness and despair that had struck my heart. Just earlier in the spring, our little girl Naomi had passed on to be with the Lord at 4 ½ years old, and now my second son Daniel was dying from rabies. Both situations could've been prevented if I would have simply listened to the Spirit of **GOD**! Immediately I gathered my wife, my first son Michael, my third son Steven, and my daughter Stephanie.

We all gathered around Daniels's bed and began to cry out to **GOD**. We wept, cried, and prayed crying out to **GOD**. I was repenting and asking **GOD** for mercy. Daniel, as he was lying on the bed running a high fever and almost delirious, informed me that he was dying, and he was barely hanging on to consciousness. He knew in his heart he said that he was dying!

After everyone disbursed from his bed with great overwhelming sorrow, I went into our family room where we had a wood stove. I opened up the wood stove which still had a lot of cold ashes from the winter. Handful after handful of ashes I scooped out of the stove pouring it over my head, saturating my body, with weeping and tears of repentance and sorrow running down my face, and then I laid in the ashes.

The ashes got into my eyes, mouth, and nose and into my lungs, making me quite sick. I did not care, all that mattered was that **GOD** would have mercy on us, and spare my son, and all our loved ones from the rabies virus.

As I lay on the floor in the ashes, crying out to **GOD** with all I had within me, you could hear the house was filled with weeping, crying, and praying family members. All night long I wept and prayed, asking **GOD** to please have mercy on my stupidity. I prayed that He would remove the rabies virus not only from my son but everyone else that had been in contact with this raccoon.

I also asked **GOD** to remove the virus from the raccoon as a sign that he had heard my prayers. I continued in this state of great agony and prayer till early in the morning (about 16 hours) when suddenly the light of heaven shined upon my soul. Great peace that passes understanding overwhelmed me, I got up with victory in my heart and soul.

I went upstairs to check on my son Daniel. When I walked into his bedroom the presence of **GOD** was all over him. The fever had broken, and he was resting peacefully. Our whole house was filled with the tangible presence of **GOD**. From that minute forward he was completely healed.

A couple of days later I was contacted by the state informing me that to their amazement they could find nothing wrong with the raccoon. **GOD** had supernaturally removed the rabies virus not only from my son, and those in contact with Bandit, but from the raccoon itself. Thank **GOD** that the Lord's mercy endures forever!

Psalm 34:19 Many are the afflictions of the righteous: but the Lord delivereth him out of them all.

COULD NOT MOVE or SPEAK for 2 1/2 hours

My family and I travelled out West ministering in different churches and visiting relatives in Wisconsin. We were invited to speak at a church in Minneapolis, Minnesota. The pastor actually had two different churches that he pastored. One of these churches was in the suburbs, and the other one was in the heart of Minneapolis.

The larger of the two churches was in the suburbs. I was to minister at the larger church first, and then immediately go to his other church downtown. The whole congregation was in the same service that morning. There were approximately 140 to 160 people including women, men, children, and babies in the sanctuary.

As I began to speak, I found myself unexpectedly speaking on the subject of The year that King Uzziah died, I saw the Lord high and lifted up, and his glory filled the Temple, which is found in the book of Isaiah!

The unction of the **Holy Ghost** was upon me so strong, that it just flowed out of my belly like rivers of living water. To this day I do not remember everything that I said. As I was speaking, I sensed an amazing heavenly touch of **GOD**'s presence on myself and on everyone in the sanctuary.

The spirit of **GOD** was on me in a mighty way, and yet I was aware of the time factor. To get to Pastor Bill's sister church downtown Minnesota, I was not going to have time to lay hands on or pray for anyone. If **GOD** was going to confirm his word with signs following, then he would have to do it without me being there.

It turns out that is exactly what **GOD** wanted to do! When I was at the limit of the amount of time allotted to me, I quickly closed with a prayer. I did not say anything to the pastor or anyone else as I grabbed my Bible to leave the sanctuary. My family was already loaded up and waiting for me in our vehicle. As I ran out the door I perceived something strange, awesome and wonderful was beginning to happen to the congregation. There was a heavy, amazing and holy hush that had come upon them.

By the time I arrived at the other church, their worship had already begun. As I stood up in the pulpit to minister **GOD**'s word, the Holy Spirit began to speak to me again, with a completely, totally different message. **GOD** did wonderful things in the sister church downtown that afternoon as I preached a message on being radically sold out and committed to **CHRIST**. Everyone ended up falling out of their chairs to the floor on their faces, weeping and crying before the Lord.

This is not something I have ever encouraged any congregation to do. I have seen this happen numerous times where I simply must stop preaching because the presence of **GOD** is so strong, and so real that people cannot stay in their seats. I would stop preaching, get on my face, and just wait on **GOD**, as he moved on the people's hearts.

After that service, we went back to our fifth-wheel trailer at the local campgrounds where we were camping. Later in the day, I received a phone call from this pastor. He was acting rather strange and speaking very softly in a very hushed manner.

He asked me with a whisper: does that always happen after you are done preaching? I said to him, tell me what happened. He said, "As you were headed out the door, I began to melt to the floor, I could not keep standing, and I found myself pinned to the floor of the sanctuary.

I could not move or speak." Now all the children (including babies) were in the sanctuary with the rest of the congregation. He said he personally could not move for two and a half hours. During this whole experience, he did not hear another sound in the facility. For over two and a half hours he just simply laid there not being able to move or speak a word under the presence and mighty hand of **GOD**. After two and a half hours Pastor Bill was able to finally move and to get up.

He had thought for sure that he was the only one still left in the church. Everybody must have gone home a long time ago, and that he was thereby himself. But to his complete shock and amazement, everybody was still there, laying on the floor. Nobody could move or speak for over two and a half hours! Men, women, children and even the babies were still lying on the floor, not moving, talking, or crying! **GOD** was in the house! The tangible, overwhelming, solemn, presence and holiness of **GOD** had come!

Pastor Bill asked me to come over to his house so we could talk about what happened that day in his church service. My family and I arrived. He invited us inside. He asked if this normally happens wherever I went. I informed him, no, but many wonderful and strange things do take place. It did not always happen, except when I get myself in a place of complete, absolute surrender and submission to **JESUS CHRIST**.

This submission included not putting ANYTHING else but the WORD of **GOD** into my heart. When I simply seek the face of **GOD**, by praying, giving myself completely to the word, meditation, singing, and worship, intimacy with the **FATHER**, Son and **Holy Ghost**, this was the result! **GOD** is not a respecter of people, what he does for one, he will do for others!

Sowing 80,000 cassettes and CDs.

My wife sometimes gets upset with me because I give everything away. The first book that I had printed was called "War in the Heavenlies". I had 10,000 copies printed, and I probably gave away two-thirds of them. I just can't help it. I want people to experience the fullness of **CHRIST**, to be free, to grow spiritually so I give away that which I believe will help them grow spiritually.

Back in 2001, we were doing evangelistic outreaches throughout Pennsylvania, Maryland, and Delaware. It was in my heart to leave something in their hands. The income from the church was almost non-existent, and yet somehow **GOD** kept us going. I put my **FAITH** out there to purchase CD duplicators, plus cassette duplicators.

My three sons and I began to mass-produce CDs and cassettes. Most of these messages were not from me, but other ministers, who I believed had powerful messages that would transform people's lives. These teachings were not copyrighted materials so all we did was legal. Wherever we went we began to pass out these CDs and cassettes.

It was in my heart to reach even more people, so we went to many different stores getting permission to put clear plastic bowls on their counters. On these bowls was a very nice label that declared Free Teaching Cassette! We would try to revisit those stores once or twice a month to restock them with more teachings. We estimate that within a two-year period over 80,000 cassettes and CDs were passed out. For the life of me I can only tell you that **GOD** brought the money in to do such a thing. During those years the income of the church was very little!

You might ask: did it increase the attendance of your church? No, but that was never the object. We simply wanted to see people set free and following **JESUS CHRIST**. Where did we get all the money for the CDs and cassettes? I'll be honest with you, I do not know. It had to be **GOD**.

We simply began to step out in obedience trying to fulfill the great commission. Yes, we were preaching on the streets, singing, and passing out tracts, but that just was not enough. We needed to leave something in their hands that they could listen to. We will never know on this side of heaven if what we did had any effect. When we get to glory we will discover the results. Remember **GOD**'s Word will never return void!

Isaiah 55:1,1 So shall my word be that goeth forth out of my mouth: it shall not return unto me void, but it shall accomplish

that which I please, and it shall prosper in the thing whereto I sent it.

Coming Ready Or Not!

Some years ago I was constantly running into authorities trying to prevent me from preaching on the streets. I finally researched, and gathered information, court cases, that gave me the right to be on the streets. I made up a little booklet with all the facts! And then I made multiple copies, and gave them to all our teams!

When the police, or others, approached us on public property, we were very polite, and simply handed them the book. I would inform them that we had a legal and constitutional right to do what we were doing. In this book were answered questions about different situations. For instance, if someone threw a track on the ground, they were the ones littering.

If the police became arrogant, or ugly, I would inform them that we would willingly let them arrest us, but that we would sue them in court, and we would win. So we gave them the option to arrest us, not resisting arrest, or being ugly. We told them that they needed to do what they had to do, but we had to do what we had to do. They never arrested us.

I wanted to really reach the beaches in Delaware and Maryland. Specifically, there were three different places I wanted to share the gospel with; Rehoboth and Bethany beaches in Delaware, and Ocean City Maryland.

I put on a minister collar, because they have greater respect for organized religion, and I took a handful of books. I first went to Rehoboth Beach in Delaware to the police station. I very kindly informed them that I was bringing a team of people to the beach on a specific date. We were going to be sharing **CHRIST**, but not blocking the boardwalks, yelling or screaming, or littering. We were simply going to give tracks, tapes, and CDs to anyone who wanted them.

They called for the chief of police, telling him what I had just told them. He informed me that I was not going to do this, and that they would arrest me and my team. I told them that they were going to have to do what they were going to do, but we were going to do what we had to do. Then I handed him several of my little books, informing him that if he harassed our team, we would see them in court. I was very polite, and gentle in my mannerism. As I left the police station, he was yelling at me.

I proceeded to do the same thing in Ocean City Maryland, where I got the same results. And then to Rehoboth Beach Delaware. This time it really got carried away. They called the city manager, who was a homosexual. He was extremely angry and upset. I should not have done it, but I laughed at him because he was acting so off-the-wall. I remember telling him we are coming whether he liked it or not, and he better not harass us. As I walked out the door, this man was yelling and screaming at me.

The day came, and we arrived with a van full of people I had taught and trained what to do, and what not to do. Every place we went, the police would come, surround us, and tell us we could not do that. I would inform them that we absolutely could, handing them my little booklet, and encouraging them to call their main office. In every situation, they walked away leaving us alone.

We have even done this in surrounding high schools, on the sidewalks, off school property, before school began. Once again the police came, but left us alone when we handed them our little book!

Colon Cancer will not kill me!

FAITH BASED OUTCOME INDEPENDENT

I began to experience some very disturbing symptoms in my body. I will not go into all the details, but there were approximately nine different physical symptoms.

Signs and symptoms of colon cancer
1, Red blood in your stools 2, Melena - Black Stools 3, Anemia is a low hemoglobin in blood 4, Nauseous 5, Violent bowel movements 6, Vomiting 7, Abdominal pain 8, Intestinal gas and bloating 9, Anorexia and weight loss 10, Alternating episodes of diarrhea 11, Experience constipation 12, Narrow stools 13, Chronic fatigue 14, Unexplained weight loss

One of the symptoms was almost every time I had a bowel movement; it looked as if all my innards were coming out. During this three-month period, I was so sick sometimes that I thought that I was going to die at any moment. My normal course of action is that the minute my body begins to manifest any sickness or disease, I immediately command it to go in the Name of **JESUS CHRIST** of Nazareth!

But these symptoms simply refuse to leave. I made a list of everything that was happening in my body and then I looked up these symptoms on the internet. Every one of them pointed to colon

cancer. I had gone through a similar fight of **FAITH** some years previously, with what seemed to be prostate cancer. Once again, I took hold of the Word of **GOD**. I boldly declared to the devil, myself and the spiritual world that I would live and not die. I cried out to **JESUS** for His mercy and His grace in the midst of this fight of **FAITH**. This fight was almost overwhelming and excruciating at times!

For these three months, I continued with this fight. I spoke to the symptoms commanding them to go. I kept praising, thanking and worshiping **GOD** that I was healed; no ifs, and or buts. I declared boldly that the devil is a liar. For three months every day, all day at times, declaring what **GOD** said about me. I did not invite anybody else to stand with me in this fight of **FAITH**.

Most people, if they would have known what I was going through, would have pronounced me dead and gone. Believe it or not, they are people who call themselves **Christian**'s who would've rejoiced in my death. Yes, they would've been telling people to pray, but there would have been more negative comments than the reality of **GOD**'s Word.

By His stripes, we were healed! If I were healed, then I was healed, if I was healed than I am healed and if I am healed then I is healed! For three long months, I stood and fought by **FAITH**. Many nights and days walking the floor of our church sanctuary praising **GOD** that I was healed, resisting the spirit of fear. One day I woke up and all the symptoms had disappeared, praise **GOD**. And they have never come back. Thank you, **JESUS**.

I had a friend in the medical world that sat down and discussed the situation with me. He asked me for all the specific symptoms that I had. When I finished he told me that without any doubt I had had colon cancer. Did you notice the word, **I had had, but no longer**! Praise the Lord.

Signed A $250,000 Contract with no Money

(2003)

Our congregation had dropped to approximately 30 people at this time. The church's sanctuary could sit over 700, but the Lord was teaching me how to trust him. One day as I was in prayer in our sanctuary the Holy Spirit spoke to my heart; "Begin to broadcast by satellite 24 hours a day."

FAITH BASED OUTCOME INDEPENDENT

It was about five years after we had installed our C band uplink system. We had a license with the FCC for this nine-meter earth satellite system. I had tried and tried to bring us online, but never succeeded. Now when we had just a little congregation, and no ministers, no finances, no technicians--- the Lord spoke to me, and said do it now!

I knew that I knew that I knew this was from **GOD**. I called up NPR from out of Washington DC. I told them I wanted to buy satellite time. I also contacted a company by the name of ANTEC out of Frederick Maryland. I decided to meet with both of these companies. NPR would provide the satellite time, and ANTEC would help us bring our uplink system online.

Two men from NPR met me in my office. They laid a contract in front of me for two years. It was a $240,000 contract. It was going to cost us $12,000 per month to broadcast on their satellite transponder. The Spirit of the Lord quickened my heart and said sign it. We had no ministers to broadcast with us. We had no natural source of income. And NPR was only giving us one month to do test patterns and to begin to broadcast. I signed the $250,000 contract by **FAITH**. ..

Broadcasting across the USA!
Shooting in the Dark 22,000 Miles up!

The technicians from ANTEC in Fredrick MD came to our facilities. They looked over our system and informed us that it was a good system. They asked who had installed the system for us. We told them how it all happened. Not only did we take down the extremely expensive and complicated system, but we also reassembled it with volunteer non-technical people.

They looked at us with almost unbelief. They said that the tuning of the dish was a highly technical endeavor. If it just needed a little bit of work we would be talking approximately $10,000. I asked the gentleman who was in charge, his name is John if they would bring it online and try to broadcast with it the way it was. He said he could, but there is no doubt it probably needed major work. We installed all the necessary equipment. Then he set up all his test equipment. It was 22,000 miles to the satellite that we would be broadcasting from. The dish must be perfectly tuned. I left them to do their work and went to my office.

After a couple of hours, John called me. He asked me to come to the transmission building. When I walked into the building they were crouching over the spectroscopes, waveform monitors, meters and equipment. He looked up at me with total surprise and astonishment on his face. He asked me to come over and take a look at one of the spectroscopes.

I saw perfect waves going across the screen. He said to their complete surprise that the vertex satellite dish was perfectly aligned and tuned, and we did not have to pay for an expensive retooling and re-tuning. This was completely unheard of in their industry.

Within one month **GOD** supernaturally sent us quality ministers. We began to broadcast 24 hours a day. We renegotiated our contract about halfway through. And they gave us a better price. After three years of broadcasting by satellite which went to low power TV stations, TV stations and the sky Angel network, we came off the air. ANTEC has approached us to purchase our equipment. But I believe with all my heart that **GOD** is not yet done with the Word Broadcasting Network.

Offering up the church as Isaac

We were in the country and doing outreaches in the streets of Baltimore, the Badlands of Philadelphia, and at times In

FAITH BASED OUTCOME INDEPENDENT

Gettysburg and Chambersburg, the beaches of Ocean City Maryland and Rehoboth Beach in Delaware. I wanted to reach souls. I decided to take a step of **FAITH**, so we began a church in Chambersburg.

I would hold services in the morning in Gettysburg. And do one in the afternoon in Chambers-burg. I also contacted an auctioneer to sell our 40,000 square foot facility in Gettysburg. It was to be an absolute sale. The auctioneer had convinced me this was the way to go. The number of $570,000 came to me.

I told this gentleman that the figure would be the minimum because the land was valued at over three million at the time. He reluctantly agreed. We were going to take the money from the sale, pay off all our debts and purchase a church right in downtown Chambersburg. **GOD** had other plans. On the day of the sale, many people were there. Businessmen and men that I knew were wealthy.

As the bid began, the price kept going up. We were almost at the absolute minimum price when it seemed like everybody was frozen in place. We were $10,000 from the minimum bid, but nobody could raise their hands, or open their mouths.

The auctioneer got extremely agitated. He kept telling the crowd that they were almost there. He finally came off the auction block and told me to follow him into the building. We went to my office and he told me we had **three options**.

 Number one, we could lower the minimum bid price.
Number two, we could try again to get them to respond.
Number three, we could simply take it off the auction, and proceed with the other 30 acres we were selling.

The minute he said this, the Spirit of **GOD** came up within me. I heard the Lord say this was your Isaac. Do not sell the building! I told him, take it off the auction.

After the auction, I was approached by Mennonites who are willing to purchase our property for a Bible college. They kept upping the price until they reached almost $1 million. But the Lord had said to me keep the property I'm not done here yet. Up to the moment of writing this story, we are still on the property waiting for a mighty outpouring of the **Holy Ghost**.

Afterward, Attorney kept calling threatening to sue if we did not sell. I had such peace in my heart that I was in **GOD**'s will that I told him to go ahead! Thank **GOD** they never did!

Saved from Terrible Death at the Mississippi

Many times, in my life I have had vivid experiences, perceiving that **GOD** is about to do something or that something is about to take place right before it happens! Here is just one example.

On August 1, 2007, my wife, three sons, daughter and I were traveling on Highway I 35 West. We were in our Toyota crew cab pickup truck, pulling a 35-foot fifth-wheel trailer. We were on vacation and headed for Yellowstone National Park. At the time, we were headed towards the downtown area of Minneapolis, Minnesota.

As I was driving, I sensed in my heart that we needed to get off this highway even though our GPS was taking us the shortest route to where we were headed. I have discovered and personally experienced 20 major ways that **GOD** leads and guides. All 20 of these specific ways in which **GOD** leads and guides can be discovered in the Scriptures. What I felt is what I call a Divine unction of the **Holy Ghost**. It is more than a perception or a feeling. It is more like an overwhelming urgency that flows up out of your belly.

I informed my family that something definitely was wrong, that there was an urgency in my heart, and we needed to get off this highway I 35 W. immediately. This is the only time that I have experienced the urgency to get off a road or highway like this. I took the nearest exit and went north towards Canada. After a while, we connected to another highway and headed west. Later in the day, we pulled into a store to take a break from driving. As we entered this facility, we noticed that there were people gathered around the TV.

We could see that some major disaster had taken place. The viewer's informed us that a bridge had collapsed over the Mississippi River earlier in the day with lots of traffic that were loaded on top of it. We could see cars, trucks, buses everywhere that had fallen into the Mississippi.

Amazingly it was the highway the spirit of **GOD** Quicken my heart to get off of, it was I 35 W! If I had not left the highway, we would have been on that bridge when it collapsed into the Mississippi River. Thirteen people died that day and (145) were seriously injured. Not including all of the terrible destruction, and the horrible nightmare that took place with all of those who were a part of this tragedy. Only **GOD** knows if we would've died or not if I had not been obedient to that **Holy Ghost** unction.

Dam at Wisconsin Dell Lake Broke

If I had not heard from **GOD**, my family and I would have been swept away when the dam broke at Dell Lake in Wisconsin!

On June 8, 2008, my family and I were in Wisconsin at Dell Lake ministering in special meetings for an Indian tribe called the Ho-Chunk Nation. We were there at their invitation. They had provided the facility and all the advertisements. We had been having some wonderful services.

It was the second night of these meetings. At the end of the service out of the blue, I heard the voice of **GOD** say: pack up your camper and leave tonight! It had been a long day and my flesh sure did not want to leave, but I know the voice of **GOD**. I told the sponsors of the meetings that I was sorry, but I would have to go back to Pennsylvania, tonight. I could tell they were extremely disappointed. They tried to convince me to stay because **GOD** was moving in such a wonderful way, but I know the voice of **GOD**.

My family members were also disappointed. They asked me why we were leaving. They reminded me that I have never canceled or shortened my commitments. I told them I understood this. But we had to leave tonight. I did not know why. I heard the Lord tell me we must leave tonight, so tonight we will leave. We arrived back at the Dell Lake campgrounds. It was beginning to rain extremely hard.

My family asked if we could simply wait until the next morning because it was late, dark and raining heavily. I said no, we must go now! I backed my truck up to the fifth-wheel trailer. I saw the spirit of **GOD** come upon my 2nd son Daniel, who does not like to get wet or even really work, begin to work frantically. I mean he really began to move like in the supernatural hurry. My boys and I connected up the 5th wheel camper, we picked up all of our equipment and drew in the extended sides of the trailer.

Everybody was wet and tired as we loaded into the crew cab Toyota truck. Then, we were on our way. I noticed as I drove past the Dell Lake dam that water was rushing by like a little river on both sides of the road. Some parts of the road were already flooded.

We drove through the night. There were times we had to

crawl because the rain was coming down so hard, fog and strong winds. All the way through Wisconsin, Illinois and Indiana, Ohio the rain came. The wind was extremely strong. We saw 18 wheelers turned over. Lots of car accidents. Trees and debris were blowing everywhere. And yet **GOD** was protecting us.

The next day when we had finally arrived back in Pennsylvania, we discovered some shocking news. There had been hundreds of twisters and tornadoes right behind us which caused a huge amount of devastation. But that wasn't the only news. The dam at Dell Lake, Wisconsin had completely and totally collapsed. Dell Lake is the largest man-made lake in Wisconsin, and this had never happened before in all of its history. The whole lake rushed out over the town. We would have been washed away in the storm. There is video footage of this disaster on the Internet.

Psalm 124:1 If it had not been the Lord who was on our side, now may Israel say;2 If it had not been the Lord who was on our side, when men rose up against us:3 then they had swallowed us up quick, when their wrath was kindled against us:

Supernatural Download on FAITH

I was up early one morning in prayer, simply speaking to the Lord and praying in the spirit when suddenly the heavens were opened to me. Within three minutes the Spirit of **GOD** downloaded into my mind forty major dimensions and aspects of **FAITH**. My mind was filled with a Revelation of **FAITH** that I had never had before. For over thirty years I have studied the subject of **FAITH**, and yet within those three minutes I perceived things about **FAITH** I had never heard, even though I had sat underneath renowned men of **FAITH** and attended a school that majored on **FAITH**.

Now each of these forty major dimensions of **FAITH** had many truths. Some of them have up to twenty-eight points. Immediately I grabbed a pen and paper. As I sat at my dining room table, I did not have to think what to write, I simply put down on paper what the Lord quickened me. Many of the things the Lord showed me I had never been taught. For instance, the Lord showed me that **FAITH** comes twenty-eight different ways.

What he gave me in three minutes, took over three days to write down. Every dimension of **FAITH** the Lord showed me I have gone to the Scriptures to make sure it is the absolute truth. Even dealing with the twenty-eight ways that **FAITH** comes, I wanted to see it in the word. Sure enough, **FAITH** does come by at least twenty-eight ways. Every dimension of **FAITH** he spoke to my heart is in perfect agreement with the Bible.

This event took place in 2008 and ever since then, revelation keeps flowing to me on this subject. I am writing a book just to share eighteen ways that **FAITH** comes. The other aspects of **FAITH** would have to be a library of books. Over 95% of what the Lord had quickened to my heart was downloaded in me within three minutes or less. Now I understand how the prophets of old penned the prophetic words of the Old Testament. It was by the **Holy Ghost**. We still have the same **Holy Ghost**.

GOD is not giving us any new revelation; he is simply causing the Revelation that is in his word to come forth. Oh Lord let it come forth!

OVERCOMING SYMPTOMS OF A STROKE!

FAITH BASED OUTCOME INDEPENDENT

*Numbers 23:19 **GOD** is not a man, that he should lie; neither the son of man, that he should repent: hath he said, and shall he not do it? or hath he spoken, and shall he not make it good?*

When the enemy comes in like a flood, if I will trust **GOD**, act upon the word, **GOD** will raise up a standard against the enemy. I'm amazed at how many modern believers are such pacifists when it comes to fighting off the enemy by **FAITH** in **CHRIST**.

You must rise up in the Name of **JESUS CHRIST** and speak against the **Circumstance** which is contrary to **GOD**'s will. If the **Circumstance** does not seem to change, you do not let go of **GOD**'s promises. You maintain a thankful and worshipful heart towards the Lord. Here is an illustration of my personal life.

The other day I was lying in bed all night long with terrible pain racking my body, yet I am fighting the fight of **FAITH**, speaking the Word, and praying quietly as I'm lying-in bed. I never allow a spirit of fear to control and dictate my actions.

The next thing I know my left hand went completely numb with my fingers all curled up. The devil said to me: you're having a stroke. Immediately I jumped out of bed, and I took my numb left arm with its curled-up fingers and began to beat it with my right hand commanding it to be healed. I knew that this **Circumstance** was not of **GOD** because by **his stripes we were healed**! I had to rise in the **Spirit of FAITH** speaking to this **Circumstance** in and by the **Name of JESUS**.

After over 40 years of practice, I know in most situations what is, and what is not the will of **GOD**. After I had commanded my arm and my hand, my body to be healed, I began to thank the Lord that it was done. Now, in the natural, my arm and my hand were still in the same condition as it was before I spoke to it in the name of **JESUS**, but I know that **GOD** Cannot Lie.

Praise the Lord, within a short period of time my left arm and hand were completely restored, and all the pain left my body. This took place back in about 2009. We should never give into the lie, or the symptoms that the enemy is trying to use against us. The minute the enemy sticks his ugly head up, we need to cut it off with the word of **GOD**.

When I was a kid, we used to fish in a favorite fishing hole. It was filled with panfish, croppies, and bluegills. The only problem is that it also had lots of mud turtles. These nasty turtles would kill anything that was in their path. Whenever we went fishing, we would always carry our 22 rifles. When these mud turtles stuck their heads up, we popped them with our 22 rifles.

We were not going to allow them to devour the fish we were trying to catch. If we had not done this, there would have been no fish left in this pond. It is the same way spiritually. You cannot allow the devil and his demonic host to simply run over you. We must rise up and overcome spiritual pacifism.

Matthew 16:19 And I will give unto thee the keys of the kingdom of heaven: and whatsoever thou shalt bind on earth shall be bound in heaven: and whatsoever thou shalt loose on earth shall be loosed in heaven.

Healed of Terrible Fungus

I Saw Through His Shoes And There Was Fungus On His Feet!

My wife and I were ministering at a church in Harrisburg, Pennsylvania, area. I had finished ministering the message that **GOD** had laid on my heart and was beginning to move in the gifts of the Holy Spirit. **GOD** began to confirm His Word with some wonderful signs and wonders. The word of knowledge, wisdom and the discerning of spirits were manifested as I surrendered and yielded to the Spirit of **GOD**. New wine began to flow as people were being touched by the **Holy Ghost**. As I was finishing up with one of the people we were praying for, I looked over at the pastor who was sitting on the front row of chairs, with his wife.

This pastor is a rather large man, in height and in weight. The Holy Spirit drew my attention to his feet. Because he is also involved in the farming industry, he was wearing a heavy-duty pair of shoes. As I was looking at the shoes, all of a sudden, I could see right through them. It shocked me, to some extent.

I could very clearly see his feet and toes. This experience was so real that it pulled me right over to him. I stood in front of this pastor, looking at his feet, and with a look of surprise on my face. I pointed down at his feet and said: "What is going on with your toes?" He said: "What?" I repeated my question.

I could see they were completely covered in fungus. I saw that even the nails of his toes were either gone or completely covered in a black, yellow, nasty fungus. I told him: "Fungus! Your toes and your feet are completely covered in fungus!" He answered: "Yes. They have been like that for many years. When I used to play football (must have been about forty-years earlier) somehow, I contracted this fungus and I have never been able to get rid of it."

I fell to my knees, right then and there, putting my hands on his shoes. I spoke to the fungus on his toes and feet and commanded that in the name of **JESUS CHRIST**, it had to go. I told the spirit of infirmity to leave his feet now in the name of **JESUS**. As I spoke the Word of **GOD**, I knew in my heart, by a gift of **FAITH**, and the gift of healing, he was healed. I told him: "It is gone! In the name of **JESUS**, it is gone and you are healed!" I got up from off the floor and by the Spirit of **GOD**, I continued to minister to others.

About a month later, I was back in this man's church ministering. I asked him: "Brother, how're your feet?" He told me the fungus was completely gone! After all those years he was now free. By the gifts of the **Holy Ghost**, **JESUS CHRIST** had revealed this need and caused him to be completely healed.

Kidney Stones Miraculously Dissolved

A precious sister in **CHRIST** who attends the church I pastor ended up with kidney stones. She began attending our church when she was a young girl with her parents. From that time to now, she got married and had three daughters and a son. One day she began to experience extreme pain in the lower part of her body with nausea and vomiting. It became so painful that she decided she better get to the doctors real quick.

She went through a serious of medical tests, with the doctors discovering that she had many kidney stones. What is a kidney stone? A kidney stone is a solid piece of material that forms in a kidney when chemicals that are found in the urine become highly concentrated. A stone may stay in the kidney or travel down the urinary tract. A small stone may pass on its own, causing little or no pain. A larger stone may get stuck along the urinary tract and can block the flow of urine, causing severe pain or bleeding.

In Pam's situation, the stones were so large that she could not pass them. Kidney stones are one of the most common disorders of the urinary tract. Each year in the United States, people make more than a million visits to their doctors, and more than 300,000 people go to emergency rooms for kidney stone problems.

Treatment for kidney stones usually depends on their size and what they are made of, as well as whether they are causing pain or obstructing the urinary tract. In Pam's situation, the doctors informed her that the stones in her body were too large for her to pass, or for what they call shockwave treatment. In this particular procedure, they use what they call a lithotripter to generate shock waves that pass through the person's body to break the kidney stones into smaller pieces to pass more readily through the urinary tract.

This treatment would not work for Pam though. The only other option they had was to literally go in with a long, tube-like instrument with an eyepiece to find and retrieve the stone with a small basket or to break the stone up with laser energy. The urologist removes the stone or, if the stone is large, uses a flexible fiber attached to a laser generator to break the stone into smaller pieces that can pass out of the body in the urine.

When my wife and I went in to visit her as she laid in her hospital bed. She explained to us her situation, the diagnosis, and the treatment they were wanting to perform upon her. She told us that she really did not want to go through this procedure and asked if we would ask **GOD** to remove the stones. Absolutely we told her that we were in complete agreement for a supernatural divine miracle to dissolve the stones.

My wife put her hands upon Pam's abdomen, with me placing my hands upon my wife's hands. We commanded in the name of **JESUS CHRIST** of Nazareth for the stones to dissolve, to depart, to be gone. We commanded her body to be healed of all the damage the stones had caused. We commanded the pain and the discomfort to be gone in **JESUS** name. When we were finished praying, we all began to praise **GOD** together thanking him for the healing that we had just spoken into existence. We left the hospital room agreeing, believing, and receiving by **FAITH** this miracle in **JESUS** Name.

From that moment forward Pam later informed us that all the pain had completely disappeared. As they were getting ready to perform the operation, she told her doctors that she wanted them to double-check once more before they carried out their procedures. She told them that after her pastor had prayed for her that all the pain and discomfort were gone. They reluctantly agreed with her request. To their shock and amazement, all the stones were gone.

They examined her urine, but there were no stones to be located. They put her through other procedures and tests, but every stone had just simply disappeared. Pam shared with them the fact that her pastor, his wife, and herself agreed together in **JESUS** name for the stones to be gone, and that **GOD** had answered our prayers. They were so upset about her sharing **CHRIST** that they quickly released her from the hospital with no comments. **CHRIST** is the same yesterday, today, and forever. If you ever did it once, he'll do it again

Empty 1000 Gallon LP Fuel Tank Heated the Church for 2 ½ Months

In the winter of 2012, our 1000-gallon LP tank ran out of gas behind the church. We had no money so I went out early Sunday morning walking through the snow, laid my hands on that tank, and ask **GOD** either to provide the money or to cause the gas to keep flowing from this empty tank. I went into the church, and simply turned on the heater's(we have been smelling the garlic in the LP, and that meant the tank was empty) simply saying okay Lord here we go. Surprisingly the heaters came on with that lovely blue-yellow flame. For the next 2 ½ months (everybody in the church would go and look at the empty gauge on the tank) our church was heated by an empty LP tank.

Dan 3:24 Then Nebuchadnezzar the king was astonied, and rose up in haste, and spake, and said unto his counsellors, Did not we cast three men bound into the midst of the fire? They answered

and said unto the king, True, O king. 25 He answered and said, Lo, I see four men loose, walking in the midst of the fire, and they have no hurt; and the form of the fourth is like the Son of **GOD***.*

My Dog Dying From Distemper HEALED

Will **GOD** answer prayer when it comes to our animals? The Scriptures declare that he knows every sparrow that falls, therefore he cares about animals. I have a collie dog by the name of Ranger. In the summer of 2013, I was in my office busy with paperwork when I received a phone call from one of the ladies of the church. She was crying and frantic with the news that my dog was being attacked by a skunk. I told her I would be right over. By the time I arrived the skunk was waddling away up the hill behind the church.

I thought everything was okay because the skunk had been after my dog but they had not come into contact. I went back to my office busy once again with what I needed to get done. As I was continuing with my office work all of a sudden my phone began to ring once again. When I picked up the phone, here it was Nancy . She was crying and yelling more than before.

She said Pastor the skunk is back, and he's in the cage with Ranger. He is attacking Ranger and biting him. This time I grab my nine-millimeter pistol, running over to the church where I had my dog in a dog kennel. When I arrived I saw my dog Ranger backed up in the corner of his pen with this large very sick, and aggressive skunk going after him.

Nancy was standing there crying and calling out for Ranger to come to her. Eventually, I was able to separate my dog from this skunk. And then I sent that skunk to his eternal destiny, wherever that was. Immediately I knew that this skunk had a real bad case of distemper. His face was all bloated with green pus, with his eyes almost bulging out of his little head.

I pulled out all my dogs' records, discovering that his distemper shots were not up to date. As I researched it on the Internet I discovered that giving him a distemper shot at this time would not help him. If he had distemper he would need a miracle, and I hoped and prayed that he did not have distemper.

A number of days went by when I began to notice that my dog Ranger was not acting normal. He was congested and breathing very hard. He seemed to be listless and acting strange. The symptoms began to get worse, and worse every day with his head beginning to shake, swinging back and forth low to the ground. My heart grew heavy because I knew that he had been infected with distemper. I prayed over him halfheartedly not really having much hope.

I finally called up one of the men in the church asking him if he would come down and put my dog out of his misery. He informed me that he would, but he could not do it to the next day.

I was up the next morning to go visit my dog one last time. As I was standing there it is like the spirit of **GOD** spoke to my heart, asking me why I did not aggressively believe for his healing. The Holy Spirit was challenging me to trust the Lord, and his word for this situation in my dog to be healed of this distemper. As the spirit of **GOD** was speaking to my heart, my **FAITH** began to rise. I called up this brother that was going to come to put my dog out of his misery on my cell phone informing him that I did not need his help and that **GOD** was able to turn this situation around.

Once I was off the phone I grabbed hold of my dog's head with both hands taking authority over this demonic attack. I commanded this virus of distemper to let go of my dog Ranger. I informed the enemy that he had no right to trespass. When I was done speaking to this virus of distemper, I began to praise and worship **GOD** that my dog was healed.

From then on I kept praise the Lord that Ranger would live and not die. All through that day, and for the next two days I kept praising **GOD** even though it looks like Ranger was getting worse. I just kept thanking and praising **GOD** that it was done, and that the devil was a liar, and that Ranger would live and not die because the virus had to obey me in the name of **JESUS**, and that the enemy was defeated. On the third day, I walked out to see Ranger, and praise the Lord he was completely normal. He was back to his old barking, jumping, tail wagging self.

That has been over two years ago, and he is healthier now than ever. Many times we give up too soon instead of aggressively taking hold of **GOD**; we lean to our own understanding. Do not give up! Do not let go! Take hold of **GOD**, trusting him in whatever your situation is. **GOD** is **Faithful**!

Healed of Gushing Bright Red Blood!

With what I'm about to share with you, there is no pride, I am not boasting on me, but **JESUS CHRIST**. Since 1975 (when I was gloriously born again and filled with **Holy Ghost**) every time I get attacked physically by a sickness, disease, or infirmity, I aggressively take a hold of **GOD**'s promise: **by his stripes, I am healed**, and that **CHRIST** has given me authority, power, and I can speak to the problem, the illness, or the disease, and commanded to go.

I DO NOT RUN TO THE DOCTORS BECAUSE I DO NOT NEED TO KNOW THEIR PROGNOSIS, MOST LIKELY IT WILL NOT BE GOOD ANYWAYS.

The answer to victory over sickness, disease, and afflictions is not by ignoring them, but by immediately rising up in the name of **JESUS** and taking authority over the attack. NOW HERE'S THE STORY!

My wife and I arrived back from Israel on October 30th, 2014. While in Israel I had been experiencing some severe digestive problems. Specifically, when it came to bowel movements. When I got home back to Pennsylvania something was going on inside of me, and it just did not seem right. I sat down on the commode one day and perceiving something was really wrong. As I was having a bowel movement I began to gush bright red blood. When I was finished I stood up, turned around and looked down, and the commode was filled with blood.

Most people would have been immediately filled with fear, called their family members, telling them what was happening, and rushed to the hospital, but this is not how I operate.

PLEASE PAY ATTENTION TO THE STEPS I TOOK TO BE HEALED!

The **1st** thing I did was examine my heart, making sure that there was no sin or rebellion in my life, and I'm not talking about being sinless. We all have sinned because anything that is not of **FAITH** is sin. I am talking about open rebellion, disobedience, bitterness, hate, evil desires, sin in my heart, or life. In order to operate in authority, you must be submitted to the authority of **GOD** the **FATHER**, **CHRIST**, the **Holy Ghost**, and the Word!

The **2nd** thing I did was that I began to talk to **GOD**, thanking the **FATHER** for putting all my sicknesses, diseases, and infirmities upon **JESUS CHRIST**, who took it all upon himself including our sins, and our iniquities.

The **3rd** thing I did was to **Speak Boldly** to the infirmity in my body, and the demonic powers. Commanding it, and them to go from my body in the Name of **JESUS**.

FAITH BASED OUTCOME INDEPENDENT

The **4th** thing I did was to now **Speak** to my body, my bowels, the intestines, the stomach, commanding them to be healed and to be made whole. I commanded the blood to stop gushing.

The **5th** thing I did is I began to **rejoice and praise GOD** that I was healed, not that I was going to be healed!

The **6th** step is that I did not allow myself to be filled with fear, neither did I go around telling everybody, or anybody about the symptoms that were manifesting in my body.

The **7th** thing I did was to continue to thank **GOD** from that moment forward that I was HEALED until I saw, felt, and experienced its manifestation! I just kept on thanking **GOD** speaking to myself that **I WAS HEALED**.

The **8th** thing I did was to **laugh out loud at the devil**, telling him that he is nothing but a liar and that **GOD** and his word is true. How long was it before you saw the manifestation of your healing? To tell you the truth, I do not remember.

Job 5:22 At destruction and famine thou shalt laugh: neither shalt thou be afraid of the beasts of the earth.

Job 8:21 Till he fill thy mouth with laughing, and thy lips with rejoicing.

The **9th** thing I do is that I endure, I stand upon **GOD**s WORD! He that endures to the end will be saved.

The word saved in Greek is the word **SOZO**! This word means: 1), cured (1), ensure salvation (1), to get well (2), made...well (6), made well (5), preserved (1), recover (1), restore (1), save (36), saved (50), saves (1), saving (1). The person who holds onto **FAITH** when it comes to divine healing no matter what the **Circumstance**, will be made whole.

The **10th** thing I do is that **I do not** let the symptoms of the sickness, affliction, and infirmity control or dictate the course of my life! Now this attack was over 5 years ago, and I have no more blood in my bowel movements, feeling wonderful, and I am doing well in **JESUS CHRIST**.

✦✦✦

Raising the Dead at Cracker Barrel!

One morning in the middle of November of 2016, my wife asked me to take her to breakfast at Cracker Barrel. "Normally we only eat at Cracker Barrel when Joanna and Randy Herndon (Joanna is the daughter of the late great Jack Coe) are staying at our church." I agreed to her request, informing her that I would love to go eat breakfast with her at Cracker Barrel. From where we pastor in Gettysburg, PA, it is about a 20-minute drive.

We arrived at Cracker Barrel around 10 AM. One of the waitresses took us to our table which was in about the middle of the restaurant. We were sitting and simply discussing the how good and wonderful **GOD** has been to us. We ordered our breakfast meal. Eventually, the food arrived, and we held hands thanking **GOD** for our food, and for his divine guidance in our lives.

We ate our food leisurely enjoying each other's company. When out of the blue two waitresses began to walk briskly down the length of the restaurant urgently asking if there was any doctor or nurse available. The way they were calling out you could tell that something urgent and tragic was going on.

In most of these similar situations, I would be immediately upon my feet heading to the problem area. One time I was at (in about 1996) Lowe's with my family shopping when a similar situation happened. One of the tellers had gone into an epileptic seizure. I immediately ran over to the counter informing them that I was a doctor (Ph.D. in biblical theology) and that I could help. In that situation, I simply leaned over the counter and laid my hands on the girl who was having a seizure and was thrashing about. I took authority very quietly commanding the devil to let her go. Immediately the seizure stopped, and she jumped up to her feet.

Now here I was in a seemingly similar situation. What is so strange though is that I did not sense any urgency in my heart to go help at that moment. It did not occur to me until after this event that for some reason I had not acted in my regular routine method. Now that I look back, I believe that **GOD** was in this. My wife and I simply sat there, talking back and forth a little bit, and finishing our meal.

Approximately 10 minutes later we simply got to our feet and began to walk towards the front of the restaurant. As we got to the opening of the entrance to the restaurant we noticed a small crowd had gathered. As we walked up to this crowd I could see that there is a woman who was leaning over the top of a rather large lady who was laying on her left side, on the floor with her body completely extended.

This lady who was laying out on the floor was completely still. There was no movement from her whatsoever. There was a very heavy blanket of silence over the whole crowd, with nobody talking. Everybody's eyes were upon the lady who was laying on the hardwood floor completely still.

When I saw this lady laid out upon the floor the compassion of **GOD** rose up in my heart, and immediately overwhelmed me. When the love of **GOD** begins the flood when your heart to this extent, the best thing to do is simply to surrender to the divine impulse at work inside of you. In my heart, it was as if the lady laying on the floor was a very personal person to me.

I had to do something and at that very moment, I was motivated to get involved. I walked over to the crowd and very gently pushed my way through. I spoke up informing them that I was a local pastor and that I would like to help. I did not have to push my way through, they simply made room for me to come through.

The woman who was bending over this lady on the floor informed me that she was a nurse. She had a hold of one of the hands of the lady on the floor. I could see that she had her fingers on her wrist, looking for a heartbeat. I knelt down next to her. This lady who was laying on the floor looked to be in her mid to late-60s. She was laying on her left side completely still. Tears began to fill my eyes, and I reached forth my hand and place it upon her cheek. I discovered that her cheek was extremely cold to my touch.

I have learned in over 40 years of moving in the spirit that you do not have to pray aloud prayer or shout at the enemy. (Them that do know their **GOD** shall be strong and do exploits) With the love of **GOD** flowing in my heart, I prayed a very simple prayer in **JESUS** name. I commanded the spirit of infirmity to go and began speaking life over her very quietly in **JESUS** name.

As I'm praying for this lady, tears were filling my eyes. I felt as if I knew her personally and that she was someone who was important to me. This is how the Holy Spirit works. **GOD** has shed His love abroad in our hearts by the **Holy Ghost**. It is in this realm that the gift of **FAITH** will begin to operate. You're not leaning on the understanding of your mind, or operating in simple human sympathy.

In probably less than a minute as I was praying the nurse spoke up very excitedly and made this statement: She Has a Pulse! As I thought about this later it became obvious to me that this lady up to that moment had lost her pulse. I continue to pray softly, as I still had my right hand on her cheek very softly. The next thing I knew this lady who was laying on the floor began to stir, and she reached up her right hand and put it on my hand squeezing it.

I knew in my heart that my job was done. The spirit of **CHRIST** had touched this precious lady, raising her from the dead. There were no fireworks, explosions, or loud shouting, but simply the gentle moving of the Spirit of **CHRIST**. The resurrection power of **GOD** manifested without people even realizing it.

I got up from my kneeling position, walking back to the crowd. My wife was simply waiting for me to complete the task. As we walked out the door of Cracker Barrel, the ambulance was coming around the corner, with its lights flashing. We simply walked out to our car and got into it. We took a minute to thank **GOD** once again for confirmed the authority and power that we have in the Name of **JESUS**, with signs following.

How To Live in The Miraculous!

This is a quick explanation of how to live and move in the realm of the miraculous. Seeing divine interventions of **GOD** is not something that just spontaneously happens because you have been born-again. There are certain biblical principles and truths that must be evident in your life. This is a very basic list of some of these truths and laws:

1. You must give **JESUS CHRIST** your whole heart. You cannot be lackadaisical in this endeavour. Being lukewarm in your walk with **GOD** is repulsive to the Lord. He wants 100% commitment. **JESUS** gave His all! Now it is our turn to give our all. He loved us 100%. Now we must love Him 100%.

Proverbs 23:26 My son, give me thine heart, and let thine eyes observe my ways
Revelation 3:16 So then because thou art lukewarm, and neither cold nor hot, I will spew thee out of my mouth.

2. There must be a complete agreement with **GOD**'s Word. We must be in harmony with the Lord; in our attitude, actions, thoughts, and deeds. Whatever the Word of **GOD** declares in the New Testament is what we wholeheartedly agree with.

Amos 3:3 Can two walk together, except they be agreed?

2 Chronicles 16:9 For the eyes of the LORD run to and fro throughout the whole earth, to shew himself strong in the behalf of them whose heart is perfect toward him ...

3. Obey and do the Word of **GOD** from the heart: from the simplest to the most complicated request or command. No matter what the Word says to do - Do it! Here are some simple examples: Lift your hands in praise, in everything give thanks, forgive instantly, gather together with the saints, and give offerings to the Lord, and so on.

*John 5:30 I can of mine own self do nothing: as I hear, I judge: and my judgment is just; because I seek not mine own will, but the will of the **FATHER** which hath sent me.*

4. Make **JESUS** the highest priority of your life. Everything you do, do not do it as unto men, but do it as unto **GOD**.

*Colossians 3:1-2 If ye then be risen with **CHRIST**, seek those things which are above, where **CHRIST** sitteth on the right hand of **GOD**. 2 Set your affection on things above, not on things on the earth.*

5. Die to self! The old man says: "My will be done!" The new man says: "**GOD**'s will be done!"

*Galatians 2:20 I am crucified with **CHRIST**: nevertheless I live; yet not I, but **CHRIST** liveth in me: and the life which I now live in the flesh I live by the **FAITH** of the Son of*

GOD, *who loved me, and gave himself for me.*

Romans 6:8 Now if we be dead with **CHRIST***, we believe that we shall also live with him:*

6. Repent the minute you get out of **GOD**'s will—no matter how minor, or small the sin may seem.

Revelation 3:19 As many as I love, I rebuke and chasten: be zealous therefore, and repent.

7. Take one step at a time. **GOD** will test you (not to do evil) to see if you will obey Him. *Whatever He tells you to do: by His Word, by His Spirit, or within your conscience ... Do it!* He will never tell you to do something contrary to His nature or His Word!

Matthew 12:50 For whosoever shall do the will of my **FATHER** *which is in heaven, the same is my brother, and sister, and mother.*

2 Kings 5:14 Then went he down, and dipped himself seven times in Jordan, according to the saying of the man of **GOD***: and his flesh came again like unto the flesh of a little child, and he was clean.*

ABOUT THE AUTHOR

Dr. Michael and Kathleen Yeager have served as pastors/apostles, missionaries, evangelists, broadcasters and authors for over four decades. They flow in the gifts of the Holy Spirit, teaching the Word of GOD with wonderful signs and miracles following in confirmation of GOD's Word. In 1983, they began JESUS is Lord Ministries International, Biglerville, PA 17307. Doc has authored over 185 books to date.

Websites Connected to Doc Yeager

www.docyeager.com

www.jilmi.org

www.wbntv.org

FAITH BASED OUTCOME INDEPENDENT

<u>Some of the Books Written by Doc Yeager:</u>
"Living in the Realm of the Miraculous #1"
"I Need **GOD** Cause I'm Stupid"
"The Miracles of Smith Wigglesworth"
"How **FAITH** Comes 28 WAYS"
"Horrors of Hell, Splendors of Heaven"
"The Coming Great Awakening"
"Sinners In The Hands of an Angry **GOD**", (modernized)
"Brain Parasite Epidemic"
"My JOURNEY To HELL" - illustrated for teenagers
"Divine Revelation Of **JESUS CHRIST**"
"My Daily Meditations"
"Holy Bible of **JESUS CHRIST**"
"War In The Heavenlies - (Chronicles of Micah)"
"Living in the Realm of the Miraculous #2"
"My Legal Rights To Witness"
"Why We (MUST) Gather!- 30 Biblical Reasons"
"My Incredible, Supernatural, Divine Experiences"
"Living in the Realm of the Miraculous #3"
"How **GOD** Leads & Guides! - 20 Ways"
"Weapons Of Our Warfare"
"How You Can Be Healed"
"**GOD** Still Heals"